ACTORS AND ACTING IN SHAKESPEARE'S TIME

John Astington brings the acting style of the Shakespearean period to life, describing and analysing the art of the player in the English professional theatre between Richard Tarlton and Thomas Betterton. The book pays close attention to the cultural context of stage playing, the critical language used about it, and the kinds of training and professional practice employed in the theatre at various times over the course of roughly 100 years – 1558–1660. Perfect for courses, this up-to-date survey takes into account recent discoveries about actors and their social networks, about apprenticeship and company affiliations, and about playing outside the major centre of theatre, London. Astington considers the educational tradition of playing, in schools, universities, legal inns and choral communities, in comparison to the work of the professional players. A comprehensive biographical dictionary of all major professional players of the Shakespearean period is included as a handy reference guide.

JOHN H. ASTINGTON is Professor in the Department of English and the Graduate Centre for the Study of Drama at the University of Toronto. He is the author of *English Court Theatre, 1558–1642* (Cambridge, 1999), and has published articles and chapters in many books and journals including *The Cambridge Companion to Shakespeare*, *The Cambridge Shakespeare Library*, *The Oxford Handbook to Early Modern Theatre* and *The Oxford Dictionary of National Biography*.

ACTORS AND ACTING IN SHAKESPEARE'S TIME

The Art of Stage Playing

JOHN H. ASTINGTON

CAMBRIDGE
UNIVERSITY PRESS

CAMBRIDGE UNIVERSITY PRESS
Cambridge, New York, Melbourne, Madrid, Cape Town, Singapore,
São Paulo, Delhi, Dubai, Tokyo, Mexico City

Cambridge University Press
The Edinburgh Building, Cambridge CB2 8RU, UK

Published in the United States of America by Cambridge University Press, New York

www.cambridge.org
Information on this title: www.cambridge.org/9780521140775

First published 2010

Printed in the United Kingdom at the University Press, Cambridge

A catalogue record for this publication is available from the British Library

Library of Congress Cataloguing in Publication data
Astington, John.
Actors and acting in Shakespeare's time : the art of stage playing / John H. Astington.
p. cm.
ISBN 978-0-521-19250-7 (hardback)
1. Theater–England–History–16th century. 2. Theater–England–History–17th
century. 3. Shakespeare, William, 1564–1616–Stage history–To 1625. 4. Shakespeare, William,
1564–1616–Stage history–England. 5. Acting–History–16th century. 6. Acting–History–17th
century. I. Title.
PN2589.A88 2010
792.0942′09031–dc22
2010025719

ISBN 978-0-521-19250-7 Hardback
ISBN 978-0-521-14077-5 Paperback

Contents

Illustrations

Acknowledgments

The preparation of any larger study draws on a long period of reading, thought, and conversation, the consequences of which are cumulative, and hard to disentangle retrospectively. I am grateful for the help, encouragement, and criticism of colleagues in the theatre history seminar of the Shakespeare Association of America over a long period, including those of people I can no longer thank in person: Tom King, Herb Berry, and Scott McMillin. In the immediate period of the planning and writing of this book I have been grateful for the help and advice of Catherine Belsey, Susan Cerasano, Roslyn Knutson, Lucy Munro, Roger Bowers, Alan Nelson, David Kathman, Chris Matusiak, Andrew Gurr, Lawrence Manley, Peter Blayney, Martin Butler, Helen Ostovich, Marta Straznicky, and Eva Griffith. I would like to thank David Beasley, Librarian of the Goldsmiths' Company, Penelope Fussell, Archivist of the Drapers' Company, and D. E. Wickham, Archivist of the Clothworkers' Company, for their ready and courteous help in research matters. My own university granted me an administrative leave in 2007–8, during which much of my writing was done; I am grateful to the Master and Fellows of Corpus Christi College, Cambridge, for the award of a Visiting Fellowship during that period, allowing me to work in pleasant and supportive surroundings, the former haunts of Marlowe and Fletcher. Sarah Stanton of Cambridge University Press has provided steady encouragement and wise guidance of the project. To my wife Janet, who has endured my obssession, my thanks for her patience and support.

Introduction: the purpose of playing

In calling the school he founded in 1619, built and endowed with the money he had partly earned from acting, the College of God's Gift, Edward Alleyn recognized that talent on the stage is not entirely a matter of conscious human disposition, as is also the case in any of the arts. One cannot become a good actor simply by wanting to be one. We still speak of a gift for music, without which the most advanced and meticulous technical skill will not produce an outstanding player or composer. That human gifts for one accomplishment or another came from God was widely recognized in Shakespeare's time; even Dogberry in *Much Ado About Nothing* modestly defers to his creator the credit for his superior deductive powers. Alleyn's establishment was not to be a school for the arts or a dramatic academy – and the lack, largely speaking, of such institutions in England before the later seventeenth century will form one theme of this book – but an academic school for middle-class boys, in the tradition of such charitable foundations from the early Tudor period onwards, to produce, eventually, the future lawyers, clergymen, and civil servants the nation required. God's gift to Alleyn was not to be rewarded by fostering similar gifts in others, save as a part of his professional life as an active player in one of the leading theatre companies, and his consequent influence on his junior colleagues and apprentices, which was largely over by 1600. The player's role as an instructor will provide a second major theme of the study that follows.

In becoming the benefactor of a school perhaps Edward Alleyn, like many modern donors to educational institutions, was recognizing his own lack of an advantageous start in life, in terms of social rank and opportunities, at least. Elizabethan England was, of course, quite different from modern Western societies in the ways in which its educational systems worked and in how they served social and cultural structures. Modern measures that correlate the formal educational experience within populations to economic attainment and to social and political development will not fit the conditions of sixteenth- and seventeenth-century England. University education in Shakespeare's day, for example, was restricted to a very small percentage of the population, entirely male, determined largely by rank and social expectations. University education was the very rare exception among contemporary actors – the actor-playwright Thomas Heywood spent some years at Cambridge, without graduating, and a number of other playwrights either were university graduates or had experience as students – but all players would have experienced at least a few years of schooling, of one kind or another. It is frequently assumed that the boy William Shakespeare attended Stratford Grammar School (although no contemporary document confirms his attendance), where he would have learnt to read and compose in Latin; although we cannot be certain about his schooling it is likely that he first acquired his evident familiarity with classical authors in his teenage years, rather than later. Ben Jonson certainly attended Westminster School, where he was taught by William Camden, and he may have been admitted to Cambridge, although he did not attend for long, while Cave Underhill, a leading comic actor after the Restoration, was a pupil at the famous Merchant Taylors' School in London before the civil wars. At the very least even the youngest actors had to be literate, in order to read the scripts they had to learn. Good memory – a gift of God commented on by several contemporary educational theorists – was, and is, a secondary requirement of any successful actor.

Gifts in the arts frequently run in families. The Bachs and the Mozarts are the eminent musical examples, in whom nature and nurture combined to produce eminence over several generations. The stimulus provided by early exposure to sophisticated music-making by one's parents or other close relations gives a notable edge to any latent talent. A child's interest in imitating adult behaviour not infrequently leads on to an artistic career in the same area as that of the parents. In modern theatrical families – the Redgraves, or the Cusacks, for example – women and men are equally distinguished; in the early English theatre, framed by inherited cultural conventions, there was no outlet for female talent in performance, although in contemporary continental Europe families of performers formed a notable part of theatrical organization, and women became leading players and managers. While the genetic circumstances were the same, then – individual gifts and aptitudes were as likely to be inherited from a mother as from a father – in Shakespeare's theatre, at least in the matter of performing on the stage, it is the paternal line only which can be observed. Richard Burbage, Shakespeare's leading colleague for twenty years or so, was the son of James Burbage, an actor, manager, and prominent figure in the theatre from the 1560s onwards. Many sons of actors became actors themselves, but daughters also frequently married other actors, and widows of actors remarried to yet other actors, so that lines of descent and family relationships within the profession were often complex and intricate. Other leading figures of the theatre, however, had no family background or particular early training to do with the stage. Richard Tarlton, the famous Elizabethan clown, was not born into the theatre and did not, so far as we know, pass on his talents to any descendants. The genius of William Shakespeare, player as well as playwright, simply arose and was eclipsed in one generation, although, like Alleyn, Shakespeare in later life might not have encouraged younger people to take his own career as a pattern. His colleague John Heminges, for example, although he trained many young men for the theatre, sent his own son to Oxford.

Most actors never achieved the financial success in the theatre which gave them the choice of retirement, while others evidently loved the stage too much to leave it: Shakespeare's colleague John Lowin, a prominent and well-rewarded performer, continued acting until late in life, his career stopped by political change rather than his own free choice. The pleasure of continuing to do what one was expert at doing, and which gave pleasure to others, must have sustained many actors less eminent than Lowin. A passion for the creative act of performance lies at the centre of the actor's art. Talent, will, and technical refinement – the last the part of acting that can be trained and improved – were all required of Shakespearean players. The particular configurations and proportions of those elements must have varied, as they still vary. If talent was in God's hands, the will and the acquisition of experience might have found a number of channels to fulfilment.

In the course of a written legal suit in the mid 1660s the minor actor William Hall claimed that he had 'served an apprenticeship in the art of stage playing'; a similar phrase, the art of a stage player, is used by the actor William Trigge in 1631 to explain what he was to learn from his master John Heminges, veteran member of the King's company, and the phrase was used proudly by a group of players in 1597 who had, they claimed, 'of long time used and professed the art of stage playing'.[1] Apprenticeship was a legally recognized system of training in any skilled occupation, and its regulation had been established in the early Elizabethan period by the Statute of Artificers of 1563. In London it was overseen generally by the city authorities, and particularly by the individual companies of trades and occupations which controlled much of the commerce of the city, from the small-scale to the large. Yet the word 'apprenticeship' could also mean, as it still may, simply a period of training, applied more loosely than the statutory requirements of formal apprenticeship stipulated by law. Of the two men named above we know that Trigge was certainly legally apprenticed, although as a grocer rather than a player, since Heminges was a freeman of the Grocers' Company, one of the ancient and rich 'great companies' of the City of London. Hall, of whom we know less, may simply have meant in his statement that he had spent some time as a minor player on modest wages with an acting troupe willing to give him a try-out season or two. Legally binding apprenticeships, on the other hand, were usually served for terms of seven years upwards, in adolescence and early manhood, with the ten years between the ages of fourteen and twenty-four representing the central band of experience for the majority of apprenticeships.

In the English theatre before the civil wars and the Restoration, then, when boy actors played female roles on the stage, apprenticeship was a convenient system for attaching suitably talented boys to a company. John Heminges, Trigge's master, was a member of the King's men, the leading acting company for nearly forty years, and William Trigge served his apprenticeship by playing a variety of female characters in that company's plays during the 1620s. We do not know that Hall followed a similar route, and it is clear enough that not all players had begun as boys or teenagers, as it is also clear that not all boys who apprenticed continued to perform as adult actors. One might, therefore, have trained for the stage without continuing a lifelong career in the theatre, and one might have entered the profession without having begun as a boy player, and perhaps without having 'apprenticed' in any sense of that word. If a boy apprentice had demonstrated talent early, and continued to develop it, as an adult he probably had a better chance of finding a permanent place in an acting troupe than did someone entirely unconnected with the company, although he still would have had to buy his position as a sharer, committing himself to the investment of production capital which the leading players of a troupe jointly managed, sharing the dividends from what we now call the box office. We do not know if those in charge of the management of acting troupes did any active scouting, in the fashion of modern professional sports teams, but rising stars occasionally moved from one troupe to another, and some kind of negotiation is likely to have prefaced such transfers.

What made a good actor, and what kinds of qualities might players charged with recruiting new colleagues have been looking for? As in the modern theatre, actors would have had a variety of individual physical and vocal characteristics, with the common requirements of strong and clear oral delivery and a suitable stage presence: an ability to command an audience's attention in a manner suited to character and the situation within a given scene. What makes a 'well graced actor' – Shakespeare's phrase – is rather mysterious, but actors and directors know it when they see it and hear it, as do audiences. Attempts to define the qualities that distinguish the good player from the merely competent tend to sound vague. Contemporary gestures in this direction include the following passage by Thomas Heywood, like Shakespeare an actor, a sharer in an acting troupe, and a playwright:

Actors should be men picked out personable, according to the parts they present; they should be rather scholars, that though they cannot speak well, know how to speak, or else to have that volubility that they can speak well, though they understand not what, and so both imperfections may by instructions be helped and amended; but where a good tongue and a good conceit both fail, there can never be good actor. (*An Apology for Actors* [London, 1612], E3ʳ [modernized])

The voice and the judgement can be improved by training, in Heywood's opinion, but there should be enough to work with, and both a good tongue and a good conceit (or intelligence, as we would say) would be an excellent combination. As to the 'personable' qualities of the performer, Heywood hints at the individuality of appearance and behaviour that makes any good player interesting. Although it may sound as if he is suggesting careful auditioning to suit the parts in a given play, his own practice – that of a member of a repertory company with a permanent core of performers – cannot have bent too far in that direction; new plays would have been cast from the company strength, and Heywood's own voice, face, and physique, however he may have appeared (no representation of him survives), would have been lent to a variety of differing parts over the course of his career. The truly useful actor would bring range and variability, as aspects of his talent, to the troupe he served. Burbage, who is likely to have played the very different roles of King Lear and Volpone at roughly the same age, no doubt had a range of skill at least the equal of that of Alleyn, of whom Thomas Heywood wrote that he was 'Proteus for shapes, and Roscius for a tongue, / So could he speak, so vary'.[2] The surviving head-and-shoulders portrait supposed to be of Burbage does not tell us a great deal about his person, and one cannot read much from the face; perhaps a neutral expression is an asset for Protean changeability in performance. Later, better, and more reliable half-length portraits of the leading actors John Lowin, at the Ashmolean Museum in Oxford (Figure 1), and of Richard Perkins, at the Dulwich Picture Gallery (Figure 2), give a far clearer sense of innate character, and of physique: Lowin large, bluff, even coarse, where Perkins is slim and long-faced, sensitive and melancholic.[3] Neither of the portraits seems to show its

1   Portrait of John Lowin, 1640. Anonymous British artist, oil on canvas

subject costumed for stage roles, although Lowin *may* be dressed and posed as if he were delivering a prologue: a black cloak was supposedly the traditional dress of the player addressing an audience before the perform-ance proper, and Lowin's right hand holds his hat, removed in deference to the observers, as in a playhouse when the performer acknowledges the presence of the audience.

The art of stage playing as the basis for an extended and busy professional career was a relatively recent option when Alleyn had his great artistic and financial success. Although since the later Middle Ages smaller troupes of players had made their living from a combination of private patronage – providing entertainment for the households of great lords and monarchs, and performing commissions for special events – and public performances,

2 Portrait of Richard Perkins, late 1640s. School of Gerard Soest, oil on canvas

collecting what they could from audiences at occasional performances at improvised playing places in town halls, inns, or at fairs, the late sixteenth-century metropolitan theatre with its large permanent playhouses and varied daily repertory was the result of at least fifty years of continuing enterprise, in which the elder Burbage, James, was a leading figure.[4] The theatre of late Elizabethan London was considerably changed from that operating at the start of the Queen's reign: its playing companies were larger, and its productivity, in terms of shows available to audiences, was enormously increased. By 1600 the opportunities available to anyone naturally gifted in the art of acting were far wider than they had been a hundred years before. How many mute, inglorious Alleyns there may have been in earlier centuries is impossible to calculate, but by the later half of the sixteenth century not only did dramatic writing change radically, to the actors' great advantage, but the entire organization of public performance was also thoroughly changed. Theatre was a central cultural phenomenon of late Elizabethan London, with an international reputation, and the consciousness of everyone involved in its production or consumption was raised to new levels. Even actors on the fringes of the profession, or away from the hub of London, working in provincial and touring troupes, must have thought rather differently about their art by the time the seventeenth century began.

Considered in comparison with such an increase in standing and self-regard, the total membership of the profession probably did not expand at the same rate. The population of actors in London in the first decades of the seventeenth century must have stood between a hundred and fifty and two hundred people, calculating that estimate on the basis of principal actors or sharers in licensed troupes, minor or junior actors (hired men), and boys. In addition to this number there were more actors spread across the country as a whole as members of touring or local groups, and although the size of such companies may have been smaller than those of their metro-politan colleagues, the total number of people involved could easily have matched the London figures, and probably exceeded them. In addition English actors formed troupes in continental Europe, some of them spend-ing extended careers there. Perhaps around five hundred people continu-ously involved in acting in the English professional theatre before the civil wars is not an exaggerated estimate. Equally, it is apparent from sixteenth-century records from across the country that professional players were numerous a century earlier; we know less detail about their activities and their identities, but that there were a good many of them is clear from the material collected by the Records of Early English Drama project, and is also suggested by early Elizabethan anti-theatrical polemical complaints about the proliferation in the performing and viewing of plays. The profession of playing as it was practised by Richard Burbage and Edward Alleyn was based on the work of preceding generations of actors.

It seems reasonable to think of an established community of theatre people in London by the year 1600, most of whom knew or knew of many of the others, even outside their immediate colleagues in any given company. Letters to Edward Alleyn from his wife while he was on tour, for example, give news not only of the London household, but also of the ups and downs of professional colleagues.[5] Gossip is one leading off stage activity of actors and their circle. Although daily performance combined with frequent learning and rehearsal of new plays for an ever-changing repertory would have left most actors with little free time, I think that when chance afforded the opportunity they would have gone to see other actors at other playhouses, with a critical eye for both strengths and weaknesses: actors today remain both fiercely competitive and communally supportive. Actors who were also playwrights, Shakespeare and Heywood, notably, seem to have been well aware of the plays performed by companies other than those to which they belonged, and alluded to them in their own writing. Although theatre troupes of Shakespeare's time were nominally permanent in their member-ship – Shakespeare's own troupe notably so – there was in fact a fair amount of fluidity, particularly available to talented actors, and one's rival today might be one's partner tomorrow. Changes in the patronage of troupes, or crises over financing and management, gave rise to periodic rearrange-ments of personnel. Sickness, death, and retirement at one end of profes-sional careers, and particular brilliance and appeal to audiences at the other, meant that individually and collectively actors had an eye to the state of the profession, and to where their own skills and those of their colleagues might appear to the best advantage.

The community of the professional theatre was supported by a variety of communities of theatre-goers, and other enthusiasts of the theatre. There are many indications of a vigorous amateur theatre during Shakespeare's lifetime, not only within the pedagogical and festive contexts of school and university drama but also in other communities, certainly including, for example, apprentices, sailors, lawyers, and aristocratic families. The appren-tice Ralph in Beaumont's satirical theatre comedy *The Knight of the Burning Pestle*, even before his adventitious starring role as grocer errant (possibly a theatrical in-joke aimed at the player-grocer John Heminges, and his string of apprentices) was to have played Hieronimo with a shoemaker for a wager, an acting contest based on one of Alleyn's most famous stage roles. Shakespeare's theatre comedy *A Midsummer Night's Dream* includes a man who claims knowledge of how to play 'Ercles' vein, a tyrant's vein', as well as the quieter tones of a lover. Falstaff, preparing to play the role of one of his actor colleagues, King Henry IV, promises to do it in 'King Cambyses' vein', the style of a generation before Shakespeare.[6] Amateurs in the French sense, lovers of the theatre theatrical, were particularly taken by the style of Marlowe and his imitators during the late 1580s and early 1590s, and by the showy histrionics it encouraged: Pistol, in Shakespeare's *2 Henry IV* and *Henry V*, adopts a mangled extravagance in vocabulary, syntax, and gesture, full of half-remembered quotation, and originally, perhaps, some imitation of Edward Alleyn's stride and commanding posture.

Schoolboy players and gentleman amateurs were still welcome at court in Queen Elizabeth's reign, and all pre-Restoration royal visits to Oxford and Cambridge featured plays presented to the monarch by student performers.

All such groups would have disdained playing for money at a playhouse, but their standards, at the best, were quite high. The play so admired by Sir Philip Sidney, *Gorboduc*, was staged as an amateur show, for example. Boy players might well step over the amateur boundary when they were organized into troupes giving regular performances for paying audiences of plays written by professional playwrights: the singing boys of the choirs of St Paul's Cathedral and of the Chapel Royal were so professionalized, one might say, at various times between the 1570s and the first decade of the seventeenth century, and the practice of 'boy' or 'children's' playing was revived thereafter in various forms. Famously, in the Folio text of *Hamlet* (1623) the 'children' are spoken of as serious rivals to the adult actors. In what sense such companies were regarded as training grounds or 'nurseries' of acting talent, to use a contemporary term, is a matter examined at more length in what follows, but they generally do not seem to have had a close relationship with the adult troupes, who recruited their own boys, the specialists in female parts within a predominantly adult troupe, largely independently. A company of boys of roughly the same age performing in such a play as Marston's *Antonio and Mellida*, for example, as they did, cannot have had the same range of vocal production, of differentiated physique, as an audience would have experienced at similar plays performed by adult troupes.

Enthusiasm for the theatre during the years considered in this book no doubt produced many conversations and discussions about the art of acting, carried on in taverns, at street corners, and in domestic groups. Actors themselves, as I have suggested, are likely to have discussed their common work with colleagues and friends. In Shakespeare's day there was no equivalent of the modern newspaper reviewer, so that not only do we today lack anything resembling a contemporary critique of a performance but Tudor and Stuart theatre-goers did not experience any common public discourse about theatre, with the exception of what was carried on in plays themselves, and in the corresponding printed texts which sometimes followed their performance. Although there would have been a lively tradition of talk about plays and players, then, our impression today, based on surviving texts, is that contemporary dramatists were the chief critics and theorists of the arts of theatre, performance included. A range of playgoers certainly recorded their presence, at the very least, at performances of various kinds, and their testimony is usefully collected by Andrew Gurr in the book *Playgoing in Shakespeare's London*. Detailed comment of a kind which illuminates performance is rare, however, so that it is particularly impressive to read the account of Henry Jackson, from Oxford in 1610, of a performance of *Othello* by the King's men, in which a purely theatrical experience, the moving effect of the face of the murdered Desdemona lying on the bed, is vividly recalled.[7] This, of course, was a performance by a boy apprentice, whose name we do not know. Richard Burbage, playing the title part, goes unmentioned. Simon Forman, who went to the Globe in 1611, at least, and saw three plays by Shakespeare – *Macbeth*, *The Winter's Tale*, and *Cymbeline* – gives full, if rather eccentric, accounts of plot and dramatic event, and notices the presence of certain characters – Autolycus, for example – but mentions no actors by name, and makes no remarks about the immediate and particular effects of their performances.[8] The language that those most intimately involved in stage playing used about their art, oddly limiting although much of it was, is the subject of the next chapter.

CHAPTER I

Shadows, jests, and counterfeits

If we shadows have offended,
Think but this, and all is mended,
That you have but slumb'red here
While these visions did appear.
A Midsummer Night's Dream, 5.1.423–6

Attitudes to the theatre have always varied, and the sixteenth and seventeenth centuries in England saw a wide range of views expressed about its artistic and moral status. Though it was highly regarded by many, its popularity made suspect, in certain eyes, any pretensions it might have to being an especially serious or meaningful human endeavour, while certain stripes of religious fundamentalism, by no means solely 'puritan', regarded its appeal to the senses and its arousal of pleasure as morally corrupting. The moral debate about theatre, which can seem rather unsophisticated and wearisome to us, certainly affected the varying views as to the pedagogical value of theatre and performance, which will be examined at more length below.[1] However genuinely felt the various moral attacks on the theatre may have been, they tended to rehearse old arguments dating back to the early church fathers, and they were parodied notably by Ben Jonson, in a hilariously meaningless stage argument between the hypocritical puritan Zeal-of-the-Land Busy and a puppet, manipulated by the puppet-master Leatherhead, following Busy's noisy interruption and attempt to stop the show, near the end of the play *Bartholomew Fair* (1614).

Busy ... my main argument against you, is, that you are an abomination. For the male among you putteth on the apparel of the female, and the female of the male.
Puppet *You lie, you lie, you lie abominably.*
Cokes Good, by my troth, he has given him the lie thrice.
Puppet *It is your old stale argument against the players, but it will not hold against the puppets; for we have neither male nor female amongst us. And that thou may'st see, if thou wilt, like a malicious purblind zeal as thou art!*
(The puppet takes up his garment) (5.5.83–91)[2]

Busy, 'confuted' by this comic mooning, collapses and joins the party. In so far as the episode raises serious anxieties about theatrical shows, cross-dressing was certainly among them. Busy's words about women dressing as men evidently did not apply to the professional stage of the time, other than fictionally: the fictional Viola in *Twelfth Night*, played by a boy or young man, disguising herself as her brother, for example. Yet the same performer, or rather the series of performers who played the role over the course of forty years of the play's production before the civil wars, certainly first appeared on stage in a woman's dress, appropriately padded, and with a wig of long female hair. This cultural habit had evidently grown out of another anxiety about the display of the body on stage, which any conventional stage performance entails, and the taboos of shame and modesty surrounding female bodies in particular. The confidence and control required of any performer in demonstration of character were probably also at odds with cultural attitudes about the virtuous reticence of women, even under a commandingly performative female monarch. For a woman to display the skill of a good actor had traditionally been regarded as too 'bold'. As late as the 1630s the excoriation of women appearing on stage continued, and the author of the compendious *Histriomastix*, William Prynne, suffered an ancient, painful legal punishment for his tactless criticism at a time when the French-influenced court was nudging English theatrical practice towards the European norm.

The ambiguities surrounding performance were not dispelled by some of the aesthetic language used to address the art of playing in the sixteenth and seventeenth centuries. Diderot's famous later paradox concerning acting gives one kind of voice to the pleasurable consciousness we have about theatrical performance: we are deeply affected by its truth, if it is a good performance, while knowing it to be a controlled pretence.[3] Two kinds of things have excited us, as it were, after a successful play: the characters' life, and the actors' skill in creating it. Actors must possess a similar double consciousness, believing deeply in their parts, yet remaining technically detached, aware moment by moment of the necessary mechanics connected to their function as performers: entering on cue, moving to the positions expected by the lighting designer and the stage manager, and so forth. If one latches simple-mindedly onto the pretence inherent in acting, it is an easy step on the part of the unsympathetic to represent it as an art of untruth, of lying, and hence as devilish, connected with deceit in real life, as if all actors were trying to do to audiences what Iago does to Othello. Reductive as that may be, there is in fact something uncanny and unsettling about powerful acting, and even Hamlet, an enthusiastic defender of the value of theatre, finds the moving recounting of Hecuba's grief by the player, though deeply affecting, to be 'monstrous' – unnatural and disturbing, like the phantom of his father, an emanation from a world outside the known and familiar.

Sixteenth-century actors, in character, had to utter some fairly dismissive opinions about acting. Duke Theseus in *A Midsummer Night's Dream* thinks that even good actors, which it is not his luck to experience, are fairly lightweight: 'The best in this kind are but shadows', he says (5.1.210). (The term 'shadows' is significantly and ironically picked up by Puck in his final address to the audience, quoted in the epigraph above, when he speaks almost, but not quite, as actor rather than character.) In *The Third Part of King Henry VI* the Earl of Warwick rouses his colleagues in the midst of battle by urging them to enter the stage, as it were:

> Why stand we like soft-hearted women here
> Wailing our losses, whiles the foe doth rage,
> And look upon, as if the tragedy
> Were played in jest by counterfeiting actors?   (2.3.25–8)

Both terms applied to playing are dismissive, particularly here, but they were widely used, notably by Shakespeare himself. *The Oxford English Dictionary* locates the first use of 'counterfeiting' in connection with acting in the middle of the sixteenth century: a translation of Erasmus tells of 'Men like players counterfeted and disguysed'. Modern usage of the word immediately suggests falsity; this was *one* of the sixteenth-century senses of 'counterfeit', but it could also simply be used neutrally to mean to make or manufacture, especially if artistic technique was involved in the making. Its theatrical use, however, certainly seems invested with uncertainty about what it is that is being made. In referring to an assumed identity, as well as a costumed disguise, Falstaff in *The Merry Wives of Windsor* ironically congratulates himself on 'my admirable dexterity of wit, by counterfeiting the action of an old woman', and escaping arrest (4.6.110–11). Edgar, in his assumed 'poor, bare' role as the incoherent Poor Tom, fears that his growing sympathy for Lear's suffering will give him away: 'My tears begin to take his part so much, / They mar my counterfeiting' (*King Lear*, 3.6.60–1). (Once we realize these lines have a specifically theatrical sense, we notice the pun on 'part': taking another's part makes one forget one's own lines.) Malvolio, manipulated into giving a grotesque performance, and then treated as if he were insane, is further taunted by lines which probe the various levels of pretence and impersonation going on by the fourth act of *Twelfth Night*: 'Are you not mad indeed, or do you but counterfeit?' he is asked (4.2.113–14). His interrogator, Feste, 'counterfeits well' in his own assumed role as Sir Topas the parson (4.2.19). A particularly densely packed exchange which uses the word occurs during the tricking of Benedick in *Much Ado about Nothing*; he overhears a staged conversation about Beatrice's love for him:

Leonato By my troth, my lord, I cannot tell what to think of it but that she loves him with an enrag'd affection; it is past the infinite of thought.
Don Pedro May be she doth but counterfeit.
Claudio Faith, like enough.
Leonato O God! counterfeit? There was never counterfeit of passion came so near the life of passion as she discovers it.   (2.3.99–106)

The joke is that the account itself is a counterfeit. Beatrice's love – or at least her admission to it – is the speakers' invention. When, in the progress of the comedy, she does indeed reveal her love for Benedick it must remain a 'counterfeit', an actor's performance (as the succession of male performers in the role were themselves counterfeit women), but it also must, if we are to be properly affected by it, approach 'the life of passion', the real thing. This final phrase of Leonato's requires some further examination, which I take up below.

Warwick's words about playing 'in jest', performing and speaking actions and words which are not entirely committed, or are hypothetical, also seem to debase the value of the currency of acting. 'Jesting' is, like 'counter-feiting', distinct from the real or the true. The little poem attributed to Sir Walter Raleigh, 'What is our life?', rehearses the common analogy between life and theatre (like Jacques's famous set piece of the 'seven ages' in *As You Like It*), but ends with the ironic dividing line between stage performance and human existence: 'Only we die in earnest, that's no jest.' One stage player in his time might die many times, where each individual person does so once only, irreversibly. 'A queen in jest, only to fill the scene' is merely, the bitter Queen Margaret reflects, the outward sign rather than the genuine thing (*Richard III*, 4.4.91), while Hamlet ironically mocks Claudius for taking the reflected image for what it is reflecting. Speaking of the players in *The Murder of Gonzago, or The Mousetrap*, he proclaims 'they do but jest, poison in jest'. How could such formalized actions and speeches be confused with anything in the real world?

The play in *Hamlet* also raises the question of 'passion' and its contem-porary usage.[4] Largely confined these days to refer to the passion connected to erotic desire – although we still speak of being 'passionate' about other things, surfing (in the sea or on the web) or cooking, for example – the word has a long and rich etymology, stemming from a Latin verb meaning to suffer, undergo, or endure: hence the phrase the Passion of Christ, to refer to Jesus' suffering during his arrest, torture, and death. During Shakespeare's lifetime the word could refer to deep or strong feeling of any kind, so that it is of particular interest in the context of stage performance, where convincingly simulated deep feeling is especially impressive, and can arouse sympathetic feeling in an audience. After the actors have arrived in Elsinore, in 2.3 of

Hamlet, the prince asks for a demonstration: 'Come give us a taste of your quality, come, a passionate speech' (2.3.431–2). It turns out that he has a particular recollected speech in mind, about the death of Priam and the grief of Hecuba at the fall of Troy, significantly recalling a murdered king and his widow's lament. Elizabethans might indeed have called Hecuba's reported 'sudden burst of clamour' a 'passion': the word could also refer to an emotionally wrought lament on stage, as it does, ironically, at the close of *A Midsummer Night's Dream*, for example (5.1.315).

The Hecuba speech itself, which Hamlet begins and the leading player takes over, is not only, as Polonius remarks, 'too long', but as a piece of writing is stylistically rather stiff and bombastic; it is usually cut, to some degree, in modern performances of *Hamlet*. As a vehicle for a performer, however, it allows the player to enlist his feelings so that he turns pale 'and has tears in's eyes' (2.2.519–20), deeply impressing at least the chief member of his immediate audience. What the player achieves at the climax of the speech is something resembling what the famous actor, director, and theorist Konstantin Stanislavski nominated 'emotion memory', by which process the performer recalls strongly felt experiences from his or her personal life to inform the performance of a fictional character: so, for a modern performer, Lear's grief at the loss of Cordelia might be coloured by the actor's own feelings to do with the death of someone close to him.[5] Hamlet's phrase for such a phenomenon is 'a dream of passion': once again something that closely resembles reality, a display of emotional reaction which stimulates sympathetic feeling, but which is ultimately insubstantial or illusory. Hamlet particularly is comparing *acted* grief and compassion with his own feelings at the death of his father: he is hardly a disinterested observer of the actor's performance. His soliloquy which follows the end of the actor's speech and the departure of the players is a mixture of gratitude – for the comfort offered by the display of sympathetic grief – and discomfort, at the very facility of acting and at its uncanny ability to be both deeply involving while remaining technically detached.

> O, what a rogue and peasant slave am I!
> Is it not *monstrous* that this player here,
> But in a fiction, in a dream of *passion*,
> Could force his *soul* so to his own *conceit*
> That from her working all his visage wann'd,
> Tears in his eyes, distraction in his aspect,
> A broken voice, an' his whole function suiting
> With forms to his *conceit*? And all for nothing,
> For Hecuba!

What's Hecuba to him, or he to Hecuba,
That he should weep for her? What would he do
Had he the *motive* and the *cue* for *passion*
That I have? He would drown the stage with tears,
And cleave the general ear with horrid speech,
Make mad the guilty, and appall the free,
Confound the ignorant, and amaze indeed
The very faculties of eyes and ears.   (2.2.550–66; my emphases)

The monstrosity of the theatre (see the first emphasis above) would become truly apparent if fictional emotion and real emotion, such as Hamlet's own grief and anger, were to come together, and in the resulting storm of expression the stage would be drowned in a terrible flood of tears destroying the world around it, carrying away both the righteous and the sinful. The allusion to God's condemnation of the world in Noah's flood is not accidental, and it is an implicit reminder of the recurrently invoked moral function of theatre and performance, which Hamlet picks up again in addressing the players about their command performance, two scenes later.

The words I have emphasized in Hamlet's speech all bear on performance, whereas the words of the last quoted line address reception by an audience: it is our faculties of vision and hearing on which an actor works, affecting our perceptions and our associated mental judgements. The sense of the word 'soul' in the fourth line quoted is, we might say, expressive of the full extent of being, as apparent in the individual personality, apprehended through voice, movement, physiognomy, and even characteristic dress. (The 'wickedness' of disguise perceived by Viola in *Twelfth Night* (2.2.27) is precisely that it conceals the soul of the person, in Hamlet's sense.) The soul of an actor is one thing and that of his character another, although for Stanislavski and his school the two must be related. Hamlet's version of what it is the actor does is both strenuous and intellectual: that the soul must be 'forced', rather than coaxed, say, is characteristic of the monstrous or unnatural side of Hamlet's view. Yet that 'conceit', in the modern sense of mental conception, should lead the process marks it as a conscious and humane achievement. Sympathetic imagination concerning what it must have been like to experience the confusion and shocking violence of the destruction of Troy – even if the characters and events were never more than a 'fiction' – invests the actor in the moment of performance, affecting his facial expression, gesture, vocal tone, and rhythm, and producing the 'soul' of the sorrowing Aeneas, whose story he is telling. The actor, were he asked to respond to Hamlet's observations, would be unlikely to concede that what he did was 'all for nothing', unless all acting is for nothing. The art of acting is to provide a physical something, visible, audible, and memorable, to give force and body to what on paper is merely 'a speech'.

Hamlet's choice to enlist performance to reflect on the events of his own life, then, is not without a certain distrust of its effectiveness. Though 'the purpose of playing' may be 'to hold ... the mirror up to nature' (3.2.20–2), we can remember that Hamlet has previously identified the mirrored image as tricksy and insubstantial, which is perhaps why he himself seems to protest too much in instructing the players in what they are to do (3.2.1–45). Generally the 'advice' to the players repeats certain old nostrums about the cultural function of the stage, and boils down to rather platitudinous direction (don't overplay it, but don't underplay it either), although it also recognizes the artistic importance of technique, through which emotional force is shaped so that it engages and moves an audience rather than appalling them or driving them mad, say (even if, we may note, that is precisely what he wants the performance to do in respect of certain members of the Elsinore audience). '[I]n the very torment, tempest, and, as I may say, whirlwind of your passion', Hamlet advises, repeating a crucial word, 'you must acquire and beget a temperance that may give it smoothness' (3.2.5–8). Not, then, so carried away by the force of emotional sympathy that one cannot keep a critical and editorial eye on the likely effect of what one is doing, and remaining detached enough from real jealousy, anger, or grief that one can exercise 'discretion' (3.2.17) in its artistic representation. If there is something monstrous at the heart of acting one must at least avoid monstrosity at the surface level, and if nature is to be copied, then 'the modesty of nature' (3.2.19), precisely its avoidance of extremity and grotesqueness, must remain a chief check on staginess and false exaggeration.

Shakespeare's contemporaries, then, might have talked, as we do, of 'natural' acting, in which technique gives the illusion of disappearing. If one probes the term 'natural', however, particularly in its recurring appearances in discussions of the effect of performance over the course of the last four hundred years, one soon discovers its variability. The 'natural' is in the eye of particular beholders at particular culturally determined moments, and striking new performers with a technique at odds with established conventions – the beginning David Garrick or Edmund Kean – tend to draw the 'natural' epithet to themselves, when successful, condemning older styles to being nominated the artificial, the stale, and the stagey, and having in turn to make way in time for new views of 'the natural'. Particularly from a modern point of view, still somewhat in thrall to the theory of a hundred years ago, we must avoid aligning the 'natural' with the naturalistic, the attempt at an unmediated recreation of the surface of life in performance.

Early modern actors certainly aspired to being lifelike, and the 'life' created by a representation, in the theatre or the other arts, was a measure of approbation. 'Lively' acting, similar to what the player achieves in *Hamlet*, is described by Julia in *The Two Gentlemen of Verona*. In her disguised role as the youth Sebastian she tells Silvia of having played a woman's role, supposedly before Julia herself, 'at Pentecost', and dressed in one of her borrowed gowns. The subject, once again, was a lament from classical mythology appropriate to Julia's own situation, the abandonment of a woman by a faithless male lover:

> ... at that time I made her weep agood,
> For I did play a lamentable part.
> Madam, 'twas Ariadne passioning
> For Theseus' perjury and unjust flight;
> Which I so lively acted with my tears
> That my poor mistress, moved therwithal,
> Wept bitterly ... (4.4.165–71)

Yet one can be like life in many different ways, or can hold the mirror towards nature at various angles, so to speak. No one would have expected, as no one really now expects, the character of John Falstaff to be particularly lifelike in the sense of reflecting a kind of person as commonly experienced in everyday existence. Falstaff is a magnificent exaggeration based firmly enough on common human characteristics of conniving self-interest, but combined with unusual powers of charm and verbal resourcefulness: a kind of monster, in fact. Any convincing performance of the part is likely to persuade an audience that Sir John is drawn from human life but is larger than its everyday confines, in spirit as in body. The actor in the role has precisely to overstep the modesty of nature in that respect. The force of exaggeration and caricature is apparent in many comedies of the period, particularly so in the plays of Jonson, a number of which were first played by Shakespeare and his colleagues.

Returning to Hamlet and his actors, we may notice that 'the modesty of nature' is particularly invoked with reference to a matter central in the art of playing, that of the match between the vocal and visual expressiveness of the performance. The latter aspect Shakespeare's contemporaries frequently summed up in the word 'action', as does Hamlet: 'suit the action to the word, the word to the action, with this special observance, that you o'erstep not the modesty of nature' (3.2.17–19). Action, with its frequently matched alliterative partner, accent (for skill in which Hamlet's performance of the start of the Aeneas speech is commended by Polonius, 2.2.466–7), together form the central terms in whatever we might tentatively call a theory of acting in the Shakespearean period, and the young page Moth is taught both in preparation for a formal address he is to deliver to introduce a masque in *Love's Labour's Lost*: 'Action and accent did they teach him there: / "Thus must thou speak," and "thus thy body bear"' (5.2.99–100). This may reflect actual instruction of contemporary young performers, in schools or in theatres, where the body was regarded as complementary to and in balance with the purely auditory effect of the voice. Heywood, cited in the Introduction, says nothing about this complementarity, perhaps showing the prejudice of his academic background, although skill in 'action' alone, rather than the possession of a particularly 'good tongue', might have been a relative strength in comic performers especially. That said, most of the famous stage fools of the period were renowned for their verbal wit as much as for physical clowning.

In the dumb show, a silent emblematic or explanatory episode within a spoken play, action is all; such a show prefaces the spoken play in *Hamlet*, and during it the player Queen, discovering the body of her poisoned husband, is instructed by the stage direction to make *'passionate action'* (3.2.135 ff.) Quite what this might originally have looked like is hard to say exactly, although we may be drawn to think of heroines in distress in early silent film, and the ludicrous effect such century-old conventions have in the modern eye. The limits, for any actor at any time, are plain: distress and outcry have to be indicated, as in dance, with movement, pose, and expression only: raised arms, contorted facial mask, hands lowered to cover face, and so forth. The subtlety and force of such expressive movement is a challenge to the skill of the individual performer. One of the most celebrated moments in modern acting, after all, was the 'silent scream' produced by Helene Weigel in the role of Mother Courage in Brecht's play named for the character. In *Titus Andronicus* the mutilated Lavinia (like the player Queen, an apprentice part) can no longer speak after act two, so that her action becomes language, which her father determines to translate: 'Speechless complainant, I will learn thy thought; / In thy dumb action I will be as perfect / As begging hermits in their holy prayers' (3.2.39–41).

Once the actors of *The Murder of Gonzago* begin the spoken part of their performance we can observe how hard it is to follow the prince's advice, since there are many words and little obviously required action arising from them. The individual speeches are long, and simultaneously rhetorically elaborate and cumbersome. Very little in the way of 'natural' expression, gesture, and movement is immediately suggested by their rhythm, and what formalized gestures might have marked the speeches, and how elaborate or continuous these may have been, are matters about which we can only speculate, with some guidance from Hamlet's warning to the players not to 'saw the air too much with your hand, thus' – actorish mannerism to disguise a vacuum. Certainly Shakespeare removes the style of the play from that of *Hamlet* itself, composing it in an antiquated, awkward, and repetitive rhymed verse: deliberately achieved bad writing, which he did not usually impose on his fellow actors. The words o'erstep the modesty of language by some distance, so that it is hard to imagine an accompanying language of gesture – action which should be suited to the word – being anything other than rather stiff, formal, and unbending, the style, perhaps, of an older generation of actors who had to cope with texts far more cramped and less gesturally suggestive than Shakespeare's own.

Action was not only produced as the accompaniment to speaking on the stage, but also was a silent indication of reaction, continued organically in playing a scene with one's partners, as the following passage from *King John* makes clear:

> Young Arthur's death is common in their mouths,
> And when they talk of him, they shake their heads,
> And whisper one another in the ear;
> And he that speaks doth gripe the hearer's wrist,
> Whilst he that hears makes fearful action
> With wrinkled brows, with nods, with rolling eyes.
> I saw a smith stand with his hammer, thus,
> The whilst his iron did on his anvil cool,
> With open mouth swallowing a tailor's news ...   (4.2.187–95)

Too many nods and rolling eyes could easily become ludicrous, but the flow of action and reaction, so to speak, was expected as a part of performance; seeing the open-mouthed listener was as important to the audience as hearing the tense tones of the speaker. Action could certainly also include grotesque caricature and parody, as no doubt it often did in the performance of comedy, rather than simply the 'temperate' accompaniment to speech recommended by Hamlet. In *Troilus and Cressida* Ulysses reports on the mocking skits of Patroclus, performed for the benefit of Achilles: 'with ridiculous and awkward action, / Which, slanderer, he imitation calls, / He pageants us' (1.3.149–51).

The term 'action' might primarily indicate bodily movement and gestures with the limbs: Lear might raise his arm, or both arms, and look upwards, or look and reach in invocation to wherever he imagines the goddess Nature to inhabit, when he begins his curse on Goneril, 'Hear, Nature, hear' (*King Lear*, 1.4.275). Individual modern actors might feel such gesture to be something of an overstatement, or cliché, but an audience would not find it unsuited to the word when skilfully performed. Yet 'action' commonly included, I believe, the smaller and more subtle movements of the body, including the inclination and turn of the head, the intensity of the gaze, and the cast of the mouth, in speech or silence. The word 'gesture', which we would freely use for movement of the limbs, particularly, on stage, does not often occur in the Shakespearean vocabulary. It is used significantly in *Othello*, however, and there it refers especially to the varying expressions of the face. Iago is deceiving both Othello and Cassio, the one to believe that he is watching a conversation about Cassio's supposed affair with Desdemona, and the other, innocently, not knowing he is being watched, into laughing at Iago's teasing him about his involvement with Bianca. Iago urges Othello to watch Cassio carefully during the encounter he is about to manage:

> Do but encave yourself
> And mark the fleers, the gibes, and notable scorns
> That dwell in every region of his face,
> For I will make him tell the tale anew:
> Where, how, how oft, how long ago, and when
> He hath, and is again to cope your wife.
> I say, but mark his gesture.   (4.1.81–7)

As Othello retreats and Cassio enters, Iago notes: 'As he shall smile, Othello shall go mad; / And his unbookish jealousy must conster / Poor Cassio's smiles, gestures, and light behaviors / Quite in the wrong' (4.1.100–3). The 'gesture' which follows certainly involves some movement, as Cassio facetiously acts out how Bianca has embraced him, but what Othello principally observes is laughter and smiles on Cassio's part, the last a purely facial 'gesture', or action, and the first a non-verbal vocalization with associated sympathetic movements of face and body.[6] Cassio's laughter is likely, for example, to get increasingly energetic as the little scene progresses, up to Bianca's entry (see 4.1.103–45).

In short, facial expression, the major medium of actors' expressive physical language always, even when fixed within the form of a theatrical mask, was included in the action that was to accompany accent. The face, in fact, is at the centre of the business of suiting action to word, since its movement in speech is in organic relationship with what is being spoken. We watch speech as well as listen to it, and observe its nuances of meaning through the accompanying expressions of the eyes, the tension or relaxation of the lips, and the movement of all the sympathetic facial muscles we might use during the production of vocal sound, as well as punctuating or following it: frowns, raised eyebrows, smiles of all varieties. Othello, concealed at the rear or side of the stage, cannot hear all the speech between Iago and Cassio, but he interprets it through what he sees of it, through the prejudiced lens of Iago's lies. The audience must see what he sees, but see that he is seeing falsely.

It has sometimes been claimed that passages in the plays of Shakespeare's day which describe facial reaction in detail are amplifying what the audience could *not* perceive for themselves: visibility in the theatres, in other words, was not good, and only the larger aspects of 'action' could be read by much of the audience. I find this altogether unlikely as a general rule, the more so after watching daylit performances in the rebuilt Globe on Bankside, London, where actors' facial expressions can be seen quite well at a distance. Some members of the audience can see more than others at any given moment, but any actor wanting to signal a significant facial reaction might easily do so with a turn of the body or head, to take in the whole sweep of the house. Conditions in the artificially lit indoor theatres and playing places of Shakespeare's time are harder to reimagine, and no modern experiments with reconstructions of such places have so far tried very hard to recreate the quality, colour, and luminosity of early modern theatre lighting, provided chiefly by candles. It may be that it would have been harder to see detail on such stages than at the daylit Globe, although the indoor theatres were smaller and more intimate. Their stages also appear to have been lit, as were eighteenth-century theatres, by two suspended candelabra over right and left downstage, and actors may be presumed to have been used to 'finding their light', and assuring that they were in a good position to be seen, especially at important moments. 'Your face, my thane', says Lady Macbeth, 'is as a book, where men / May read strange matters' (*Macbeth*, 1.5.62–3). Richard Burbage, whom we may reasonably guess to have been the first Macbeth, would have wanted audiences to read the strange matters visible in the character's face, and, we may take it, would have given them full opportunity to do so. Testimony from the period also confirms that audiences carefully watched faces, as did the observer of the Oxford performance of *Othello* cited in the Introduction.

The classical oratorical tradition defined by the texts of Quintilian and Cicero, which I will address at more length below, distinguished three aspects of effective live delivery of a speech: *vox*, or voice; *vultus*, face or facial expression; and *vita*, literally life, although 'animation' might be a better translation, suggesting the full force of the various strands of expression working together. The arts of oratory, chiefly connected in classical times to legal pleading and political speeches, took early notice of actors and the stage: Quintilian's work specifically recommends to aspiring orators some careful observation of the theatre. Through classically based school training in oratory, the law courts, the church, and the playhouse remained associated throughout the Renaissance, and the language drawn from oratorical techniques might apply to successful pleading, preaching, or playing. The three 'v's in Latin became the two 'a's, action and accent, the first term in English including, as I have suggested, both *vultus* and *vita*, facial expression and the gesture and movement accompanying it.

'Accent' covered both a clear pronunciation and an appropriate musical modulation of the voice, corresponding to the rhetorical structure, syntax, and emotional colour of the speech. *Vox* could also refer to the manner of speech appropriate to an assumed character, and in *Twelfth Night* Feste makes a joke of it, reading out Malvolio's letter to Olivia in a crazy rhythm and pitch. When challenged, he replies (since Malvolio has been treated as being deranged): 'I do but read madness. And your ladyship will have it as it ought to be, you must allow *vox'* (5.1.294–6). The prominence Thomas Heywood gives to the voice as the chief qualification of a good actor is indicative of the high place of vocal skill in the theatre of the period, and his equal stress on 'a good conceit' returns us to the language of Hamlet. The musicality of the voice should be governed by conscious intelligence in controlling its effects artistically. The 'conceit' of the player in *Hamlet*, controlling the 'soul' of Aeneas' retelling of Troy's destruction, produces, Hamlet notices, 'a broken voice': the vowels caught by the contraction of the throat, an effect of sympathetic emotional distress.

Individual vocal characteristics of tone, pitch, and colour would have differentiated the 'good tongues' of the members of an acting troupe, matching their differing faces and physiques. The chief vocal distinction in a troupe like Shakespeare's or Alleyn's would have been between on the one hand the bass, baritone, and tenor ranges of the men, the predominant group, of ten to twelve individuals, and on the other the treble voices of the three or four boys required to play female roles: few plays required more than that number to play principal women. Puberty, Hamlet suggests, would have spelt the end of the useful career of the boy player; speaking to the boy of the travelling troupe, who has grown taller since his last visit to court (and who subsequently plays Gonzago's queen), he says: 'Pray God your voice, like a piece of uncurrent gold, be not crack'd within the ring.' The 'cracking' of an adolescent voice would also spell the end of his commercial usefulness to the troupe: he could no longer attract gold as the accomplished and attractive performer of such a part as Juliet, say, and a younger substitute would take his roles, as still happens in choral groups. Yet not every career in female impersonation on the English Renaissance stage ended with the change of voice. Not a few younger actors continued to play female parts until their late teens or early twenties.[7] If male puberty arrived a little later in the sixteenth and seventeenth centuries than it does today, one cannot plausibly stretch the average age much beyond a year or two later. In the fourth century BC Aristotle thought that puberty for boys arrived at fourteen,[8] while the Old Shepherd in *The Winter's Tale* dates the start of unruliness in male youth, the beginning of such trouble as 'getting wenches with child', at ten (see 3.3.59–63).

Logically, then, some 'female' voices on stage in Shakespeare's theatre were not unbroken trebles, but lighter adult male voices, perhaps trained to attain, or retain, higher registers. The individual vocal and accompanying physical characteristics would have had to be suitable to allow such a lengthened career in female roles – boys who turned into husky giants would have been found other roles or theatre jobs while they were still attached to the company by agreement. Yet perhaps more roles than we have thought, and more of the senior, demanding female roles, were played by male actors in their later rather than early teens, with considerable stage experience, with stronger if tonally light voices, and with more breath power than mere 'boys'. Cleopatra mocks her likely enactment by a boy performer as a 'squeaking' Cleopatra, with a constricted and insufficiently powered voice (*Antony and Cleopatra*, 5.2.219–21). The performer speaking this can hardly himself have been squeaking, and the part as a whole, like a good number of Shakespeare's female roles, calls for a full and commanding voice, as well as a good deal of time on the stage. Aristotle is particularly interesting, in the light of cracking and squeaking, on the change in the male voice which arrives with puberty: 'At about this same time [fourteen] firstly the voice begins to change, becoming rougher and more uneven, no longer high-pitched but not yet deep, nor all of one pitch, but sounding like ill-strung and rough lyre strings: what they call "goat-voice".' But bleating Cleopatras might have learnt to control their changing voices, as Aristotle goes on to suggest: 'if they help to check it through exercises, as some do who are engaged in the choruses, the voice remains the same for a long time and the change that it undergoes is altogether slight'.[9]

Training connected with the theatre in classical Greece, to retain higher vocal tones within a chorus, prolonged a performer's career in that range beyond the onset of adult manhood. Some performers' careers in the theatre of Shakespeare's day suggest that similar training of a 'female' voice was adopted in appropriate cases, and that the experienced and skilled players of female parts – in some troupes at some times – were not exactly boys, but rather youths and young men, with correspondingly larger physiques and breath power: they could produce a more sustained stage voice than the average twelve-year-old performer. Physique, voice apart, must partly have determined which boys, beginning as actors before puberty, followed such a path. The growth of taller, heavier bodies and large facial features would have disqualified some adolescent players from continuing as convincing stage women; hair colour and complexion may also have figured. Francis Flute, cast as Thisby in the play staged within *A Midsummer Night's Dream*, pleads 'Let me not play a woman; I have a beard coming' (1.2.47–8). His name suggests that he has been so cast because of his lighter voice (where Bottom is a *basso*), while his beard, such as it may be, might have been shaved. Even after shaving, however, dark beards are more visible than light ones, and the conventional 'fairness' of the female face in the stock con-temporary language of erotic praise, both employed and mocked in stage comedy, cannot have been entirely ignored in matching performer to part. Francis Flute is reassured that he may play the heroine 'in a mask', but such a solution is unlikely to have been employed on the professional stage.

Flute's ebullient partner in performance, Nick Bottom, would be willing to take on both roles, if he could divide himself, exercising a peculiar variation of *vox*: 'And I may hide my face, let me play Thisby too. I'll speak in a monstrous little voice, "Thisne! Thisne!"' (1.2.51–3). The dem-onstration, in a strangled falsetto, of a squeaking Thisby is produced by the adult male 'head voice', but there is no evidence to suggest that senior actors in the contemporary professional theatre used even well-trained versions of such a voice to take on female roles, which remained the first responsibility of their younger colleagues. Bottom, the enthusiastic amateur, wants to leap over the established conventions of representation. It is of some interest that he uses Hamlet's word 'monstrous' to describe his technique, but in *A Midsummer Night's Dream* the theatre – at least the theatre of *Pyramus and Thisbe* – is grotesquely coarse rather than marvellous and uncanny, and Bottom remains an ass in both the roles he plays.

Action and accent were expected to be complementary and mutually supportive: all the parts of expression worked together in communicating character, thought, and emotion. The varying physical aspects of dramatic expressiveness might be categorized in several ways. At the beginning of *The Taming of the Shrew*, for example, the unnamed Lord contemplates the likely success of his boy, Bartholomew, who is to impersonate the 'noble' wife in the trick to be played on the drunken Christopher Sly:

'I know the boy will well usurp the grace, / Voice, gait, and action of a gentlewoman' (Induction, 1.131–2). The separation of 'gait' from 'action' seems to create subcategories, not exactly of what physiologists would call gross and fine motor movements, but certainly movement of the whole body, in walking, from that of parts of it. The more indefinable 'grace' suggests something similar to Hamlet's 'soul', emanating from an inner apprehension of what it is like to be a gentlewoman: the spirit of the role, which will govern voice, gait, and action. The verb 'usurp' slips back into the pejorative vocabulary about performance and the deceiving nature of theatre, which takes over what is real or true by trickery, or indeed by treason. The same verb is used by Olivia in *Twelfth Night*, in an exchange where both the principal characters are disguised:

Viola Good gentle one, give me modest assurance if you be the lady of the house, that I may proceed in my speech.
Olivia Are you a comedian?
Viola No, my profound heart; and yet (by the very fangs of malice I swear) I am not that I play. Are you the lady of the house?
Olivia If I do not usurp myself, I am.   (1.5.179–86)

In this riddling exchange about true identity, a theme which permeates the play, we are reminded of the circumstances of theatre. Viola, or the performer of Viola, is indeed 'a comedian', in the French sense (*comédien* = actor), as well as being the performer of the youth Cesario ('that [person, understood] I play'). The work of the actor is to 'usurp' someone else beyond himself. Actors may have preferred another, more positive word, but their work was and is to enter into another kind of being while on stage, remaining conscious of doing so. Olivia's final line quoted above, spoken in character, suggests that even while she jokes she may not be entirely certain of her genuine self.

   She remains an observant audience for Viola's performance as Cesario in the ensuing scene, however, and after 'he' has left records how she has read the character, speech, and behaviour of the new arrival, remembering his words: '"I am a gentleman." I'll be sworn thou art; / Thy tongue, thy face, thy limbs, actions, and spirit / Do give thee fivefold blazon' (1.5.291–3). A blazon is the sign of noble identity displayed on a shield or banner: a proud outward proclamation of the bearer's honour. Cesario's heraldic devices, as it were, are the languages of stage oratory: action (or 'actions') and accent; or *vox* ('thy tongue'), *vultus* ('thy face'), and *vita* ('actions, and spirit'). The words once again describe subdivided categories: 'limbs' and 'actions' are distinct, although the admiration of 'face' and 'limbs' are also those of an erotically engaged eye. Once again, moreover, the tangible, sensory signs, those of the body and the sound and movement it produces, are accompanied by the more ethereal 'spirit', like Hamlet's term 'soul' and the Lord's 'grace', the informing and unifying inner being which brings the parts into a whole. (We might note that, evidently, all three words are central terms of religious discourse.) One of the paradoxes of acting is that one must produce the outer signs which correspond with the 'spirit' of the character, yet without somehow apprehending that spirit and taking it imaginatively within oneself voice, facial expressions, and movements will remain unconvincing, stagey, and 'usurped' in its most negative sense, like the outsized regal robes on the 'dwarfish thief' in *Macbeth*. Actors must work on both the interior and exterior of their roles: the two are co-dependent.

What Iago calls 'outward action', distinct from what is within, 'the native act and figure of my heart' (*Othello*, 1.1.61–5), might be felt to be in a problematic relationship, at least within the fictional world of the play. Iago, a committed deceiver, proclaims 'I am not what I am', but his identity is clearly defined by the play of *Othello* itself, and the job of the actor playing the role is to impress his slippery, devilish ingenuity on the audience with all the force and subtlety he can. The deceiver, a common figure in drama generally, is a performer of roles, and the insidious charm of the stage villain undoubtedly has something to do with the pejorative vocabulary associated with acting and performance in Shakespeare's England. The successful actor is to be distrusted as a creator of persuasive fictions. More immediately, outward action not entirely corresponding with sincere feeling and thought might taint the integrity of inner being. Coriolanus, urged by his mother to renew his interrupted petition for the consulship, is advised tactically to kneel and speak softly to the people: 'for in such business / Action is eloquence, and the eyes of th' ignorant / More learned than the ears' (*Coriolanus*, 3.2.75–7). Coriolanus, committed to a fierce integrity, struggles with the expediency of political campaigning, and its own kinds of perform-ance: 'I will not do't, / Lest I surcease to honor mine own truth / And let my body's action teach my mind / A most inherent baseness' (3.2.120–3). A certain strain of criticism of acting and the theatre in Shakespeare's time, we might say, moves outward from this personal moral distrust of insincere action into an unsophisticated opposition to pretence of any kind, however framed by the conventions of art and its reception.

Our usual word for what actors do is acting; the commoner term in Shakespeare's time was playing, particularly when, we have seen, it was regarded as a professional art. Yet both words were used for performing a fictional role, and Hamlet, mocking the verbose and pedantic Polonius, adds a third term, an elaborated version of the first:

Hamlet My lord, you play'd once i' th' university, you say?
Polonius That did I, my lord, and was accounted a good actor.
Hamlet What did you enact?
Polonius I did enact Julius Caesar. I was kill'd i' th' Capitol; Brutus kill'd me.

(*Hamlet*, 3.2.98–104)

Polonius might indeed have played Caesar in Latin, a university tradition I will examine at more length below. Learning Greek was a rarer accomplishment, and the Greek term *mimesis* in reference to stage playing was not widely known, but its English equivalent, imitation (and its derivatives), the copying of life, was relatively common. Ulysses, quoted above, scorns Patroclus' claim for the broad satirical sketches he puts on to be 'imitation' (*Troilus and Cressida*, 1.3.150), while Hamlet dismisses the bad actors he has seen in the past because 'they imitated humanity so abominably' (*Hamlet*, 3.2.34–5). King Henry V, urging his men into battle, suggests a very theatrical preparation for the rigours of combat, so that Burbage, we might again fairly guess, simultaneously urged his fellows into suitable stage performance in early productions of the play:[10]

> In peace there's nothing so becomes a man
> As modest stillness and humility;
> But when the blast of war blows in our ears,
> Then imitate the action of the tiger;
> Stiffen the sinews, summon up the blood,
> Disguise fair nature with hard-favor'd rage;
> Then lend the eye a terrible aspect;
> Let it pry through the portage of the head
> Like the brass cannon; let the brow o'erwhelm it
> As fearfully as doth a galled rock
> O'erhang and jutty his confounded base
> Swill'd with the wide and wasteful ocean.
> Now set the teeth and stretch the nostril wide,
> Hold hard the breath, and bend up every spirit
> To his full height.   (*Henry V*, 3.1.3–17)

The 'action of the tiger', imitated in muscular tension, facial mask, and breath rhythm, is once again inspired, we note, by 'spirit', while 'fair nature' and 'modest stillness' sound more like the temperance Hamlet advocates. Action, Henry points out, should be suited not only to word but to the exigencies of situation and the challenges of circumstance: nature also includes tigers.

The performance of a role is a representation, but Elizabethans were more likely to speak of 'presenting' a part on stage, using a shorter form of the longer word, which also carries with it some sense of bringing into being, or into the current living moment and 'presence'. Ariel, speaking to Prospero after the masque, says that he 'presented Ceres' in the show (*The Tempest*, 4.1.167–8), while Prospero, about to re-enter his old life and former role, resolves to resume his old appearance as Duke: 'I will discase me, and myself present / As I was sometime Milan' (5.1.85–6). In Shakespeare, at least, 'presentation' is a concern in the awkward shows put on in the comedies *A Midsummer Night's Dream* and *Love's Labour's Lost*, and hence subject to some parody as a rather naïve term; the actors in those entertainments seem to assume that making somebody or something present in however clumsy a fashion were enough to fulfil the aesthetic contract of a live performance. In *Love's Labour's Lost*, for example, a parade of famous and mythical characters, well-known at the time of the play's first performances from representations in tapestries, paintings, and prints, are brought before the assembled court to the accompaniment of awkward verses, some not even spoken by the represented figure; Holofernes the schoolmaster explicates the show of the boy, Moth, wrestling an inert theatrical snake: 'Great Hercules is presented by this imp, / Whose club killed Cerberus, that three-headed *canus*; / And when he was a babe, a child, a shrimp, / Thus did he strangle serpents in his *manus*' (5.2.588–91). Such a presentation is declarative rather than imitative: it relies on explication or familiarity to give it meaning, and calls on an audience's indulgence to fill in its gaps as persuasive communication. The indicative force of presentation by the player is such that it can, at least to certain minds, extend beyond human or humanized character to take in other deictic elements of a stage performance. The workmen actors in *A Midsummer Night's Dream* collectively decide that the fiction of their play requires the physicalized presence both of moonlight and of the wall separating Pyramus and Thisby, and that the only satisfactory way of accomplishing this is to have both 'presented' by actors: 'This man, with lime and rough-cast doth present / Wall, that vile Wall, which did these lovers sunder; . . . This man with lantern, dog, and bush of thorn, / Presenteth Moonshine; for if you will know, / By moonshine did these lovers think no scorn / To meet at Ninus' tomb, there, there to woo' (5.1.131–8). What action poor Snout, the wall impersonator, can suit to his stiff verses is a problematic matter, and the actor in performance is often hung about with a ludicrous and cumbersome costume provided by the ingenuity of the design department. The rigidity of mere 'presentation' is mocked by Shakespeare in Wall's moments on stage.

While the watching Hippolyta finds the performance 'the silliest stuff that ever I heard', Theseus replies that 'The best in this kind are but shadows; and the worst are no worse, if imagination amend them' (5.1.210–12). While Hippolyta sensibly replies that the audience should not have to be doing all the imaginative work in the contractual agreement of theatre, Theseus' word for the actors, 'shadows', introduces a term which is both metaphorical and analogical. *A Midsummer Night's Dream* is a play of shadows – Oberon, for example, is called 'the king of shadows', those of the wood in moonlight, by Puck (3.2.437) – as it is a play of dreaming: the shadows are the visions of dreams and magic flowers, while remaining, in the physical theatre where they are played, the pictures produced by actors on the stage. The dream of the play's title is in an important sense the collaborative dream of one's hours in the theatre, and Puck reminds us at the end that we have to wake up and go home:

> If we shadows have offended,
> Think but this, and all is mended,
> That you have but slumber'd here
> While these visions did appear.
> And this weak and idle theme,
> No more yielding but a dream,
> Gentles, do not reprehend.   (5.1.423–9)

Actors, then, *are* shadows: what they do is proverbially evanescent and insubstantial, leaving only memories and a few photographs behind, at least when their performances are in the theatre and not on film or video. Macbeth, wearily contemplating the fleeting quality of existence, brings together the shadow and the actor: 'Life's but a walking shadow, a poor player, / That struts and frets his hour upon the stage, / And then is heard no more' (*Macbeth*, 5.5.24–6). The word 'shadow', however, was also a verb in the sixteenth century, meaning to sketch, to draw, or even to reflect: to create a graphic representation. A shadow, like a counterfeit, can mean a painting or portrait: the pictures of old Hamlet and Claudius with which Hamlet confronts his mother are the 'counterfeit presentment of two brothers' (*Hamlet*, 3.4.54), a phrase which uses words that might equally be applied to a stage performance. Analogically, actors 'shadow' nature itself, portraying character and behaviour, as we still say, using another graphic analogue. The disguised Julia in *The Two Gentlemen of Verona*, contemplating the portrait she has been given by Silvia to convey to Proteus, Julia's faithless lover, has these lines:

> Come, shadow, come, and take this shadow up,
> For 'tis thy rival. O thou senseless form,
> Thou shall be worshipp'd, kiss'd, lov'd, and ador'd;

And were there sense in his idolatry,
My substance should be statue in thy stead.   (4.4.197–201)

Both the portrait of Silvia and Julia herself, disguised as she is as the boy
Sebastian, are shadows, or representations; comparing the ironic distance
between shadow and substance, the show and the real thing, she wishes
herself into the position of another shadow, the statue of herself, so then
Proteus' futile worship of shadows ('idolatry') might make at least some
kind of sense. The complexity of this oscillation between the real and the
unreal, and the substitution of the one for the other, is once again given
further range by the audience's perception that it is an actor who speaks, in
two roles: four shadows are each laid over the other, as it were (Actor–Julia–
Sebastian–Julia Statue).

A different kind of dialogue between the real and the unreal is put on the
stage in Shakespeare's *Richard II*, when the deposed King calls for a mirror
so that he may, literally, hold it up to nature and contemplate his careworn
face, as an actor might before going on stage, checking that the outward sign
is matching the inner state.[11] He examines himself with dissatisfaction and
then smashes the glass on the floor, turning to his adversary and successor:

King Richard Mark, silent king, the moral of this sport,
  How soon my sorrow hath destroyed my face.
Bullingbrook The shadow of your sorrow hath destroy'd
  The shadow of your face.
King Richard Say that again.
  The shadow of my sorrow! Ha, let's see.
  'Tis very true, my grief lies all within,
  And these external manners of laments
  Are merely shadows to the unseen grief
  That swells with silence in the tortur'd soul.
  There lies the substance ...   (4.1.290–9)

Richard's smashing of the glass is a deliberately histrionic act, a 'sport', with
a moral, and as such merely an insubstantial gesture, Bullingbrook suggests:
only the reflection of a face has been destroyed. Richard turns this remark
back on itself by observing that outward appearance, or the actor's action,
can never be more than a shadow in comparison to the substance of inner
feeling contained in the soul, though the soul itself is paradoxically silent
and insubstantial without its reflection in the 'shadow' of speech, cries,
facial expression, and movement. Only through embodiment can the actor
express inner thought and feeling.

The language of the graphic arts was commonly transferred to the art of
playing, particularly so in the case of the renowned Burbage, since he was

known also to be a painter; what is thought to be a surviving portrait of him in the collection of the Dulwich Picture Gallery (from a collection originally assembled by the actor William Cartwright) has sometimes been called a self-portrait.[12] The painter-player Burbage therefore summed up the overlap between the two modes of visual representation, and in an elegy written after his death in 1619, which employs much of the terminology discussed in this chapter, the author begins with this trope: 'Some skillful limner help me, if not so / Some sad tragedian help t'express my woe. / But, oh! he's gone that could both best; both limn / And act my grief.'[13] 'Limning' is another contemporary word for sketching or drawing (specifically the fine drawing used for preparing miniature portraits and medals); the actor's playing is both like and unlike a picture, unlike in that it moves and changes. Its skill, like that of a picture, is to convince the viewer of the validity of its illusion. As Edgar's 'counterfeiting' is challenged by a sympathy inappropriate to his assumed character of a mad beggar, so his grief at the appearance of his mutilated father disrupts his ability to maintain the correct action and accent. 'Poor Tom's a-cold', he repeats, reverting to one of his stock phrases, 'I cannot daub it further' (*King Lear*, 4.1.52). What has been a striking and alarming portrait of mental disturbance and physical wildness has sunk to a 'daub', a crude and coarse piece of representational art. The actor's own feelings, inappropriate to the role at hand, have intruded into the conceptual realm of playing, blurring intention and choice, and affecting outer expression in speech and movement.

The parallel between acting and painting is explored in one of the added scenes made for the famous older play *The Spanish Tragedy* at some time before 1602. The grief-crazed Hieronimo entertains the petition of a painter, whose skills he wants to employ in memorializing his former happiness and present misery:

Hieronimo I'd have you paint me in my gallery, in your oil colours matted, and draw me five years younger than I am … My wife Isabella standing by me, with a speaking look to my son Horatio, which should intend to this or some like purpose: 'God bless thee, my sweet son': and my hand leaning upon his head, thus, sir, do you see? May it be done?
Painter Very well, sir.
Hieronimo Nay, I pray mark me sir. Then sir, would I have you paint me this tree, this very tree. Canst paint a doleful cry?
Painter Seemingly, sir.
Hieronimo Nay, it should cry: but all is one.[14]

Looks, in pictures as in the theatre, may 'speak', but only live performance can produce the actual 'doleful cry' that Hieronimo wants his tableau to utter; the painter can merely suggest it 'seemingly'. The 'seeming' involved in painting renders it another suspect word in sixteenth- and seventeenth-century usage. Painting can deceive the viewer: an early observer of the Swan playhouse in 1596 noted that the stage pillars, a prominent feature of the accompanying drawing, although actually made of wood were painted in faux marbling so skilfully that they appeared to be of grand and expensively finished stonework.[15] The French term *trompe l'oeil* expressly spells out the intention of such technique. Another form of painting, in contemporary usage, was theatrical or personal make-up, used to decorate the face with colours and consistencies it did not naturally possess, and hence suspected by literal-minded moralists. Hamlet, affecting such a stance, berates Ophelia for the 'paintings' of womankind (*Hamlet*, 3.1.142); earlier in the same scene a revealing aside by King Claudius makes clear the sinful aspects of painting, literally and metaphorically (while also making plain to the audience that he is indeed a 'villain'): 'The harlot's cheek, beautied with plast'ring art, / Is not more ugly to the thing that helps it / Than is my deed to my most painted word' (3.1.50–2). Words with a fair outside, such as Claudius utters in concealing his guilt as a fratricidal murderer and usurper, are produced performatively, like Iago's in *Othello*, and as words may be painted so may actions. In further painted words Claudius encourages Laertes' revenge against Hamlet for the killing of Polonius, by goading him to prove that his appearance of outrage is matched by the inner spirit informing it: 'Laertes, was your father dear to you? / Or are you like the painting of a sorrow, / A face without a heart?' (4.7.107–9). It is doubtful whether a convincing portrait of sorrow, either painted or enacted, could indeed be 'without a heart', an inspiration supporting its outward form; rather Claudius' rhetoric once again suggests the potentially misleading or deceptive character of mere appearance, and the need to test it, matters which are at the heart of the entire play of *Hamlet*. English Renaissance artists who dealt in representations of nature, then (as those who practised the arts of music largely did not), had to contend with a moralistic opposition to pretence which all too easily muddied the spring of humane critical response to, particularly, the kinds of pretending involved in stage acting.

Apart from metaphorical language, Shakespeare brings the representational arts together most strikingly in the final scene of *The Winter's Tale*, in which an actor must become a statue, a memorial image of the Queen Hermione, presumed to be dead not only by most of the characters on stage but also by the audience; it is one of the rare moments in Shakespeare's plays where the listeners and observers in the theatre audience are not made aware beforehand of the ironic sense of the scene, and the result is a true *coup de théâtre*. The actor in the role, then, had to convince the first audiences that he might indeed be inert and carved from stone, at least as the scene begins; his action, paradoxically, is absolute unmoving inaction, to match his silence. Since the part of Hermione during the opening scenes of the play requires strong and compelling speech and physical presence, played, notably, in a costume that emphasizes the unmistakably womanly shape of the final stage of pregnancy, we can assume that it would have been taken by the senior boy or younger apprentice within the King's men at any time the play was performed between 1611 and the early 1640s: the statue was acted by an experienced and valued player, and the grace of its appearance, the focus of the spoken dialogue for much of the scene, is of a piece with Hermione's bearing and gesture at the start of the play, while the face, body, and dress of the actor recall a figure long absent, in the time of performance, from the audience's view.

The statue, like many of the actual funeral statues in Shakespeare's time, has been painted with colours to render it more lifelike, and must not be touched because it is still wet. It looks so much like the life that its eyes almost seem to have motion, and its mouth to breathe, but until it actually moves, as at Paulina's invitation it does, its distance from real life is cruelly apparent. The imitation of life that sculpture, painting, and playing attempt is superbly achieved, while its limitation is criticized. Once the player of Hermione is freed to move and speak, the superiority of playing over the other arts is triumphantly demonstrated, and its magical nature celebrated: 'Strike all that look upon with marvel', the actor of Paulina commands his colleague, notably including the audience. 'Start not; her actions shall be holy, as / You hear my spell is lawful' (*The Winter's Tale*, 5.3.100–5). These lines contain reassurance about the 'lawful' nature of stage enactment, even as the reviving image moves and amazes us. Like the artist Pygmalion, whose myth this scene recalls, the player is enabled to give present, breathing life to the images he creates.

Such moments as the closing of *The Winter's Tale* in Shakespeare's time could not occur anywhere but in live performance, through the intricate and deliberate speech and action of skilled actors in the presence of an attentive and expectant audience. These days film and television may take their own approaches to conveying the rich sense of the scene, although we may think it is truly designed for the concurrent living presence of performers and audience, and for the particular shared excitements of such experience. Reading Shakespeare's plays, and other drama of the period, has its own pleasures and excitements, commended by a pair of actors in the preface to the first collected edition of Shakespeare in 1623. One may also 'speak the speech', reciting the text aloud, with due attention to 'good accent and good discretion', as Hamlet does with the passage he has evidently learnt and remembered, about Pyrrhus and Priam at the fall of Troy. Once the player takes over, however, the effect of the rhetorical verses of recalled horror changes, the body and face of the speaker become a map of emotion, and the rather stiff text a newly flexible register of lament at human suffering. Only when the actors 'do it in action' does the drama yield its full force of meaning (although the quoted phrase comes from *A Midsummer Night's Dream*, 3.1.5–6, where the players are as wooden as their text, and grief remains at a hilarious distance).

Conventional sixteenth-century defences of the literary arts, under which written drama was subsumed, being a branch of poetry, in the Aristotelian tradition, claimed that they provided pleasant recreation and imaginative engagement while having a serious moral function. The theatre in particular lay open to charges that it was frivolous ('No more yielding but a dream') and, at worst, devilish, trading in the arts of deceit, a corrupting example to impressionable minds. The refutation of such charges was summed up in the Latin tag which Inigo Jones had inscribed over the stage of the theatre he built at the court of King Charles I in 1629: 'Prodesse et Delectari', to do good and to delight.[16] Both Hamlet and Thomas Heywood are equally insistent about the moral purpose of the stories told in the theatre, and of the manner of their telling, which impresses itself vividly on the imagination and memory of audiences. Plays catch the conscience, and players are 'the abstract and brief chronicles of the time', a condensed epitome of culture and outlook, while serving as reflective critics of both. Comedies, hardly designed to catch the conscience, still 'sport with human follies', as Ben Jonson put it,[17] allowing some ironic self-reflection on the part of audiences, as well, crucially, as providing health-giving and therapeutic laughter, enjoyed communally within the large group of a playhouse audience. 'Hey ho, 'tis nought but mirth / That keeps the body from the earth' the actors sing together at the close of Francis Beaumont's hilarious theatre comedy *The Knight of the Burning Pestle*. Humane enjoyment of the positive energy of life was one pleasure of the Shakespearean theatre.

What the player provides for Hamlet is a very different kind of delight from that the first audiences found in the speech and appearance of Sir John Falstaff, but we should remember that the same players took part in a very wide range of repertory; powerful tragic performance also generates a response which we can only call pleasurable, if in a differing register and degree. Burbage, as I have pointed out above, would have taken leading roles in the comedies Ben Jonson wrote for Shakespeare's company between the late 1590s and 1610 – *Every Man In His Humour, Every Man Out of His Humour, Volpone,* and *The Alchemist* – while concurrently performing in the major tragedies Shakespeare himself wrote over the same period, as well as, say, in *Twelfth Night,* in 1601 and thereafter. When we imagine Burbage's playing as Hamlet, Lear, or Macbeth, we should also think of him, say, as Malvolio, adapting his physique, face, and voice to the frosty confines of that role, a kind of parody of tragic solemnity. In the period following Shakespeare's retirement and death, later members of the King's men displayed similar range; John Lowin, for example, played the parts both of Falstaff in the histories and comedy in which he features and of Bosola, the sinister and ironic servant of the evil brothers in Webster's tragedy *The Duchess of Malfi.* Most players would have been expected to have a range of performing styles, and the 'Protean' qualities praised in Alleyn and Burbage no doubt also gave audiences pleasure when, as frequently happened, one actor played distinct roles in the same play. Virtuosity must have been encouraged, and looked for in young actors and other new recruits to the playing company's complement.

By the time the playhouses were closed by Parliamentary decree at the beginning of the civil wars in England in September 1642, the art of stage playing had been a central part of civic life in London for many years, and older actors like Lowin possessed long and rich experience of performance in front of many audiences. The old trouper Richard Baxter, in his early seventies by the 1660s, testified that he had been 'an actor in stage plays for above fifty years',[18] a career which, like Lowin's, included some unauthorized playing in the later 1640s, and had seen him act on the stages of the Red Bull, Globe, and Blackfriars playhouses. Although the gap of almost twenty years in sanctioned professional playing in England certainly broke some of the old continuities, a significant number of the people who had been young or trainee actors in the late 1630s and early 1640s were subsequently to emerge as leading players in the early Restoration theatre, in 1660 and the years following. The traditions they may have carried with them are the subject of the succeeding chapters.

CHAPTER 2

Playing and education

Is't not a fine sight, to see all our children made interluders? Do we pay
our money for this? We send them to learn their grammar, and their
Terence, and they learn their play-books?
                    Ben Jonson, *The Staple of News*, Third Intermean, lines 42–4[1]

Before the days of universal compulsory education, a fairly recent phenomenon in Western societies, a minority among European national populations was literate, and in England in Shakespeare's and Jonson's time only a
small proportion of those male children who were taught first to recognize
letters, then more complex reading and to write, went on to the rigorous
process of 'learning their grammar', in Latin, beginning at around the age
of eight, and continuing for about eight years. Following the completion
of grammar school an even smaller percentage of adolescent young men
might then attend one of the two universities for several years, many of
them leaving without taking a degree, the last path followed by Thomas
Heywood, Thomas Middleton, and perhaps also Ben Jonson.[2] Other
dramatists – Christopher Marlowe, Robert Greene, John Lyly, George
Peele, and John Fletcher, to take fairly eminent names – held Oxford and
Cambridge degrees, while Francis Beaumont studied at Gray's Inn, one of
the inns of court, collegiate communities of lawyers and law students in
London which collectively have been called England's third university of the
period, and which, incidentally, provided a significant source of patronage
for the commercial theatre of the city.

What the grammar schools and the universities taught had nothing
directly to do with the arts of drama and theatre, and actors whose sons
were destined to follow them in stage careers would not have put their boys
to school any longer than did fathers in trade occupations, who planned to
place their sons in apprenticeships at around the age of fourteen. (Had
Hamnet Shakespeare survived his boyhood, his father may have had more
ambitious plans for him than such a career.) By the age of fourteen most
boys who had followed the path laid down by contemporary educational

theorists would have learnt to read and write in English, to understand enough mathematics to 'cast accounts' (to do bookkeeping), and to read and translate simpler Latin, probably reading some of Terence's Latin plays, or dialogues based on them, along the way. William Shakespeare would seem to have got thus far along the educational track, and probably rather further. The legend that he had been a schoolmaster in the country before reaching London, which is entirely possible, would mean that he had mastered enough Latin to be able to teach it to others in the early grades of school, and that within a school of any consequence he would have been an usher, or under-master, rather than master in charge. His plays, at any rate, demonstrate that he was familiar enough with the common school textbooks of the day.

Latin, then, was the chief language of formal education of any but the youngest children in the sixteenth and seventeenth centuries, and the mastery of Latin was the mark of being 'lettered': mastery meant not only to be able to translate accurately in both directions between English and Latin, to read and understand classical Latin fluently and readily, but also to be able to write compositions in imitation of its various styles, and indeed to speak it, spontaneously, and with some rhetorical brio. Even in grammar schools conversation in English was officially banned during school hours. Shakespeare's theatre, committed to the energetic exploration of the powers of the vernacular language, and economically dependent on a widespread popular appeal, could not be further from the hermetic world of contemporary formal education. One could add that the success of the English-language drama of the day, eventually enshrined as published literature, contributed to the eventual collapse of classically based pedagogy.

Conceding the remoteness of the medium of education from most people's lives and language, sixteenth-century pedagogical principles were far from inert and rigid. The humanist project of the Dutch scholar Erasmus and his colleagues and followers was to re-establish a proper understanding of the classical languages, including Greek, in order to study the entire field of learning in a historical context. The classical works of philosophy, science, mathematics, history, oratory, and law, particularly, were regarded as the principal basis for any modern exercise of those disciplines; literature was studied primarily as a model of rhetoric. Religious reformers included the study of the original biblical languages, principally Greek and Hebrew, to inculcate informed knowledge of Scripture, and the more ambitious Elizabethan grammar schools taught their pupils at least some Greek and Hebrew, in addition to a great deal of Latin, before they began at university. Those who could withstand the rigours of the system, and had the patience to endure a good deal of tedious repetition, as not all could, emerged with at least the raw material to supply considerable comparative linguistic and critical skills. The intelligent and serious-minded boy John Milton thrived, although in later life he was critical of the narrow pedantry the system encouraged at its worst, and in the tract *Of Education* (1644) pointed out the failings within the Latin-centred system as it had developed during the preceding century and a half, and proposed a new model; other contemporaries favoured yet more native-language instruction in the earlier years of schooling.[3]

The connection between the performative arts of the stage and the select and remote realm of contemporary formal education lay in the respect for oratory that was a central part of the pedagogical project. To be able to recite Latin prose and verse aloud was a widely recognized mark of schoolboys' success in their studies, and such recitations frequently figured in the formal visits of monarchs and other notables to the city of London, and to other towns and cities. Senior schoolboys and university students were expected to acquire the ability to debate formal questions – of philosophy, or history, for example – in Latin, and such 'exercises' were also offered as public demonstrations of educational attainments: both Queen Elizabeth and King James were themselves sufficiently educated (by tutors) to follow the arguments, when they were presented with such events on visits to Oxford and Cambridge. The acquisition of proper pronunciation, clarity of enunciation, vocal emphasis and control, respect for rhythm and pitch, and the accompanying 'action' of facial expression and bodily stance and gesture, then, were all regarded as appropriate educational attainments in the mastering of oratory, as laid down by the two principal Latin authors studied in this area, Cicero and Quintilian. It is hardly surprising, therefore, that 'exercises' were not infrequently extended to include drama, in the performance of which schoolboys and students confronted the matching of word to action on the same basic terms as did the players.

In what follows I examine the place of performance within the contemporary schools, universities, and inns of court, with some separate attention to the rather special conditions of the two choral establishments in London which gave rise to something far nearer to commercial theatre than merely occasional demonstrations of scholarly achievement in oratory. One general issue to consider is the age of the performers. Schoolboy groups were generally younger, so that treble voices probably predominated; among university players broken voices were the rule, including, as we shall see, the voices of those chosen for female roles. The choirboy performers, if they included only the boy singers in the choirs of the royal chapels and St Paul's

Cathedral, necessarily all had unbroken voices; in the later phase of their commercial existence, after 1600, the composition of the Chapel troupe, particularly, changed, and their vocal and physical characteristics changed accordingly. Later commercial troupes such as '[Christopher] Beeston's Boys', so called, in the 1630s, were junior professional actors; they were neither boys, save for being under twenty-one, nor did they have connections with the school-based troupes of the Elizabethan years.

SCHOOLS

Sirrah, didst thou ever see a prettier child? How it behaves itself, I warrant ye, and speaks, and looks, and perts up the head – I pray you brother, with your favour, were you never none of Master Monkester's scholars? (*The Knight of the Burning Pestle*, Induction, 93–7)[4]

The enthusiastic Grocer's Wife admires exactly the kind of confidence and presence 'Master Monkester' – the eminent Elizabethan schoolmaster and educational writer Richard Mulcaster – tried to inculcate in his boys by putting on plays, presented both to London citizen audiences and to the royal court, at Merchant Taylors' School (the old form of spelling has been retained at the school to this day) in the 1560s and thereafter. That she admires particularly the boy playing the distinctly goofy role of Humphrey is typical of her uncertain taste, but a further level of joking was originally provided by the speaker's status: a boy player, a fellow member of the Children of the Queen's Revels, a troupe originating in the Chapel boy players.[5] Neither he nor the player of Humphrey were or ever had been 'one of Master Monkester's scholars'. Mulcaster ended his long career in the year of Beaumont's play, 1608, by retiring from St Paul's School, the second eminent London institution of which he had been headmaster.

Mulcaster's attitude to the place of theatre in the curriculum is of a piece with his enlightened views on providing a 'rounded' education, as we would now call it, even while remaining committed to the thoroughgoing training in Latin described above. He was also an advocate of regular physical exercise, and training in vocal and instrumental music, for example. In his *Positions Concerning the Training Up of Children*, published in 1581, and drawing on his experience at Merchant Taylors', he devotes a chapter to the virtues 'Of loud speaking', 'The exercise of the voice which in Latin they name *vociferatio*', drawing on Ciceronian models to extol the virtues of vocal warm-ups and exercises to strengthen the voice as an expressive medium. He says nothing directly about the performance of plays, disappointingly, but what we know to have been a deliberate part of his pedagogy is attested to in a memoir by one of his eminent pupils, the lawyer, judge, and legal theorist Sir James Whitelocke: 'I was brought up at school under Mr Mulcaster, in the famous school of the Merchant Taylors in London, where I continued until I was well instructed in the Hebrew, Greek, and Latin tongues. His care was also to increase my skill in music, in which I was brought up by daily exercise in it, as in singing and playing upon instruments, and yearly he presented some plays to the court, in which his scholars were only actors, and I one among them, and by that means was taught then good behaviour and good audacity.'[6]

'Good behaviour' is a term common to the sagacious Sir James and the garrulous Wife, and in a theatrical context it means something rather different from merely being well-behaved: showing both performative presence and expressive action suited to character, perhaps. 'Audacity' – the ability to come out of an involuted adolescent protective shell – is precisely what many modern parents hope for in encouraging their children to enrol for drama classes or to audition for the school play or musical. The educational benefit of performance was recognized at other leading schools. Mulcaster himself had been a schoolboy at Eton in the 1540s, and the school has a recorded tradition of play performances from the 1520s onwards; Eton's headmaster from 1534 to 1541 was the playwright Nicholas Udall. St Peter's College, Westminster, or Westminster School, had a tradition of playing at Christmas, instituted by a royal statute in 1560: '*Quo juventus majori cum fructu tempus Natalis Christi terat et tum actioni tum pronuncia-tioni decenti melius se assuescat*' (So that the youths may spend Christmas more fruitfully while also becoming accustomed to suitable action and pronunciation [or action and accent, in Shakespearean phrasing]).[7] The Queen also patronized the Westminster boys' performances at court, as she did those of Mulcaster's boys from Merchant Taylors' School, and those of several other London-area schools and training establishments: Eton College, St Paul's School, founded by Dean John Colet in the early sixteenth century, and the singing schools of the Chapels Royal at Windsor and at Whitehall, and of St Paul's Cathedral. The 1560s and 1570s were the peak decades of school performances at court in the Christmas and Shrove festival seasons.[8] The increasing prominence of professional playing was undoubtedly one reason for their decline thereafter, but there are also some signs of changing attitudes at the level of school governance. The governors of St Paul's School, the Mercers' Company, became increasingly strict about what they took to be the educational principles of their founder,[9] while the Merchant Taylors' Company, which had welcomed the scholars' performances in their hall during the first years of the school's existence, forbade them to be held there in 1574. That two of the prominent city schools were governed by 'Great Companies' – the leading bodies of trade and manufacture in London – is of some interest in connection both with the material of the next chapter, which shows how thoroughly involved many actors and their apprentices were in the companies and their 'brotherhood', and also with the question of the attitude of the city government, drawn as it was from prominent members of the chief trade companies, to the growing business of the professional players.

The Latin of the Westminster School statute of 1560 suggests that the pronunciation (and its matching action) the boys were to improve in staging their Christmas play was to be that of the Latin language. Some plays presented to the court were indeed those of the classical repertory: in 1564 the Queen was entertained by Terence's *Heautontimoroumenos* and Plautus' *Miles Gloriosus*. Yet the boys also performed drama in English: the court shows of *Paris and Vienna* (or *Vienne*, a treatment of a French romance story translated by Caxton) in 1572 and *Truth, Faithfulness, and Mercy* in 1574 demonstrate that their repertory was wide, and not narrowly tied to school pedagogy. The headmaster William Malim's guidelines for curriculum at Eton allow for English-language plays to be performed occasionally, so long as they are, in a phrasing that echoes Cicero, 'quae habeant acumen et leporem' (such as have keenness and wit): English comedy is specifically preferred, perhaps as being more suited to the tastes and abilities of younger boys.[10]

Dramatic activity in grammar schools was not restricted to the London area, but seems to have been widespread throughout England. The Protestant reformer and playwright John Bale visited Hitchin Grammar School in 1552, where the boys presented a variety of English-language plays on religious and controversialist subjects, under the leadership of their master, Ralph Radcliffe.[11] When Bale was later a prebendary of Canterbury Cathedral, in 1562, the King's School there was putting on plays, as they certainly were again between 1629 and 1632, and the tradition may have continued through the period when Christopher Marlowe was a student at the school (1578–80).[12] The Free Grammar School at Shrewsbury under the mastership of Thomas Ashton mounted the Whitsun play for the town in 1565, its fame such that it reached the ears of the Queen.[13] Plays were presented by schoolboys for both elite and popular audiences. The boys of the King's School at Chester presented a Terence play, more than likely in Latin, before the visiting Earl of Derby and the mayor of the city in 1578, while the scholars' play at Congleton in Cheshire on Shrove Tuesday 1621 was presented outdoors before the whole town.[14] Plays had evidently been presented at Blackburn School in Lancashire before 1590, when it was decreed that 'no English interludes or plays shall be from henceforth played or used in the same school', presumably leaving the masters free to continue performances in Latin, should they have chosen.[15] The teacher Charles Hoole, whose book *A New Discovery of the Old Art of Teaching School* (London, 1660) was based on his experiences at Rotherham Grammar School, Yorkshire, in the 1630s, has the following observations on teaching Terence's plays as reading texts in the fourth form, to boys of thirteen or fourteen:

When you meet with an act or scene that is full of affection and action you may cause some of your scholars, after they have learned it, to act it, first in private among themselves, and afterwards in the open school before their fellows; and herein you must have a main care of their pronunciation, and acting every gesture to the very life. The acting of a piece of a comedy, or a colloquy sometimes, will be an excellent means to pronounce orations with a grace, and I have found it an especial remedy to expel that sub-rustic bashfulness and unresistable timorousness which some children are naturally possessed withal, and which is apt in riper years to drown many good parts in men of singular endowments.[16]

Even when records of school plays for important occasions do not exist, then, classroom or in-school performance may have been going on as a continuing pedagogical practice, improving pronunciation and suitable gesture, and overcoming sub-rustic bashfulness, Hoole's rather charming variation on the need for 'audacity' on both the dramatic stage and the great stage of life.

There is enough evidence to suggest that the model of dramatic performance as a teaching medium in early modern grammar schools in England was both widespread and persistent, still being recommended after the Restoration. It was certainly not universally followed, some grave school governors or masters disapproving of anything tinged with frivolity, or even pleasure, and the stricter sort frowning on the bawdiness of much Latin comedy, particularly in the plays of Plautus. Yet numerous Elizabethan schoolboys, almost certainly including Ben Jonson and possibly William Shakespeare, must have followed the young James Whitelocke in taking roles in school dramatic performances, from the modest context of the schoolroom before an audience of fellow pupils to the more intimidating and grand performances before important and high-ranking people, entirely outside the school.

The theoretical underpinning of school performance was provided by the writings of Cicero and Quintilian on oratory, both, especially the first, recommended as school reading,[17] although *De Oratore*, Cicero's principal work on the topic, is long and discursive, constructed as a dialogue, and not especially easy of access, while the *Institutio Oratoria* of Quintilian, which offers a model for the education of an orator, is simply enormous, with an elaborately constructed but uncompelling system of categories. Elizabethan schoolboys, one would hope, would have been more likely to have read extracts from either work than to have known the complete texts, and perhaps to have compiled notebooks with suitable quotations, a habit commonly recommended by contemporary schoolmasters. Such a note-book collection on the general subject of delivery – speech and gesture in oratory – might have been quite compact, and the words it contained would have provided the basis for much of the language used about live perform-ance by a speaker, including that on the theatrical stage, in the sixteenth and seventeenth centuries. One might imagine the schoolboy Hamlet, or the university student Polonius, having compiled such a book: Cicero and Quintilian lie behind Polonius' praise of good accent and good discretion.

Both classical authors have an ambiguous attitude to stage performance, that is to the Roman stage at the time they wrote, between the first centuries BC and AD, regarding it as lesser than the serious business of oratory in the contexts of politics and law, and yet providing compelling models of effective and moving use of voice and gesture to affect listeners. Thus Cicero can write of 'histrionum levis ars' (the trivial art of actors), yet he quotes with approval the saying of the legendary actor Roscius 'caput esse artis, decere' (the chief point of art is to find the graceful and suitable), something rather similar to Hamlet's remarks on temperance. This partic-ular passage tellingly continues, possibly still quoting Roscius, 'quod tamen unum id esse, quod tradi arte non possit' (yet achieving this is the one thing that cannot be taught).[18] Inspiration must be found in the moment of performance, whether by the schoolboy or the great stage actor.

In speaking of vocal training and the mastery of a good voice Cicero frankly states that actors have to be a principal model, while his treatment of appropriate vocal tone and volume uses examples of poetic lines from plays: the tone proper for compassion and sorrow, for example, should be that of Andromache sorrowing for the loss of Troy, quoted from a lost play by Ennius. Thus rhetoric (verbal construction) and oratory (vocal delivery) are closely linked in Ciceronian thinking: delivery is directly related to content and style. In so far as the academic tradition had any influence at all on the professional stage of the English Renaissance such linkage was its central point. The written text was the source for accent and action, so that the Induction to Marston's *Antonio and Mellida*, played by Paul's Boys in 1599 or 1600, would have been understood to have been founded upon a non-sense, when the boy playing Piero claims 'we can say our parts, but we are ignorant in what mould we must cast our actors'.[19] A thirteen-year-old boy with access to St Paul's School should have been, and presumably was, far better educated in Ciceronian principles than to utter such a preposterous claim. The entire routine of the Induction is facetious.

Moreover, for Cicero the life of words meant for speech is inescapably embodied, and he is particularly eloquent on the expressive power of the accompanying languages of gesture and countenance which give full dimension to verbal utterance: 'Est enim actio quasi sermo corporis' (Action is truly the body's speech) is precisely the kind of pithy epithet which would find its way into a commonplace book, as a memorable touchstone from a long and complex text.[20] Similarly the memorably compressed 'imago animi vultus, indices oculi' (the face is the mirror of the soul, and the eyes its index) comes in the same section, on gesture,[21] which Cicero understands to include the subtle communications of the face, and which are to be understood and practised by the orator as thoroughly as by the stage actor. Thus bodily 'action', a centre of the actor's art, had the approval and endorsement of one of the most respected classical authorities.

Quintilian, writing after Cicero, draws on the earlier writer, while attempting to lay out an entire system of oratorical pedagogy, in which actors were to have some part, principally in teaching proper delivery ('pronuntiati scientiam').[22] The pupils were to avoid picking up the more grotesque and exaggerated vocal and physical actorly skills, appropriate to satire and broad comedy, but they were, interestingly, to learn something about emotion memory: 'qua concitatione consurgat ira' (how to arouse a feeling of anger).[23] Pupils might also learn to recite speeches from plays, exercising their memories as well as their expressive powers in speech and associated gesture.

Thus the 'exercises' of the Elizabethan grammar schools, including not only the more elaborately presented plays, but in-class performances of acts and scenes from dramatic texts, both readings aloud and memorized performance of the popular 'colloquies', Latin textbooks in the form of dialogues, the memorizing and recitation of classical verse, with proper observation of the length-based system of accent, and culminating in the debates and disputations of the senior forms, were all directed to the oral mastery of language, in the oratorical tradition. The chief interest of this system in connection with the contemporary theatre is its inescapable stress on the living, physically present speaker as a potent means of communication: in using speech and the expressive power of the body the orator's end was to persuade and move his audience, or in the Ciceronian phrase which was taken over in defences of the art of the stage, 'docere, delectare, permovere' (to teach, delight, and move).[24] The disconnect, to use a modern term, in the Elizabethan educational system was that a training in *Latin* oratory was unlikely to be able to teach or move a very large body of people. In terms of common understanding and the capacity to impress large numbers the actor had the great advantage over the university orator, although we should note that the important public language of the pulpits and of Parliament was English.

The ability to speak clearly and expressively might be regarded as one mark of a finished education, whether or not it is tied to the classical oratorical tradition, and one contemporary writer gives a lively account of the common deficiencies of ordinary communication, and the need for education to put them right.

Some there be that either naturally or through folly have such evil voices and such lack of utterance and such evil gesture, that it much defaceth all their doings. One pipes out his words so small through default of his windpipe that ye would think he whistled. Another is so hoarse in his throat that a man would think he came lately from scouring of harness [cleaning rusty armour]. Another speaks as though he has plums in his mouth ...

Some nods their head at every sentence. Another winks with one eye, and some with both. This man frowneth always when he speaks. Another looks ever as though he were mad. Some cannot speak, but they must go up and down, or at least be stirring their feet as though they stood in a cockering boat. Another will play with his cap in his hand and so tell his tale ...

There are a thousand such faults among men both for their speech and also for their gesture, the which if in their young years they be not remedied, they will hardly be forgot when they come to man's state.[25]

CHORAL TRAINING SCHOOLS

The chief business of the choir schools was to train boys with unbroken voices in vocal and instrumental music, principally the first, to sing within larger male-voice choirs in cathedrals and other ecclesiastical establishments. New pupils entered as the older boys left, so that the school was a constantly changing group, although it was also small, made up of ten to twelve boys only. Today schools connected with cathedral and collegiate choirs teach the full range of modern subjects to university-entrance level, and they include a good number of other pupils beyond the dozen or so treble boy singers. In Tudor times educational standards in choral groups may not have been that high, measuring by the scale of Richard Mulcaster, but the training did not have the duration of grammar school. Once boys' voices broke, at thirteen or fourteen, they left the choir community and either joined other schools, or in some cases may have graduated to adult member-ship of the chapel or cathedral musical community. Regular choral services and rehearsal for them was the chief business of the boys' daily lives, and in that respect they were far nearer to the condition of boy apprentices in an acting troupe, both receiving an applied training in performance concur-rently with being required to demonstrate their art at a high level of skill.

The boys singing in the royal chapels were surrounded by the leading musicians of the day: players, singers, and composers, among them, during the reign of Queen Elizabeth, Thomas Tallis, William Byrd, Thomas Morley, and John Bull, the last of whom had graduated to the rank of Gentleman of the Chapel through serving as a boy singer in the choir; Orlando Gibbons and Henry Lawes were among the members of the Chapel in the Stuart years. Such a rich and creative community, supple-mented by a large and distinguished body of instrumental players, on string and wind instruments, some of them also composers, is directly comparable to those of the leading theatrical troupes of the day, and junior membership of the court musical world must have been at once daunting and deeply impressive, likely to have been remembered for a lifetime, whatever career one subsequently followed. The boy John Bull was recruited for the Chapel Royal from the choir of Hereford Cathedral at about the age of eleven, in 1574, by the Master of the Children William Hunnis, who held a royal licence to enlist promising boy singers in such a fashion. In early 1578, when he was around the classic Aristotelian age of fourteen, Bull was moved on to an apprenticeship, technically with the Merchant Taylors' Company, but probably involving further musical study, since he went back to Hereford as organist five years later.[26] During four court seasons of Christmas and Shrove entertainments, from 1574–5 to 1577–8, however, John Bull was undoubtedly a boy performer in the plays mounted first by Hunnis and then by Richard Farrant, who was instrumental in the opening of a new teaching, rehearsal, and performance space at Blackfriars, in 1576. Bull was probably among the first performers in a theatre that attracted a London audience to the Chapel boys' shows, and perhaps, as a senior boy, he took one of the larger roles in *The History of Mutius Scaevola*, performed at court in January 1577, and no doubt also at Blackfriars beforehand.

As Queen Elizabeth seems to have encouraged such schoolmasters as Richard Mulcaster in their dramatic exercises, so she appears to have smiled on similar efforts by the masters of the choir children, who were, in effect, members of her household. The court had two male-voice choirs: one permanently based at St George's Chapel, Windsor, while the second, the Chapel Royal, moved with the monarch around the principal palaces in the London area, although the older Tudor base for the Chapel Royal was at Greenwich. The boys from both choirs appeared in plays at court at roughly the same time, in the late 1560s; Richard Farrant had been Master of the Children at Windsor from 1564, and William Hunnis Master of the Children of the Chapel Royal from late 1566, when he succeeded Richard Edwardes. Ten years later Hunnis and Farrant came to an agreement which saw the latter take over as *de facto* master of the Chapel Royal children, deputizing his responsibilities at Windsor, until his death in 1580, when Hunnis resumed his old post for a further seventeen years. Farrant's lease of rooms in the dissolved conventual buildings at Blackfriars in September 1576 was to provide a convenient base, not far from the central court of Whitehall, for the chapel boys to live and to be trained, a facility which, rather oddly, they had never officially possessed, and provision for which had never been directly granted by the royal purse: the annual fee of forty pounds paid to the Master was supposed to cover such costs, although it evidently fell considerably short of what was needed, especially as prices rose.[27]

Farrant's model for the move to Blackfriars may have been a third choral school, that of St Paul's, an establishment which should be distinguished from St Paul's School, also in the precincts of the cathedral, which was a grammar school under the governorship of the Mercers' Company. Paul's Boys, as they were commonly called, were the ten treble singers of St Paul's Cathedral choir; their voices were complemented by those of eighteen singing men. Like their Chapel counterparts they remained members of the group only until their voices changed, but thereafter they had at least the nominal right to attend their larger sister school as pupils. Their training as choristers, once again, was principally in music. Their masters in the Elizabethan years were Sebastian Westcott, until 1582, Thomas Giles, until 1600, and Edward Pierce or Pearce, who left a place in the Chapel Royal to oversee the most productive years of the boys' career as players, producing plays in direct competition with the professional troupes. The St Paul's choirboys had a long tradition of involvement in drama, under their earlier Tudor director, John Redford, a playwright as well as a musician, who enlisted the involvement of John Heywood, a minor canon of St Paul's and also a playwright and actor. In 1547, the year in which King Henry VIII died, Sebastian Westcott succeeded to the Mastership. Until his death in 1582, remarkably, Westcott remained a Catholic, but even during Queen Mary's reign he and his boys had entertained the future Queen Elizabeth,

establishing a particular favour which both protected Westcott from pros-
ecution and ejection from his position as a recusant (as it also did Thomas
Tallis within the Chapel) and saw Paul's Boys become preferred and regular
performers of plays at court. Roger Bowers has recently written that
'So elevated and so constant a degree of royal favour probably rendered
Westcott the leading producer and arbiter of taste in English drama between
1560 and the later 1570s',[28] and the fashion for the choirboy players at court
may explain the subsequent involvement of the ambitious John Lyly as their
playwright. Westcott's performers were a group of ten boy players, all with
unbroken voices. Over the years of his Mastership they included some
famous names in musical, if not theatrical, history: Thomas Morley, Peter
Phillips, and William Byrd, among others, all played as boy actors before the
Queen.

It should be apparent from my account so far that the major musical
institutions in the London area had many links. Although St Paul's
Cathedral was an important symbolic centre for worship and ritual ceremony
within the city of London, it was and is also a royal site. While coronations
and burials took place at Westminster and Windsor, royal marriages – like
that of Prince Arthur to Princess Catherine of Aragon – were sometimes
held at the city cathedral, while queens and kings could command services
of national thanksgiving or repentance to be held there.[29] Westcott held
a royal licence, of 1560, authorizing him in 'the taking up of certain apt
children that may by his good education be framed in singing so as they may
be meet to serve us [i.e., the Queen] in this behalf when we shall call
for them',[30] as did his successor Thomas Giles, 'to take up children to be
brought up in music to be made fit for her Majesty's service, the same to be
found out in any place within the realm of England or Wales'.[31] Paul's Boys,
like their colleagues in the Chapel, were regarded as being in royal service,
and they might have had a variety of regional origins; the Master's chief
sources of enquiry, no doubt, were the choirs of other cathedrals around
the country.

Dramatic activity at St Paul's, then, was incidental to being brought up in
music. It provided a kind of vocal exercise different from singing, encouraged clear pronunciation (equally essential in vocal music, if differently
achieved, depending on the particular demands of the notes being sung),
and promoted 'audacity', allowing for some exercise of individual characteristics outside the group discipline of the choir. One would guess that the
Paul's shows usually traded on the performers' ability to sing and play
instruments, which they were taught as part of their training, and that
escaping from the chief repertory of church music provided another holiday

for the boys. Drama, in terms of the brief of a musical education, expanded performers' range, particularly since, although the boys' ages spanned a mere four to five years, they would have been called on to play a full range of age in dramatic characters, older and younger, as well as male and female parts, with no distinction in voice range.

As Richard Mulcaster used the company hall of the Merchant Taylors, for some years, to display his scholars' theatrical accomplishments to a wider audience, so Sebastian Westcott, probably at some time in the late 1560s or early 1570s, began to open the rehearsal and teaching space used by his choirboys to audiences, for payment, as the court play or plays for the court holiday season were prepared: by 1575, when the city administration complained about it, it had become a well established practice. In so far as the arrangement was commercial the profits either defrayed the Master's costs or went to the cathedral coffers; there is no sign that the Dean and Chapter disapproved of Westcott's activities. Although the playing spaces at Paul's and at Blackfriars (after 1576) are frequently called theatres in general histories of the Elizabethan stage, we should be clear that neither was a permanent theatre building, with a fixed stage and seating, unlike the later and distinct Blackfriars theatre established in 1596, which was to become the leading performance space of the city. Westcott's and Farrant's performing spaces were, like many other contemporary places, temporary conversions of an indoor hall or chamber used most of the year for other purposes: at Paul's and Blackfriars they were chiefly schoolrooms, used for choral and musical practice, and for the teaching of academic curriculum. Roger Bowers has identified the premises used for performances at Paul's as the Almoner's House, a wooden building of fairly modest dimensions, in the church yard by the south transept of the cathedral; the plays were opened to a necessarily small audience within a rectangular room, no doubt with a stage positioned across the width of one end.[32] The acoustics there were probably quite different from the larger chambers used for the festival seasons at court, but part of the boys' training would have included the control of breath and vocal volume which would have allowed them to adjust to such circumstances.

The Paul's and Chapel choirboys who gave performances to paying audiences in London in the later 1570s were not professional players like the contemporary James Burbage and his fellows. Their plays were mounted in the holiday seasons of Christmas and Shrove, and their training in drama lasted for only a few weeks annually, at the turn of the year, as against their constant business of learning and performing music. Roger Bowers puts the matter this way, speaking of Paul's Boys: 'Though

evidently accomplished [Westcott's] choristers were never more than intermittent actors, and never did they become transformed from a professional
liturgical ensemble to a professional "theatre company".[33] In stage acting
their advantages over a group of boys from a grammar school, of similar ages
and abilities, lay in their constant training and practice as a mutually
supportive performing group; when they left the choir stalls for the stage
they knew one another very well, as did the actors in contemporary professional troupes. If the disciplines of spoken drama were rather different,
ensemble work, with meticulous attention to timing and rhythm, was the
basis of the boys' training. Further, their lives were lived in close proximity
with one another, and with the Master and his associates, in the Almoner's
House. Westcott's will of 1582 left the contents of the house, where he lived,
to his successor; they included 'a chest of violins and viols to exercise and
learn the children and choristers there', and five bedsteads, with mattresses,
blankets, bolsters, and coverlets, 'such as are accustomably used for the ten
choristers'.[34] Paul's Boys slept two to a bed.

Since Masters could recruit boys who were already talented in singing, it
is likely that most children arrived either in the Paul's or Chapel establishments already literate, and able to read music. Other training beyond the
practice and theory of music was supplemented by ushers and assistants.
Probably the boys in the Tudor period were taught at least some Latin, to
keep them in reasonable step with their contemporaries in grammar schools,
apart from its advantages to them as musicians likely to be reading and
singing texts in languages other than English. The royal commission of 1604
to Nathaniel Giles, master of the Children of the Chapel after Hunnis,
provides for the boys that 'when the voice or voices of the said children after
three years' service shall become insufficient or unmeet, to be placed for
their better advancement in any college, hall, or school of the foundation
of the king or any of his predecessors'.[35] This amounted to scholarship
support – at least on paper – at such schools as Westminster, and perhaps
also at university colleges. Individually, much must have depended on
family background and, where musical talent continued past puberty, on
patronage. By the eighteenth century both the educational remit of the
Chapel Royal and the prospects of the boys sound rather reduced. When he
became Clerk of the Cheque in 1752 William Lovegrove compiled notes on
the responsibilities of those whom he paid:

The Master's duty is to teach [the boys] to sing, to play upon the harpsichord or
organ, writing, arithmetic, and [to] compose.

They are to attend the service of the Chapel daily throughout the year, where his
Majesty resides, Kensington excepted.

When their voices break and they become unfit for the Chapel his Majesty gives thirty pounds to the parents or friends of each boy, to place him out apprentice.

If they behave well, and their voices turn out useful, they are frequently admitted Gentlemen of the Chapel Royal.[36]

No chorister we know of subsequently became an adult professional actor, with the exception of Nathan Field, who was recruited from St Paul's School to the Children of the Chapel in 1600, yet whether he was ever a singer (he turned thirteen in October of that year) is in some doubt. The early years of the seventeenth century are marked by increasing activity in the choirboy theatrical troupes, to exploit their evident skill and popularity, and in the case of the Chapel leading to a distinct division between the singing boys and an acting troupe which had arisen from their traditions, solely devoted to professional playing.[37] The Blackfriars venture of 1576–84 was marked by an earlier attempt to professionalize, and the common figure behind both enterprises was Henry Evans, a scrivener with no internal connection to either the Chapel or St Paul's. The disgruntled landlord of the Blackfriars property leased to Farrant in 1576, Sir William More, later complained that his tenant 'pretended unto me to use the house only for the teaching of the Children of the Chapel but made it a continual house for plays'.[38] This statement was made in a legal submission, and like many such another statement is probably exaggerated for effect: it is highly unlikely that any of the children's troupes ever acted 'continually'.

Circumstances certainly changed after Farrant's death in 1580, however, when some kind of merger was made between the two choral groups in their presentation of plays, with the collaboration of William Hunnis, resuming his role as Master of the Children of the Chapel, Henry Evans, whose interests were doubtless financial, the writer John Lyly, and Lyly's court patron the Earl of Oxford, whose own performing troupe (of adult actors) may at some stage have been involved with the choir children in performances, at court and perhaps also at Blackfriars. The culmination of this enterprise (such as it was; it seems not to have been very carefully planned) came in 1583, when Blackfriars would have come closest to being 'a continual house for plays', and which circumstance led More to reclaim the lease, early in the following year. The combined boy troupe, directed by Lyly himself, produced his own *Campaspe* at court, 1 January 1584, followed by *Sappho and Phao*, 3 March 1584,[39] and probably the first, at least, was seen by a paying public at Blackfriars during Christmas 1583–4, before More put an end to performances on his property.

Whatever the ambitions of the venture may have been, recorded dramatic activity by the Chapel children disappears during the later 1580s and the decade of the 1590s, while Lyly continued his association with Paul's Boys solely, who remained active for a further six years, continuing to play, as they did throughout their career as performers of drama in London, for a short season in the converted Almoner's House chamber. Under their Master Thomas Giles, between New Year's Day 1588 and Twelfth Night 1590 they presented three more of Lyly's plays at court: *Gallathea*, *Endymion*, and *Midas*; at least the first two of these were likely also to have been shown for London audiences at St Paul's. Lyly was probably also involved in the imperfectly understood polemical and satirical drama Paul's apparently staged in the 'Martin Marprelate' affair of 1589, an exchange between radical puritan critics and defenders of the established church. Whatever their role, it was enough to see their performances restrained for the next ten years or so, rather indicating their prominence in contemporary culture; to be closed down, they must have been regarded as influential on the formation of opinion.[40]

The surviving plays by Lyly are not only by far the most distinguished dramatic works produced by boy companies up to 1590, influential models on subsequent dramatic writing generally, but in their published form they provide an opportunity to compare theatrical demands with what we know of performing resources: the ten or twelve boys aged roughly ten to fourteen of the two respective choirs. In 1584 the combined group may have been larger (twenty-two or more), or it may have been an 'all-star' team of traditional size, constituted of the best actors from each institution. As is the case with plays written for the adult troupes of ten to a dozen principal actors, Lyly's plays have more roles than available boy players, necessitating doubling of the shorter roles: *Endymion*, for example, has twenty-seven parts. Modern editors of the plays have speculated that one or two adult actors – graduates of the choir, or older musicians connected with the choral community – may have taken certain roles, and while that is certainly possible, part of the fun may have been a deliberate play with the limited palette, so to speak, of the performers, in voice, gender, and physique.[41] Chiefly, Lyly's plays still impress with their brilliant and sprightly rhetorical effects, calling for clear, paced, and witty delivery, and demanding a high level of control over articulation and rhythm, what George Hunter has called a 'concentration on enunciative clarity'.[42]

A question that might be put is which style came first: did Lyly write his plays for choirboy performers because their acting was markedly sharp and energetic, and they could be relied upon for acute rhythmic sense and crisp phrasing, or did his particular antithetical way with dramatic speech set the boys a challenge which they had to do their best to meet? We might think, in other words, that 'boy' performance was always characterized by the ironic brio and grace of delivery Lyly's drama requires, and that the plays were written to match performative strengths. Alternatively we can consider that Lyly was writing for the court, where he hoped to rise, and presenting the Queen and her circle with witty and sophisticated variations on legends and myths, played by troupes which had always received court favour, whether or not they were especially successful in Lyly's plays in particular. We might read back too much, in short, from literary style alone.

From the end of the 1590s, for rather less than a decade, the famous London choir schools revived the practice of public playing once again. (They may have continued to produce festival drama in their own communities in the interim.) Plays at Paul's were under way by 1599, and the Chapel followed in the next year. Appearances of both troupes at court resumed in 1601, and continued in the new reign, which began in March 1603. The boys' performances in London probably increased in frequency, and playwrights also working for the adult professional theatres, largely, provided their plays, which were written generally in the same conventions and styles as for adult players. The management of the Chapel children seems to have been aiming from the start at establishing professional playing, a step achieved by early 1604 with the founding of the Children of the Queen's Revels, essentially a professional troupe run by a consortium of adults, with a body of performers entirely separate from the singing boys of the Chapel, a circumstance which was underlined by a renewed commission to Thomas Giles in 1606, insisting that the boys he recruited should be choristers only, and not involved in plays, 'for that it is not fit or decent that such as should sing the praises of God almighty should be trained up or employed in such lascivious or profane exercises'.[43] Thus was closed a long history of occasional playing by the Chapel boys. From the end of 1600, in fact, the performers called the Children of the Chapel became something considerably different from the earlier performing troupes directed by Westcott, Hunnis, and Farrant. The then Master of the Chapel children, Nathaniel Giles, was a party to the changes, which finally left him with only his choral responsibilities for the majority of his long career, until 1634.

Thomas Giles, who was not related to his namesake, and, from August 1600, Edward Pierce, who moved from a position in the Chapel Royal, were Masters at Paul's. Performances there continued to be mounted under the same conditions as in earlier periods, before small audiences in a temporarily converted indoor chamber, although Pierce did enlist commercial partners in Thomas Woodford and Edward Kirkham. The Chapel boys, by contrast, acquired a playhouse: a space designed for an audience solely to watch stage plays. This had been set up in 1596 within another chamber at Blackfriars by the Burbage family, who were looking for an alternative to their Shoreditch playhouse, the Theatre; the Blackfriars venture was frozen, however, by local opposition, and the opportunity for the owners to rent it was no doubt welcome, particularly after the building and opening of the Globe in 1599. The Chapel initiative involved Henry Evans, a veteran of the first Blackfriars enterprise, and he and Giles set about establishing a separate group of twelve boy players, one or two of whom were singers, but which also included boys recruited from grammar schools: the preferred age seems to have been about thirteen years old. We know the names of fourteen boys who were recruited or acted with the troupe in 1600–1, and of these, three – Nathan Field, John Underwood, and William Ostler – remained with the company in its subsequent metamorphoses and went on to adult professional careers. In some ways, then, the group that became the Children of the Queen's Revels three years later was from the start an apprentice-based rather than a choir-based troupe, and hence belongs in the next chapter, where I will give it some further notice. Yet for five or six years from the turn of the century one could say that the Chapel and Paul's ventures each supported the other, and created a fashion for playgoing and for playing style which is noticed in *Hamlet*. We have no evidence from this period that the Paul's plays were acted by any performers other than the ten members of the choir, as they had traditionally been, while the Blackfriars plays did not, at least at first, entirely sever the connection with the Chapel Royal proper.

In September 1602 the visiting Duke Philip-Julius of Stettin-Pomerania went to a Blackfriars performance by the Chapel troupe, and Frederick Gerschow, from his entourage, made notes about the occasion.[44] The performers were identified by Gerschow as the Queen's singing boys, who were taught the arts of music by their teachers, and for an hour before the play there was a recital on the organ and on string and wind instruments, and a fine solo song by a treble vocalist. These performers, at least, were the boys trained by Giles and his associates. The fifteen-year-old Nat Field is likely to have taken a principal part in the play which followed, which concerned a chaste royal widow of England – not a subject which matches any of the Chapel repertory we now know. Gerschow writes that plays could be seen at Blackfriars once a week; later testimony suggests that performances were held as many as three times a week.[45] The 'season' was generally that of the legal terms and the residence of the court in London: from the time of Gerschow's visit, in mid September, until roughly six months later. Even at its most intense, then, the commercialization of the choirboy troupes was not on the level of the adult troupes associated with Henslowe, whose relentless activity in preparing and performing plays we can observe through the entries in the *Diary*. Even so, as many as seventy-five perform-ances could have been given in a continuous six-month season of three shows a week. If the list of surviving plays we can connect with both troupes up to 1606 is some kind of guide to the frequency of their performances, then the Chapel children were more prolific (as we might otherwise expect), averaging three or more new plays each year. The average at Paul's would seem to have been around two new plays each season; older repertory was evidently repeated, but how frequently is impossible to say.

The plays written for the boys by leading playwrights do not show obvious signs of concession to performing skill, although some of them make reference to the status of the actors. Jonson's *Cynthia's Revels*, for example, first acted early in the revived career of the Chapel boys in late 1600, begins, in the version printed in 1601, with a facetious induction, featuring three boys quarrelling over who is to deliver the prologue. The ensuing play, about true and false courtly behaviour, features a number of pages – boy roles – but also male and female would-be wits, and a male and female pair of stern censors, all cast in the mould of similar figures in *Every Man Out of His Humour*, a play acted by the adult performers of Shakespeare's company in the preceding year. In terms of their genre, and the practical challenges of bringing them to life on stage, the parts of Amorphus in the boys' play and Fastidius Brisk in the adults' are not very different: they are both caricatures, and a witty boy player could be as effective in such a role, one would think, as could an adult actor. There is no allowance in Jonson's writing, in other words, for a different approach to playing the play, although there are signs he took notice of the theatrical context: there are a number of songs in the play, and a masque, featuring dancing to music, towards its end. The boys themselves no doubt enjoyed the ridiculous song Amorphus has written in praise of his mistress's glove, which in the fourth act he sings, possibly deliberately badly, and equally possibly to ridiculously awkward music. He then points out its accomplish-ments of composition theoretically: 'Why do you not observe how excel-lently the ditty is affected in every place? That I do not marry a word of short quality to a long note? Nor an ascending syllable to a descending tone? Besides, upon the word "best" there, you see how I do enter with an odd minim, and drive it through the breve, which no intelligent musician, I know, but will affirm to be very rare, extraordinary, and pleasing' (4.3.288–94). This has the ring of the parodic in-jokes of school skits and sketches, and perhaps the first performer allowed himself to guy certain mannerisms of one music master or another.

In respect of being suited to the limits of the troupe formed by Giles and Evans, Jonson's play as we have it does not seem very carefully thought out. Like Lyly's plays there are more parts than actors: twenty-three, plus three mutes, to be managed by a company of twelve players. Even with quick shifts of costume it seems impossible to manage a number of scenes without fifteen or more performers on the stage, although within the larger organization of the Chapel after 1600 it was probably easy enough to draft supernumeraries for minor roles.

A similarly casual attitude to the number of performers in the troupe marks other plays written for the boys in the first decade of the seventeenth century. To take quite a different style of play, in the first published text of Chapman's tragedy *Bussy D'Ambois* (1607), performed by Paul's Boys in or about 1604, there are twenty-three roles and several extras to be presented by a company of ten; the second scene requires fifteen actors to be on stage simultaneously, and the eighth scene sixteen. The practical options at Paul's, evidently, were either to cut and adapt the text or to find half a dozen more performers from among the local community, which no doubt could have been done. Chapman makes no concession at all to lesser abilities in playing, if lesser they were: his play is unrelentingly rhetorical, featuring long aria-like speeches in highly wrought blank verse. His characters, if a little hampered by the verbal weight of their speeches, are fiery and passionate, including the leading female role, Tamyra, whose adulterous affair with Bussy is at the centre of the drama. Four major male roles – Bussy, Monsieur, Guise, and Montsurry – must be cast with equally strong actors, who have to sustain relentless pride, aggression, and assertiveness, as they play out a battle of shifting conflicts driven by political ambition, aristocratic honour, and the power of innate will; at least half the strength of Paul's Boys, in other words, had to be up to very demanding parts. Although not without some of the irony which marks the near-contemporary play *The Revenger's Tragedy* (*c.* 1606), played by Shakespeare's troupe, *Bussy D'Ambois* keeps up a relentless tension, and is made for playing with all stops out. To think that Chapman was deliberately designing work that his performers could not pull off, creating a distancing mismatch between the material and the medium, is to assume too much: the vocal and physical effect would have been different from a performance of the play by adult troupes, as happened later in its stage history, but within the limits of their own style the Paul's performances could have been entirely compelling and moving.

Tragedies of political ambition and adulterous passion were not the kind of exercises that humanist schoolmasters had in mind for improving pronunciation and action, and the close relation of a convincing performance of *Bussy D'Ambois* to choral service in one of the great cathedrals would be hard to defend theoretically. The burst of activity at Paul's and the Chapel at the turn of the century had a long history but a short future, as the stricter views of King James and his bishops about the proper activity of choral scholars came into effect. At St Paul's the rather lax and permissive deanship of the aged Alexander Nowell came to an end with his death in 1602, and firmer discipline by the new administration no doubt had a part in closing down playing at the Almoner's House, finally, four years later, two years after the Children of the Chapel were formally separated from the young professional troupe at Blackfriars. The choirboys' career as players for the court and city was over.

UNIVERSITIES

In relatively recent times, even before the establishment of university drama departments, which happened considerably later in Great Britain than in North America, university performers have made the transition to professional careers on the stage without further training. F. R. Benson, active in (extracurricular) drama as an undergraduate at Oxford in the 1880s, went on as actor-manager to run the company at the Shakespeare Memorial Theatre; more recently the old universities have produced such diverse entertainers as Michael Redgrave, Jimmy Edwards, Peter Cook and Dudley Moore, Ian McKellen, John Cleese, and Michael Palin. The influence of George Rylands at Cambridge on the founding directors of the Royal Shakespeare Company in the 1960s and 1970s – Peter Hall, John Barton, and Trevor Nunn – is well known. There was no such connection between the universities and the professional stage four hundred years earlier, although there was a lively internal culture of dramatic entertainment, and there is evidence that some members of the universities, at least, had an eye on the growing theatrical culture based in London. Otherwise university connections with the court were strong: the university chancellors were leading statesmen,[46] monarchs made formal visits to the universities, when they were entertained by plays, and the royal Offices of the Revels and the Works collaborated with university groups in supplying costumes and expertise, as they did when amateur or professional players visited the court.

In collegiate universities, as Oxford and Cambridge have remained, local culture within individual colleges was and is very significant, and the larger and richer colleges with traditions of sponsoring dramatic performances had both more personnel to draw on – more fellows and students to provide a casting pool for performers, for example – and larger and more convenient places in which to set up stages and to accommodate audiences. The surviving hall at Trinity College, Cambridge, completed in 1608, was constructed, it has been argued, with an eye to providing the college and the university as a whole with a theatrical space that could match the capacity and impressiveness of Christ Church Hall at Oxford, which has stood since 1529.[47] At the time of Queen Elizabeth's visit to Cambridge in 1564, before Trinity's Jacobean hall was built, plays presented for entertainment were staged in the grand surroundings of the antechapel of King's College Chapel, a daunting space for the voices of amateur actors to conquer.

If theatrical shows were favoured by college authorities – a matter about which there was some controversy, particularly at Oxford – then it is not surprising to find that the larger colleges led the way in the mounting of drama, committing time and money to production, theatrical equipment, rehearsal, and writing original plays, often in Latin but occasionally in English. At Cambridge St John's, Trinity, and Queens' colleges were the chief centres of theatrical energy, particularly in the seventeenth century. At Oxford most of the older and larger colleges had some traditions of dramatic performance, but from early in the Elizabethan years Christ Church became the major focus of dramatic shows put on for such important occasions as visits by monarchs and other prominent figures; it was also the largest college community, although St John's College also retained an active theatrical tradition. William Laud, Archbishop of Canterbury and Chancellor of the university at the time of the royal visit in 1636, was both a graduate and former President of St John's, Oxford, and he wrote with pride about a play he arranged to be staged there for the royal party that 'the college was at that time so well furnished, as they did not borrow any one actor from any one college in town'.[48] Given such self-congratulation, we might well ask whether Laud himself had acted as an undergraduate, as a number of leading figures in the church he led had certainly done.

Theatre production in the universities was in certain respects a continuation of the school tradition, with the same pedagogical justification of its utility in building confidence and improving delivery in oratory. Many university students came from schools with dramatic traditions – Eton, Westminster, Merchant Taylors', and Shrewsbury, for example – and those who had been leading lights in school performances were no doubt welcomed into the theatrical fraternity within individual university colleges. There would have been more of an overlap in the age of school and undergraduate communities in the sixteenth and seventeenth centuries than there is today. The terms of modern admission to Oxford and Cambridge dictate that most new students are at least eighteen or nineteen by the time they arrive (the current fashion for a 'gap year' of travel or work between school and university adding another year to the average), and in their early twenties by the time they complete bachelors' degrees. The equivalent early modern community was, first, entirely male, considerably smaller in number, and younger. Laud went to Oxford from school when he was almost sixteen, and he was twenty when he graduated as BA. If the records are right, the precocious John Fletcher, the dramatist, entered Corpus Christi College, Cambridge, at the age of eleven, graduating as BA when he was fifteen, and MA at eighteen.[49] This was unusual progress, but it does indicate that at least a few members of university colleges were pre-adolescent when they began their careers. Laud's age at entry is a more indicative average, as is the length of his undergraduate career.

College drama seems to have been firmly connected to seasonal festivals, as it was in other communities and households in the sixteenth and seventeenth centuries, notably to Christmas and its days of communal feasting. Like some schools, certain university colleges recognized in their written statutes the annual production of a play within the community; it was to be a traditional part of the annual cycle of terms and vacations. Apart from formal plays, facetious speeches and shows, parodying the formalities of the educational establishment, were common, as were 'misrule' traditions, in which the junior members of the community were given temporary leave to set up mock authority. The ceremonies of the 'Christmas prince' elected at St John's College, Oxford, in 1607 were recorded in detail: his reign ran from All Saints' Eve, 31 October 1607, to the following Shrovetide, and included plays, mock ceremonies, and processions.[50] Merton College, Oxford, had an annual tradition of the election of a 'King of Beans', and similar practices, whether recorded or not, no doubt went on in many other colleges in both universities.[51]

In most colleges where formal drama was produced the entire community seems to have been involved in the enterprise, and certain places invested a good deal of effort into mounting plays, which were undoubtedly regarded as public occasions, to which a wider audience was invited, and which reflected on the honour and reputation of the hosts. Queens' College, Cambridge, had a remarkably elaborate stage and scaffold (seating) structure, carefully stored from year to year, which was annually put up in the hall (a building which survives today) when plays were put on there.[52] Its form was rather different from contemporary playhouses in London, with consequences for staging that I will turn to below. The chief difference in terms of performance between school and university plays lay in the age range of the performers, and the consequent difference of visual and aural effect on an audience. School or choirboy performers were all within a few years of one another, the majority with unbroken voices, but including a physiological range of the taller and the shorter, the slighter and the beefier, no doubt to deliberate comic effect on occasion, but on the whole a group which was generally miniaturized, or indeed a troupe of 'apes', as Paul's Boys are called in a play they themselves acted,[53] imitators of human action who are yet not entirely human, like puppets.

The casting for plays at Oxford and Cambridge, of which there is far more surviving evidence from the latter, in terms of lists and other references, used the full range of age of college communities, from newly admitted undergraduates in their mid to later teens, who were frequently cast in female roles, to senior fellows in their thirties. Evidently the number of characters and the genre of the play governed the application of this general rule, but it certainly seems that, especially in ambitious productions, players came from the entire academic community: they were not simply undergraduate groups. Their communal function, therefore, cannot have been insignificant, while in their effect they must have more closely resembled professional performances by troupes such as Shakespeare's, in which adult bodies and voices appeared and were heard alongside the slighter and lighter bodies and voices of younger men. One difference is that the majority of university performances were in Latin, with a few in Greek, and some in English, calculated for a learned audience of peers who could follow what was being said. When Polonius played Julius Caesar at the university, he had probably learnt Latin lines to speak. A play called *Caesar Interfectus* (*The Assassination of Caesar*) was indeed acted at Oxford in 1582. As the Caesar play indicates, Latin plays were not restricted to the classical repertory of Terence, Plautus, and Seneca, but included original compositions and adaptations, in genres and styles which corresponded with the English repertory of the contemporary professional stage. The ambitious three-part play *Richardus Tertius*, for example, acted at St John's College, Cambridge, in March 1579, antedates by a whole decade the various dramatizations of the rise and fall of King Richard III on the public stages, which culminated in Shakespeare's ambitious and highly successful treatment of about 1592. The Cambridge play shows similar ambition, and features an enormous cast which, unlike the practice within the professional theatre, was not, with minor exceptions, doubled: each role was played by one actor, and the principal part, Richard himself, appeared on each of the three successive nights of performance. The actor was John Palmer, a graduate and fellow of St John's, who was then in his later twenties. Palmer had his own rise and fall, subsequently becoming Master of Magdalene College and Dean of

Peterborough, before dying in debtors' prison in 1607; there is probably no truth to the story that he never got over playing the tyrant, however, continuing to display Richard's arrogance and chutzpah in private life.[54] Some roles *did* prefigure future careers: the man playing the Bishop of Ely, Lawrence Stanton, went on to become Dean of Lincoln Cathedral in 1601.[55]

Palmer acted in the company of nearly fifty of his colleagues: the casting and rehearsal of the play must have consumed the energies of a good part of the college community for some weeks. However successful the performances, the entire production must have been long remembered in college memory, no doubt giving rise to such stories as Palmer's continuing Richardism. Academic practice seems to have been, as I say above, to cast actors in one part only, but the epic demands of *Richardus Tertius* were such that one or two people in small roles changed parts on successive evenings. One of them was the poet Abraham Fraunce, author of *The Arcadian Rhetoric*, a graduate of Shrewsbury School and protégé of Sir Philip Sidney; in 1579 he was about twenty years old.[56] In the long list of roles only two were female: Queen Elizabeth, widow of King Edward, and Queen Anne, Richard's wife (who appears only in the third part of the play). These were played, respectively, by Leonard Shepard and Thomas Gargrave: Gargrave was eighteen at the time of the play, and Shepard probably a year or two older. Although they had entered the college in the same year, Gargrave was only twelve at the time, and Shepard had graduated as BA in 1577, and was to enter the church a couple of years after playing the Queen. We have no idea of their appearance, but they were certainly both grown men with broken voices at the time of the play, and they were probably chosen for their ability to speak their parts, in Latin, clearly and confidently. Playing the role of a victim of brutality evidently had no lasting effect on Gargrave, who was executed for murder sixteen years later.[57]

Gargrave had perhaps recommended himself for the part of Queen Anne by having played a female role in quite a different play, *Hymenaeus*, acted at St John's at some time in the twelve months or so preceding the performance of *Richardus Tertius*, and hence when he was around seventeen. The play, again in Latin, but a comedy, was adapted from a story in Boccaccio's *Decameron*, in the tradition that Shakespeare was to draw on for the comedies of his middle career. Gargrave played the female lead, Julia, and Thomas Pilkington, who was probably a couple of years older, Julia's maid, Amerina. The young male leads, including Ferdinandus, taken by Abraham Fraunce, then roughly nineteen, were about the same age, necessarily giving the performance rather different dynamics from similar comedy on the professional stage, where the ages of the players of the leading lovers would have been separated by at least a few years, and often a decade or more.

Similar Cambridge comedies from twenty years later – directly contemporary with the romantic comedies of the public theatres in the second half of the 1590s – *Silvanus* and *Hispanus*, acted successively, again at St John's College, in the early months of 1597, show similar patterns of casting. Recently admitted undergraduates were chosen for the leading female roles: the youngest members of the college community, about sixteen, or perhaps younger. Yet age was not the only criterion; Thomas Heblethwaite, who played both Panthia in *Silvanus* (who appears in male disguise, like Viola in *Twelfth Night*) and Silvia in *Hispanus*, was probably nearer to eighteen or nineteen, and would have been cast for his playing skill as much as his relative youth.

A particular loss among the many academic plays no longer surviving is *Palamon and Arcite*, an elaborate and spectacular two-part English play written by Richard Edwards for Queen Elizabeth's visit to Oxford in 1566, and performed before her in Christ Church Hall. As its title indicates, it was an adaptation of the story told in Chaucer's *Knight's Tale*, and hence comparable with Shakespeare's late collaboration with John Fletcher, *The Two Noble Kinsmen*. Although there is not a great deal of surviving information about the casting of plays at Oxford, we know a certain amount about this occasion, when the part of Emilia, for whose love Palamon and Arcite are rivals, was played by a schoolboy rather than an undergraduate: Peter Carew, the son of the Dean of Christ Church, George Carew. Queen Hippolyta, the wife of Theseus (as in *A Midsummer Night's Dream*), was played by John Rainolds of Corpus Christi College, and both actors were rewarded after the show, as a surviving account of the occasion relates: Rainolds was given nine angels (gold coins) from the Queen, and 'the lady Emilia for gathering her flowers prettily in the garden and singing sweetly in the prime of May received 8 angels for a gracious reward by her majesty's commandment'.[58] The actors entertained the Queen in other ways during her visit, their skill on the stage being a sign of their general confidence and facility in oral delivery. John Marbeck, who played the youthful Palamon at the age of thirty, also delivered Latin speeches during the public ceremonies for the Queen in the streets. The young Carew had also mastered Latin and Greek speaking, as he demonstrated on 1 September, before the presentation of the play in which he played the woman:

This day in the morning the queen's majesty keeping her chamber one master Peter Carew, a fine boy, made an oration to her in Latin with two Greek verses at the end, which the queen liked so well that she sent for Mr. Secretary [William Cecil] and willed the boy to pronounce it the second time, and said before he began 'I pray God, my boy, thou mayst say it so well as thou didst to me'; and when he had ended she said 'This boy doth as well as many masters of Cambridge.'[59]

A put-down of the other place (and Cecil's university), always welcome locally, was deftly contained in royal commendation. John Rainolds, the Hippolyta, was almost seventeen in September 1566; he had a long subsequent career at Oxford, converting from Catholicism to become a leading puritan, and in doing so turning against the university stage, and playing generally, conducting a polemical war with the Oxford dramatist William Gager throughout the 1590s, which culminated in the publication of Rainolds's book *The Overthrow of Stage Plays* in 1599.

Entertainment for royal visitors, occasions which continued at both universities from 1564 to 1642 (until Oxford became the wartime royal court for the next four years) called forth the greatest efforts in production and experimentation, in which Oxford led the way, building a fashionable Serlian theatre with perspectival changing scenery within Christ Church Hall for King James's visit in 1605, an enterprise in which Inigo Jones appears to have been involved.[60] An ambitious programme of four plays, all but one in Latin, was presented in the temporary theatre, managed by a consortium of four colleges – Christ Church, Magdalen, New, and St John's – drawing each on their own pool of potential actors, no doubt, but also 'having authority to make choice of actors and pen men to help pen them, out of the whole university'.[61] Some original authorial work may have been called on, but far more 'pen men' would have been employed in the copying out of parts for the many actors to learn. Samuel Daniel's *The Queen's Arcadia* was the English entertainment that concluded four successive nights of theatre, on 30 August. Similarly ambitious in its style of presentation was a play presented in the same place thirty-one years later, William Cartwright's tragicomedy *The Royal Slave*, before King Charles and Queen Henrietta Maria. A proscenium stage was erected, filled with scenery designed by Inigo Jones; elaborate 'Persian habits' were provided for the players, and the performance included songs and dances composed by Henry Lawes. The university succeeded in appealing to current court taste, so that it was remounted at Hampton Court with professional players, the King's men, taking over the roles. 'But', the Oxford University historian Antony Wood reports with satisfaction, 'by all men's confession, the players came short of the university actors.'[62]

Oxford's experiments with *avant-garde* forms of staging might be compared with the quite distinct layout of the theatre structure at Queens'

College, Cambridge, which preserved a convention which was perhaps widely followed in Cambridge plays. It certainly *was* common, as was the case at Queens', for the seats for the highest-ranking members of the audience to be placed behind and above the stage, in a gallery facing the rest of the audience. The Queens' layout, however, provided for actors' entries from the side (rather than the rear, the position of the tiring-house in London playhouse stages), from two stage houses which were entirely independent and did not communicate one with another, save by moving over the stage.[63] The consequence was that an exit by any actor had to be followed, when the character reappeared in the action, by re-entry from the same place. The consequences for the traffic of characters – leaving with X and subsequently entering with Y – would have been very complex to work out, and we do not have anything like a surviving prompt book to show how it may have been managed. It was a quite distinct academic convention, on the face of it considerably cumbersome compared with the flexibility of staging practices at such a theatre as the Globe, but we have a very limited understanding of how it was used by actors.

University performers, if they could rival the standards of the London players, could also be tedious, even to the learned King James, whose own schooling had equipped him to follow Latin dialogue without difficulty. The length of many college entertainments could be daunting, sometimes starting at the relatively late hour of nine, and continuing until one in the morning. Enjoyed as holidays within a community of people who knew one another well, and fortified by eating and drinking, amateur performances might have been assured of a certain welcome, and indulgence. When they had to meet the scrutiny of outsiders and decorum had to be maintained, the standards of judgement became stricter. One notably low point of university playing was reached in 1621, when an enthusiastic group of performers from Christ Church, Oxford, visited Woodstock Palace to entertain the King with a Latin play, *Technogamia*, first performed in the college three years earlier, and perhaps still including a fair proportion of the original cast (no indications of casting for either performance survive); 'but it being too grave for the king and too scholar-like for the auditory (or, as some say, that the actors had taken too much wine before), his majesty after two acts offered [= attempted] several times to withdraw'. Persuaded to stay, he went to sleep, 'in despair', according to one of the many satirical verses the occasion provided.[64]

Any comparison between the academic plays and players of Shakespeare's time and the contemporary professional stage must take notice of the remarkable group of three '*Parnassus*' plays, written in English, and performed successively at St John's College, Cambridge, at some time in the period between Christmas 1598 and the same season five years later. Witty and satirical, they are filled with references to contemporary university, literary, and theatrical culture. Since they were written for an audience who would laugh at the jokes, they make clear that Cambridge university men at the turn of the sixteenth century were well informed about the public theatre of the day, and were, perhaps, less uncritically than the egregious dramatic character Gullio, fans of the new writers William Shakespeare and Ben Jonson. We have no information about the casting of the plays, but in the final, longest piece, *The Return from Parnassus, Part Two* (published in 1606), two members of the college got to play the parts of Dick Burbage and Will Kemp, the famous tragic and comic actors, who audition out-of-work graduates as possible recruits to the Chamberlain's men, Shakespeare's troupe.

The *Parnassus* series began as a relatively simple idea in the short first play, *The Pilgrimage to Parnassus*, in which two young men determined to follow the Muses travel a route laid out by an academic map through the lands of Logic, Rhetoric, and Philosophy. They encounter a series of characters devoted to less rigorous guides: Madido is devoted to Horace, and strong drink; Stupido to puritanism; Amoretto to Ovid, and sensuality; Ingenioso, a failed writer, has cynically turned to money-making. The cast of nine would have had fun both with the caricatures and with the rather innocent idealism of the seekers after enlightenment, and as a half-serious examination of the difficulties of arduous study it would have had immediate appeal to an academic community in a holiday mood. Its success, evidently, led to the sequel plays, featuring the further adventures of the two pilgrims, just as happened in the commercial world of playwriting, and the urge to squeeze the founding idea of all its juice, probably by a variety of college authors, led to progressively longer and more loosely connected dramatic structures; the jest snowballed for a number of years, so that *Pilgrimage* has 720 lines, *The First Part of the Return from Parnassus* is somewhat more than twice as long, and the *Second Part* has 2,225 lines, the length of plays for the commercial stage. The lively dialogue of the longer plays sustains the rather *ad hoc* continuity of the scenes, and demands a range of witty comic playing which, however subtle it may have been in every respect, was undoubtedly fun to undertake, and to watch. An audience which knows the actors well as colleagues, pupils, and friends – or indeed as enemies – is at once more forgiving and more sharply critical of an entertainment in which they are complicit, in a way quite different from the temporary community experienced among audiences of the commercial theatre.

The continuing jest is that Philomusus and Studioso, the young pilgrims, returning from the heights of learning, attempt to make a living in the world, under a variety of unsatisfactory patrons and in a range of employments. Their turn to the stage occurs in a relatively brief pair of scenes later in the *Second Part of the Return*, when Burbage and Kemp suddenly enter, discussing the possible bargain to be had in taking on a pair of impoverished students: 'if we can entertain these scholars at a low rate, it will be well; they have oftentimes a good conceit in a part' (4.3.1753–5).[65] 'Conceit', the word used by Hamlet and Thomas Heywood, perhaps indicates that the intellectual and imaginative grasp of university actors exceeded their technical skills. Kemp, indeed, apart from finding university men 'proud', thinks them rather stiff and unnatural in matching action to word: ''tis good sport in a part to see them never speak in their walk, but at the end of the stage, just as though in walking with a fellow we should never speak but at a stile, a gate, or a ditch, where a man can go no further' (4.3.1757–61). He has once seen 'a parasite' in a Cambridge comedy, 'who made faces and mouths of all sorts' (4.3.1761–3): an ironic critique, from a master of mugging. Burbage thinks 'A little teaching will mend these faults' (4.3.1764), and when Philomusus and Studioso arrive they are auditioned, by having them copy the actors' style of speaking, and by reciting a little of the opening soliloquy from Shakespeare's *Richard III*, which had already turned into a byword for 'acting'. Kemp's model for copy is a mock oration, with a ridiculous antithetical construction, providing a parody of excessively pompous 'academic' style. The students are both told they have promise, and 'will do well after a while', but after the actors leave they scorn an offer to earn their living by 'the basest trade', reverting to the dismissive attitude towards playing which classical oratorical texts, as well as ingrained cultural and class attitudes, encouraged.

To take this little dramatic encounter too seriously would be a mistake. It is a jest, and the famous actors were played, probably in a deliberately 'actorish' style, by a pair of undergraduates or junior fellows who had perhaps seen the living men on stage, whether on tour in Cambridge or at playhouses in London during university vacations. The observations in both directions, of professionals on amateurs, and the reverse, are facetious, and not to be relied upon as more than an indication that the university actors had their eyes open to the style of the professional stage. How they valued it no doubt varied, but the *Parnassus* plays are certainly testimony to its prominence in the cultural life of the intellectual centres of the country.

That some disenchanted or impoverished undergraduates left the universities to become professional players is certainly possible, if unlikely.

Most undergraduates were minors, under the age of twenty-one, and subject to parental discipline; they came overwhelmingly from families with higher social expectations than the profession of player would have satisfied. Many people went to university without completing a degree, but a good number of them moved to the inns of court in London, where they transferred to purely legal studies, and where dramatic activity also flourished.

INNS OF COURT

The so-called 'inns' of court were, and are, reminiscent in some ways of university colleges: they have halls, for communal eating and assembly, chapels, and residential and study accommodation within enclosed precincts. The four chief Elizabethan establishments, Gray's Inn, Lincoln's Inn, Middle Temple, and the Inner Temple, are still the chief inns of court, and are to be found in the same locations as they were in Shakespeare's day, on the western side of the city of London, outside the boundary of the walls, and stretching northwards from the Temple, south of Fleet Street, to Gray's Inn, north of Holborn. They were unlike universities in that they did no formal teaching: the community of working lawyers who lived there had no responsibility to train the young men who arrived as students, who were expected to follow their own course of reading the laws and commentaries on them, and observing the courts in action, eventually graduating, if they did so at all, by proving their knowledge in disputations, moots, and public readings adjudicated by the benchers, the senior lawyers of each inn. This process took some years, and by no means all the people who took up residence at the inns at one time or another (including such literary figures as John Donne, Francis Beaumont, John Marston, Thomas Lodge, and Thomas Campion) graduated as lawyers, or took up careers in the law. The inns of court also functioned as a kind of fashionable 'finishing school' for young men, particularly those of noble or gentry families, who could perhaps pick up a smattering of knowledge of the laws of land tenure, as likely to be useful, but who could also associate with older figures in the world of politics and power, many of whom had honorific membership in the inns – 'networking' in modern parlance.

The general acquisition of the gentlemanly accomplishments within the chief centre of fashion in the land was another end in view. Even the puritanical and earnest Simonds D'Ewes, who took his law studies seriously, paid for attendance at fencing and dancing schools; other young gentlemen took classes in singing and playing the viols.[66] Dressing fashionably, not in the cap and gown of Cambridge and Oxford scholars, and wearing one's hair and beard, once one grew one, *à la mode*, were among the expectations of the more casual 'students', and they were generally tolerated by the governing bodies of the inns. As George Whetstone put it in his dedicatory epistle, addressed to the inns of court, prefacing *The Mirror for Magistrates* in 1586: 'Your chiefest discipline is by the purse. Those that are disposed, study laws; who so liketh, without check, may follow dalliance.'[67] The inns of court lay not in small, isolated market towns, as did the universities, but between the twin poles of fashion and power, the city of London and the district of Westminster, where the old medieval royal palace housed the principal law courts and the Parliament, and the newer palace of Whitehall the monarch and her or his central administrative body, the Privy Council. Young men living in the inns could fancy themselves as being at the very heart of the nation's pulse. They also expected to take part in the pleasures afforded by metropolitan life, and the luxury and leisure economies the city fostered. Prominent among these were the playhouses, which were much frequented by inns-of-court men. At any one time there were between two and two and a half thousand students resident at the various inns in the years between 1558 and the civil wars, so that they made up an important constituency within theatrical audiences.[68]

Because many of the students at the inns of court went there after a year or so at university rather than directly from school, the average age of students was rather older, corresponding more closely to the ages of modern university students. Abraham Fraunce, an actor while at Cambridge, and probably also at Shrewsbury School earlier, was a committed student of the law, and had a long and successful career as a lawyer. After completing his Cambridge MA he was admitted to Gray's Inn in 1583, when he was almost twenty-four, being called to the bar five years later. His involvement in whatever revels Gray's Inn may have sponsored during those years seems eminently likely. As in the university colleges, seasonal festivals were a chief focus for festivals and games that featured a good deal of role-playing, at least. There were traditional elections of a 'Christmas prince', a younger member of the community who wielded temporary authority with a facetious machinery of government – ministers, ambassadors, and attendants – dispensing legislation and decrees in rhetorical styles which echoed, and mocked, the formulae of real proclamations and statutes. The oral delivery of such things, when they were read out in the mock court, no doubt also sent up the style of the learned bench, and perhaps even targeted recognizable peculiarities of the voices of senior members of the inn. Broad parody governed such games of misrule, to the general delight of a community in a holiday mood. The last and most fully recorded of such events was that at

Gray's Inn in the winter of 1593–4, when the 'Prince of Purpoole', young Henry Helmes, presided over elaborate revels which included a visiting performance of *The Comedy of Errors*, and a masque, performed by the law students themselves at court before the Queen.

Although such residents of the inns as Abraham Fraunce (Gray's Inn) and Sir James Whitelocke (Middle Temple) had acted in Latin drama at school and university, dramatic activity at the inns of court after the mid sixteenth century seems to have involved playing in English only, although the theoretical defence of it was no doubt the familiar one of training in confidence and delivery for public speaking. The practice of the law involved knowledge of and oral facility in three languages – English, Latin, and Law French, the last a relic of Norman rule, beginning in the eleventh century – but the young gentlemen of the inns who were principally involved in the mounting of plays seem, like their contemporaries working in the commercial theatre, to have written and performed their pieces in the native language. The most renowned of these was *Gorboduc*, a moralized tragedy on the breakdown of rule and civil order following a divided succession (like *King Lear*), of particular interest to serious-minded legis-lators, and hence at a far remove from the holiday hilarity of the Gray's Inn revels. It was singled out by Sir Philip Sidney in his *Defence of Poesy* (c. 1582) as the major achievement in native English tragic writing to date, a judge-ment made on the basis of reading rather than performance, although Sidney had entered Gray's Inn in early 1567, at the precocious age of twelve, and may have heard something from members of the audiences of the play's first performances. The play, written by Thomas Sackville, later the Earl of Dorset, and Thomas Norton, was acted first before their fellows at the Inner Temple in the Christmas season of 1561–2, and then before the Queen at Whitehall on 18 January 1562. Both occasions were important, since the former was distinguished by the presence of Sir Robert Dudley (Earl of Leicester from 1564), already a leading figure in Elizabethan politics, and a patron of the Inner Temple. He was the guest of the 'mighty Palaphilos, Prince of Sophie, High Constable Marshal of the Knights Templars, Patron of the Honourable Order of Pegasus', another Christmas prince.[69] The first audience of *Gorboduc* may not have been in a particularly sober mood, at least at the beginning of the performance.

We have no indication of the identity of the first actors beyond the announcement on the title page of the text published in 1570 that it was played before the Queen 'by the gentlemen of the Inner Temple'. If the play was cast in the fashion of the university plays, one man to one part, seventeen performers were required for the speaking parts, including two playing female roles. The play also included five dumb shows, with accompanying music and sound effects, one preceding each act and calling on six or seven performers each. Assuming that a team of that number might have changed costumes during the playing of each act (the shortest, act three, approaches two hundred lines, and the others are all three hundred lines or more), then a total of twenty-five performers would have been needed. The chief demand on those with lines to learn and speak was the rhetorical style of the dialogue, written in fluent blank verse but featuring rather static set speeches of some considerable length, a test not only of the variations in pitch and rhythm in delivery which might retain an audience's attention and guide them through long syntactical constructions, but also of one's partners on stage, required to maintain attention and focus on the speaker, and to avoid distracting scratching of noses. If wandering eyes in the audience catch minor signs of inattention on stage the fabric of performance begins to disintegrate. In the second scene, for example, each of the three counsellors Arostus, Philander, and Eubulus gives his own advice on King Gorboduc's proposition to divide his kingdom between his two sons: each has an uninterrupted speech of between seventy and a hundred lines, one following another. A legal audience would have recognized these as 'pleadings' – the statement of a case, and the reasons for arriving at certain conclusions from the stated premises – and probably the actors called on something of their courtroom manner in delivering them. They remain, none the less, enormously difficult speeches to sustain and animate; the end of the act, and *'the music of cornets'* which plays during the ensuing dumb show, were probably greeted with some relief by audience and actors alike.

A second original piece, also presented before the Queen and court and surviving in print, is *The Misfortunes of Arthur*, another pseudo-historical play examining the decay of civil rule. A far less distinguished piece than *Gorboduc*, although apparently taking the earlier play as a general model, it was mounted by Gray's Inn in early 1588 at Greenwich Palace, and probably also at Gray's Inn Hall. The play proper was preceded by an introduction, in which three Muses led in 'five gentleman students ... in their usual garments': in legal robes, that is to say. They are prisoners of the Muses for overstepping their usual commitment to the law, and their denunciation is answered by a speech from one of their number, pleading their case, that they have ventured outside their usual territory only to please the Queen. Thus the prologue is turned into a situational game, and a compliment. A modern editor has suggested that these captive lawyers were the various authors of the entertainment, which seems possible; far less likely are the suggestions that they took roles in the play which follows, or that the entire show was cast with eight actors only.[70] The conditions of academic casting were such that there was no compelling need to double roles, and I think it far more likely that theatrical shows of all kinds put on by institutions of learning involved relatively large numbers of people when circumstances required it: a festive offering, in this case to the Queen, demonstrated the widely shared goodwill of the community which had created it by involving more people in the creation. The cast of *The Misfortunes of Arthur* was probably similar in number to that of *Gorboduc*: twenty speaking parts, with three female roles, but also some silent costumed figures for the dumb shows and 'a number of soldiers' (single rather than double figures more likely, I think). Whether Abraham Fraunce, in his late twenties and coming to the end of his residence in Gray's Inn, may have been persuaded to take a role in the play, on the basis of his earlier prominence on the academic stage, we cannot determine.

Gorboduc and *The Misfortunes of Arthur* were the product of special events, and there is no sign that play production at any of the inns was an annual expectation, as it was at some Cambridge colleges. The talents of the law communities were such that they could rise to the occasional production of plays, with large casts and quite elaborate staging, but none of the inns appears to have maintained a regular tradition of production for its own, local audience. Ambitious productions of drama such as those discussed above seemed to draw out the serious side of the lawyers; it was Cambridge which was to produce a famous satire of the legal profession, if in Latin: the Clare College two-part play *Ignoramus*, a great success when played to the King in 1616. The students of the inns evidently relaxed more when music took a larger part in their shows. The production of masques was a long tradition of the inns, evidently connected with their Christmas celebrations, as was the masque of *Proteus and the Adamantine Rock*, taken to court by the Prince of Purpoole and his revellers at Shrovetide 1595. Masques, evidently, could demonstrate the law students' accomplishments in singing, perhaps, and principally in dancing: the dramatic components of masques were traditionally briefer and more formal, employing more set speeches, encomia, and orations, than those of plays proper. The central feature of the masque was a spectacularly costumed series of dances, and Henry Helmes distinguished himself in dancing before the Queen in 1595. Ceremonial dancing was, in fact, one of the ancient rituals of a number of the inns, observed at certain gatherings and feasts, although it was a good deal more stately than the showier figures the young men of the community demonstrated in masque dancing.[71]

Masques specifically produced by the inns for the monarch included two for the marriage of Princess Elizabeth in 1613, the Middle Temple and Lincoln's Inn collaborating to mount a masque written by George Chapman and designed by Inigo Jones, and the Inner Temple and Gray's Inn together putting on a piece written by Francis Beaumont, both at Whitehall. In 1634 all the inns collaborated on the extravagant production of *The Triumph of Peace*, written by James Shirley, designed by Jones, and with music by William Lawes, and featuring, as the 1613 productions also had, an elaborate costumed procession to Whitehall before the perform- ance. The *Triumph of Peace* procession, in the dark of a February evening, featured hundreds of people lit by torches, the masquers in spangles and plumes riding on horses and in chariots, and moving from Holborn east- wards to the city, through the walls at Aldersgate, down to St Paul's, and then processing westwards through Ludgate and along Fleet Street to Charing Cross, and then Whitehall. Thus the lawyers traced a symbolic connection between their own territory, that of the city authorities, and the court, in a theatrical parade that cost many thousands of pounds to mount. Ten years later the symbolism and the name of the show must have looked considerably ironic.

Such a grand event was unusual, and it was certainly not universally approved. One famous resident of Lincoln's Inn was the lawyer William Prynne, whose encyclopaedic anti-theatrical polemic *Histriomastix* had appeared in 1633, and for which he was savagely punished. Although his views may have been extreme they were not entirely disapproved of among his colleagues, and the growing puritan strand of resistance to a culture sponsored by the Crown had some support within the inns. Where it predominated, the older traditions of communal festival were increasingly under attack.

As I have pointed out above, the law communities were important consumers of dramatic entertainment as much as producers of it. *The Comedy of Errors*, played by professionals, was seen at Gray's Inn Hall in 1595, and the famous account by John Manningham, in a diary kept while he was a resident of the Middle Temple, tells of the performance of *Twelfth Night*, by Shakespeare and his fellows, in the hall there, 'at our feast', 2 February 1602. While individual law students went to the playhouses, then, the inn as a body might commission visiting performances by the professional players. That such visits were commoner than has hitherto been realized, and that they were sustained up until the time of the wars, will be revealed in the records to be published in the forthcoming Records of Early English Drama volume dedicated to the inns of court, edited by Alan

Nelson, the leading scholar of the academic theatre of the Shakespearean period. As a student in the inns between the 1550s and the 1640s, then, one was far more likely to be an observer of dramatic performance than a participant in it. The higher one's social rank, the truer that was likely to be; it was all very well for schoolboys and students to appear in plays, but it was not an amusement for gentlemen. Drunken skits, in hall among one's fellows at Christmas, might be allowable, as might dignified costumed dancing in a masque at court, but for those touchy about their social standing (as certain aristocratic families were not), after a certain age, the association of playing with vulgarity and 'baseness' was a strong disincentive to amateur acting. Such attitudes hardened as the professional theatre in London grew and became fashionable, particularly after the first decade of the seventeenth century. It is significant that the last elaborate production of a play sponsored and cast from within the inns of court took place in 1588. Thereafter the culture of the professionals took over in London, and the smart young men resident at the inns took to appearing prominently in the audience, at the Blackfriars, Cockpit, and Salisbury Court playhouses, rather than on a stage.

CHAPTER 3

Apprentices

Teache a child in the trade of his way, and when he is olde, he shal not departe from it.

Proverbs, 22.6, Geneva Bible (1560)

Thomas Dekker's play *The Shoemakers' Holiday* (1599) gives a romantic account of the rise of the fifteenth-century Lord Mayor of London, Simon Eyre, a member of the Shoemakers' Company. The world of trade depicted in the play is a mixture of down-to-earth handicraft, with a workroom of labourers engaged in cutting and stitching leather in the manufacture of shoes, and rather magical investment, as their master Eyre makes a killing by buying up, on a tip, the cargo of a newly arrived ship. Its accuracy as a portrayal of a bourgeois world lies in the mixture of the small-scale and domestic with the considerable wealth and power that characterized work and trade in London particularly throughout the sixteenth and seventeenth centuries.[1] Within traditional crafts and industries – the cloth trade, for example, which had been at the centre of English economic output from the fourteenth century onwards – the scale ran from the small sheep-farmer who did his own carding, spinning, and weaving to the great merchants who traded in the international market of finished cloth, buying and selling in quantity at substantial rates, extending and incurring credit and debts. A successsful career in a trade was one principal path of social mobility on the part of the able and the reasonably lucky; Dekker's legend of Eyre is to that extent based on the contemporary world in which the play was performed. The political significance of trade in London, especially, was that the great bodies of trade and manufacture, the companies, collectively contributed the efforts, skills, and wealth of their senior members to the city administration, the Court of Aldermen, led by the Lord Mayor, the post which is Simon Eyre's final accomplishment in the play. His 'holiday' is a Shrove Tuesday feast for all the 'prentices' in London, celebrated towards the end in typically exuberant fashion.[2]

Apprentices were trainees in the various crafts and trades, attached to a master for an agreed period of years, and serving him with their labour in return for practical instruction, board, clothing, and lodging in his house. They became temporary members of a family, in fact, and so the apprentice Ralph is treated by the Grocer and his Wife in Beaumont's play *The Knight of the Burning Pestle*. The apprentice–master relationship was legally binding on both parties, following the consent to the initial agreement of the child's parent or guardian, and it was regulated by statute and custom. The famous early Elizabethan legislation which attempted to subsume all older practice was called the Statute of Artificers (1563); it was meant to apply to the entire realm, while in London the Mayor's Court and the individual companies oversaw the regulation and enforcement of the apprenticeship system within the city. Professional stage players, who never had the status of a trade recognized by statute or custom, none the less employed the legislative framework of apprenticeship to attach boys to certain adult members of their troupes for training, and they did so in various ways, examined in what follows. Yet like his counterparts in choirs, any boy playing-apprentice quickly saw his training transformed into learning by practice, through memorizing and acting parts in plays before paying audiences. Like any other apprentice a boy player was expected to increase the output of the collective working community to which he was attached, and his particular contribution was the performance of female roles, many of which, evidently, were extremely challenging, as they remain to modern adult female performers.

When apprentices completed their term of training in their early twenties they were recognized as independent masters of their crafts and trades, free to set up workshops of their own and earn a living from their expert work. In London they paid a fee and took an oath to uphold the standards of the company and the statutes of the city, and then they became freemen, full members, or 'brothers', of the company to which their master belonged, as well as citizens of London, a status belonging only to adult males who were freemen of London companies, with the addition only of those to whom freedom was granted honorifically, as it still can be. Shakespeare, then, lived in London for much of his adult life, but he was never a citizen, unlike a number of his fellow actors. They had not gained such status by apprenticing as players, however, but by training first under master grocers, goldsmiths, weavers, and so on, and becoming at least nominal members of such companies. Having done so, they were then legally enabled to take on their own apprentices, and it seems to have been a widely recognized latitude of the system that members of companies were free to practise

trades other than that in which they had graduated, and to train apprentices
in the disciplines and technical knowledge of what they were actually doing,
especially if the particular trade had no traditional controlling company of
its own. Thus men who were technically freemen of the Drapers' Company
made their living variously as booksellers, printers, and musicians; John
Heminges, citizen and grocer of London, made his by playing in a series of
theatre companies, culminating in the King's men. After a certain point in
his career he seems to have stopped taking stage parts, while remaining a full
member of the troupe and being one of the principal master actors to whom
boy apprentices were attached. Presumably he could then devote his time to
training them privately – it seems quite likely that they lived in his house –
in the times when they were not at the playhouses working with the entire
troupe in performances. All Heminges's boys were, technically, trainee
grocers. John Shank, a freeman of the Weavers' Company, was the other
chief master and instructor of the King's men's apprentices, so others were,
as far as the records went, aspiring weavers.[3]

Formal binding as an apprentice on the books of one London livery
company or another was only one of several models of theatrical apprenticeship, which was adapted in a number of ways to suit the special conditions
of the profession. When an apprentice haberdasher completed his term of
service under a master and took his freedom he would have looked to setting
up an independent business, with a shop, his own apprentices, and possibly
some hired workmen. He would have needed some money to establish
himself, but might have borrowed it until profits alowed him to repay it. A
'freeman' player, so to speak (since the city administration did not recognize
any such category of person), would have been seeking not to set up on
his own, but to become a full member of a playing troupe, on the most
advantageous terms possible. To become a 'sharer', one of the core group of
ten to a dozen actors who collectively ran the costs of production in paying
for scripts, costumes, properties, and playhouse rentals, and then divided
any profits from performances, he would have required capital of two kinds.
That is to say that on becoming a sharer one had to pay a sum of money
into the joint stock of the company, but one also would have had to be
regarded as a good enough player to be likely to improve that stock through
successful performances attracting paying customers. It would have been
quite clear, after seven or so years' attachment to a company as an apprentice, whether the stock of talent was popular with audiences and one's
fellows; if one had talent but lacked money or credit one would otherwise
have had to work one's way up the financial hierarchy gradually. In the
later years of the King's men the system of sharer-actors became rather

inflexible, and the talented younger men were driven to complain to the Lord Chamberlain about a structure which was not rewarding them at a rate which matched their stage skills and value to the company. Actors, unlike grocers, actually worked from day to day as a 'brotherhood' (a term that more traditional trades reserved for their dispersed membership) and in doing so they had to strike a balance among collective and individual efforts, talents, and rewards.

In the sixteenth and seventeenth centuries apprenticeship was regarded as a route to independent adulthood, and the charitable placing of orphans in suitable trades both by guardians and parish overseers was a recognized step in securing their future, giving boys (especially) a secure place within a household for their formative years and the eventual means of earning a living and making a way in life. The apprentice Ralph in *The Knight of the Burning Pestle* is practically an adored favourite son of his master's family; he is, we learn in the second act, 'a fatherless child' (2.96). Philip Henslowe became the guardian of his deceased brother's children in 1595; his nephew was placed as an apprentice dyer, within Henslowe's own trade, not in the unpredictable theatre, we might note.[4] On the other side of the country, in 1597, the orphaned Robert Stole, aged fourteen, living on the charity of the parish of Bridgwater, Somerset, was apprenticed by his overseers to a group of travelling players, to whom the parish paid a fee of two marks, one traditional part of the formal agreement accompanying apprenticeship;[5] Henslowe had paid two pounds to one Mr Newman, his nephew's master. The young Stole did not enter a settled household – although he would have been bound to one of the actors only – but a travelling community, and his future was subject to the uncertainties faced by all working actors. Perhaps he had some talent, but he made no mark on any of the subsequent theatrical activity known to modern scholars. The poor prospects of careers in the performing arts were recognized by the governors of Christ's Hospital, a charitable school housed in the buildings of the former Greyfriars Franciscan community north of St Paul's, and run by the city of London to educate orphaned children and then establish them in apprenticeships. In 1589 the governing body decreed that 'Henceforth none of the children of the Hospital shall be put apprentice to any musicianer, other than such as be blind, lame, and not able to be put to other service.'[6] If a musician's future was regarded as insecure, 'other service' is unlikely to have included going on the stage.

Robert Stole's age at apprenticeship, fourteen, was a common average, although boys were apprenticed both earlier and later, with corresponding adjustments to their terms of service. Apprentices were expected to serve a minimum of seven years, and were not to be freed until they were at least twenty-one. The preferred age for freedom within London, at least 'on the books', was twenty-four, but many men gained freedom before that. The apprenticeship bond itself was recognized by various forms of written agreement, in which parents or guardians were involved, with the payment of a fee to the new master. Many apprenticeship indentures to musicians and instrument makers survive from the city of Bristol, between the 1540s and the 1630s, for terms of seven to ten years; in some cases the master committed to providing his apprentice at the completion of his term with an instrument on which he had been taught to play.[7] Figure 3 shows a surviving indenture of apprenticeship from 1612, in which John Risley, son of Paul Risley of Chitwood, Buckinghamshire, acknowledges his apprenticeship for a term of nine years to Thomas Havers, merchant taylor of London, as well as merchant of the staple and merchant of the Levant, Turkey, and French Companies, 'to learn his art', a phrase which makes clear the width of seventeenth-century usage, and demonstrates the kind of claim that the phrase 'the art of stage playing' represents. Players also had a body of professional knowledge to teach young men, just as did the more traditional bourgeois trades.

Havers dealt in foreign trade, and Risley was entering upon a career that might lead to considerable prosperity through business. He undertook to serve his master faithfully, keep his secrets, 'his lawful commandments every where gladly do', to do him no damage nor waste his goods. Further, in the style of patriarchal edicts, 'he shall not commit fornication, nor contract matrimony within the said term', is forbidden 'to play at the cards, dice, tables, or other unlawful games', to buy or sell, to haunt taverns, and 'to absent himself from his said master's service day nor night unlawfully'. Any visits to playhouses would have to have been requested and approved, but the general tone of the document suggests that the theatre was not high among Havers's interests. On his part the master undertakes, convolutedly, that 'his said apprentice in the same art which he useth by the best means he can shall teach and instruct', providing him during the term of his bonds with food and drink, clothes, lodging, 'and all other necessaries, according to the custom of the city of London'.[8]

Firm patriarchal control and careful training during the early to middle teens of any capable and ambitious apprentice would presumably have led to a certain loosening of discipline as young men developed into productive and profitable business partners for several years before gaining their freedom. Havers's business, for example, might have involved some travel and foreign postings for those he thought responsible and able enough. By the

3 Apprenticeship indenture of John Risley to Thomas Havers, 1612. Print on vellum. British Library MS c.106.cc.3

end of one's apprenticeship, any master might have hoped, one would be a hard-working intern rather than a dependent student; the economic calculus of apprenticeship was to provide relatively cheap expert labour and energy towards the end of its term. Once again, theatrical apprentices would have been subject to a rather different trajectory, particularly if they rapidly developed bodies and voices quite unfit for the principal apprentice roles of female characters and did not otherwise expand their range or demonstrate particular talent in performance. The horizons of such young men would have closed in as they got older, relegated to bit parts and theatrical odd jobs, and after serving out their term facing, at best, subsistence existence as hired players, without any continuing contractual connection with a company.

The legal status and the corporate protection offered by freedom in one of the London companies were considerable advantages in working at any trade within the city. Sons of freemen could claim their own freedom 'by patrimony', it being assumed that sons would have been trained in the family business of their fathers. Richard Burbage could therefore have claimed membership of the Joiners' Company, to which his father James belonged, although he never appears to have done so. Rather late in his life, and towards the end of his stage career, the actor Ellis Worth claimed freedom of the Merchant Taylors' Company by partimony, as the son of Henry Worth, 'late Merchant Taylor deceased'.[9] The advantage of a playing apprenticeship under such men as John Heminges, Robert Armin, or Andrew Cane would have been eventual freedom of a company, and of the city of London, providing at least some kind of safety net in the event that one did not emerge as a particularly succesful player. These men had all gained their status through regular London apprenticeships, however, turning to the stage as adult freemen, and without, in Andrew Cane's case, ever relinquishing the practice of his first trade as a goldsmith.

The last well-known male apprentice player of female roles was Edward Kynaston, the subject of a relatively recent film, *Stage Beauty* (2004), who carried the old tradition on at the newly reopened Cockpit playhouse for several months in 1660. Samuel Pepys, who saw him perform, thought he made a beautiful woman in appearance, but sounded rather odd. Kynaston was then seventeen; he was soon moved into male roles, beginning an eminent stage career, as actresses were admitted to the acting troupes. Kynaston's master, John Rhodes, was a member of the Drapers' Company, and had never been a player, other than in the odd extra part while working in the wardrobe at the Blackfriars playhouse. Throughout the Commonwealth period his chief business was as a bookseller, although he retained interests in the theatrical enterprises in which he had involved himself before 1642.[10] Kynaston's parents or guardians, from the relatively remote county of Shropshire, who apprenticed the boy Edward to Rhodes at the relatively early age of eleven, must have been intending to launch him in the trade of bookselling in London. When Rhodes sensed the political and cultural winds changing in 1659 he must have set to work, as well as he could, in training his evidently talented and suitably attractive sixteen-year-old apprentice in the suspended art of playing the woman's part. Rhodes had probably been biding his time for some years, and selecting his trainees with an eye to their future worth on the stage: his second famous apprentice was the renowned actor Thomas Betterton. During the 1650s Rhodes's book-shop remained in part a rehearsal hall devoted to the traditional arts of the pre-war theatre.

The model of freedom by patrimony, under which sons followed their fathers' trades, trained as youths in the family firm, was exemplified in numerous theatrical groups. Richard Burbage began acting at about the age of fourteen, and perhaps first played in female roles, trained and over-seen by his father, James. Other actor sons include a number who trained in the older theatre and resumed playing in the new theatres of the Restoration after 1660 as older colleagues of Kynaston: William Cartwright the younger, son of William the elder, whose joint careers spanned almost a hundred years of playing, from the 1590s to the 1680s; Theophilus Bird, son of William Bird (alias Borne); and Charles Hart, who is reported first to have played women's roles at the Blackfriars with the King's men, and was probably the son of William Hart, actor at the Rose and the Fortune. The eminent Burbage family of actors and theatre investors might be compared with the more obscure clan formed by the actor Robert Browne, lead player of Derby's men, and his wife Susan: they married in 1592. Their enterprise at the Boar's Head playhouse in Whitechapel hardly seems to have been a great success, but following Robert's death in 1603 his widow remarried to the actor Thomas Greene, a principal comic player at the Red Bull playhouse, opened about 1605. At his death in 1612 Greene's substantial investments in the Red Bull passed to his widow, who subse-quently (1623) was engaged in litigation with the acting troupe of the Bull to claim what she saw as her proper share of profits. One of the subjects at dispute was the money due to her son, William Browne, who had been playing as a hired man with the troupe, possibly since about 1615. In that year he was only thirteen, however: the age of apprenticeship, and suited to the playing of female roles. He had possibly learnt something from his stepfather Greene, who had died when he was ten, but the leading member of the company by 1615 appears to have been Ellis Worth, and he may have undertaken the supervision of the teenaged Browne, before the players ran into troubled times. The two men were reunited in Prince Charles's troupe, founded in 1631. Browne, at any rate, trained for the theatre as part of a theatrical family, and when he died, relatively early, at the age of thirty-two in 1634, he left an apprentice whose wages from the company, probably for playing female roles, were to be paid to his estate.

William Browne's widow shortly remarried, to the John Rhodes who was later the master of Kynaston; Browne's sister Susan was married to one of his actor colleagues, Thomas Bond, a beneficiary of Browne's will. His mother, widow of two actors and remarried to a rather obscure third, remained an investor and property-holder in playhouses, and continued managing her business, with increasing difficulty, until her death in 1649. William Browne left no children; this particular dynasty, like the Burbages in that respect, did not produce a generation that spanned the twenty-year gap in the English professional theatre. William's elder brother Robert Browne, named after his father and heir to whatever fortune their mother may have amassed by the time of her death, had been chosen for training in a traditional city career rather than a life in the theatre. At the time his brother began as a young actor, Robert was apprentice to the haberdasher Robert Holden, gaining his freedom in 1618, when he was twenty-two. There are signs that Holden's business was at least partly involved in theatrical costuming, however, and perhaps Browne followed him in that particular specialization, involving himself in his father's livelihood at a remove.

That groups of actors functioned as larger families, taking seriously the word 'brotherhood', which members of London trade companies used about their mutual relationships, is shown not only by the pattern of such intermarriages and kinship bonds apparent in the extended clan of Robert and Susan Browne, but also by signs of charitable support and relief. One of the boy actors in the newly formed Prince Charles's troupe in 1631 was the thirteen-year-old Robert Stratford. He appears not to have had, as others of his peers did, a formal bond of apprenticeship with any of the adult actors (of whom William Browne was one), but to have been a kind of adopted son. His father was the actor William Stratford, who had died in August 1625 when his son was seven, probably as a victim of the bad plague outbreak of that year, notably cruel in the parish of St Giles Cripplegate where the Stratfords lived. Stratford senior had earlier acted at the Fortune in a company that also had included Andrew Cane and Richard Fowler, both members of the new 1631 troupe. Since Cane had two apprentice actors to look after by that year, perhaps young Stratford became Fowler's boy; he certainly appears to have been given support and training to earn his living as his father had, although we know next to nothing of his subsequent career, and he would still have been a young man when theatre business was brought to a stop in 1642.

Gaps in our knowledge, reminders of which create a rather depressing but cautionary refrain in studies of the early modern theatre, make it difficult to be confident about describing any normative pattern of theatrical apprenticeship. We know very little about Burbage's apprentices, for example, but that he certainly took some on is attested to by the gratitude of his pupil Nicholas Tooley, who in his will of 1623, a few years after Burbage's own death, writes warmly and affectionately of his old master and of his family, a sign of the close personal bonds apprentices enjoyed, at best, as part of their training. Tooley was never in Burbage's class as a performer as far as we can now tell, but aside from the question of the pupil's innate talent the best performers are and were not necessarily the best teachers, as is also true to a degree in music. Edward Alleyn *did* have one eminent trainee, at least for a time, to whom we will come below; significantly, he did not retain him. Talented pupils do not always accommodate themselves to other strong talents.

The varying trajectories of theatrical apprenticeship might be appreciated, first, by considering the linked careers of John Shank and Thomas Pollard, both specialists in comic playing. We have Shank's assurance that Pollard trained under him; they both were members of the same eminent company, the King's men, Pollard for practically his entire career, and also, towards the end of Shank's time, legal antagonists, as Pollard, in the company of two other younger colleagues, tried to get hold of a larger slice of the troupe's profits through shareholding in the company's theatres, of which Shank was supposed to have cornered a disproportionate part through some shady dealing after the death of John Heminges in 1630. The documents recording this quarrel, submitted to the Lord Chamberlain for arbitration and preserved in the records of his office, are known as the Sharers' Papers, and they reveal a good deal about the later economic organization of the King's men's company.[11] At the date of the dispute, 1635, Pollard was hardly a young man, and no doubt the source of his disaffection was that he was a prominent and successful player without the fitting financial substance to match his established stage career. He was not to know that the theatre had only seven more years of commercial life, but one way or another his complaint appears to have borne fruit, and he was reputed to have died rich, in retirement in 1653. Thomas, son of Edward Pollard, had been christened at Aylesbury, Buckinghamshire, late in the year of 1597, so was fifty-five at his death, and thirty-seven in the mid 1630s, the time of the sharers' dispute.[12] If he had been apprenticed to Shank at around the common age of fourteen – we have no records of the transaction, but Shank specifically names Pollard as one of the 'boys' he has trained – the younger man had been on the stage since about 1612. Shank, obviously, was older, and in his written submission to the Lord Chamberlain he calls himself 'an old man in this quality', having served, he claims, both the second Earl of Pembroke and Queen Elizabeth, before entering the King's men about 1613, bringing Pollard with him as a specialist in female roles; under the terms of a full apprenticeship Pollard might have expected to be a freeman player about 1619–20.[13]

In his will, made at the very end of 1635, in the last few weeks of his life, Shank names himself a 'citizen and weaver of London'.[14] His apprentices, then, may have been bound to him under the regulations of the Weavers' Company, although there are no records to show it, and Pollard, for example, never seems to have claimed freedom of the Weavers. Shank *may* have acquired his own status by serving in his youth in the workshop of a weaver, and learning to work a loom, as Tarlton had served his own time with a genuine haberdasher, Ralph Boswell, and Armin with a goldsmith, John Kettlewood, all of them taking up stage careers as adults following earlier apprenticeship in quite distinct trades.[15] Yet Shank claims to have been a member of the Queen's men, and his connection with that troupe may have begun as a boy, before he was technically a 'servant' of the Queen, as an apprentice player under one of the brothers John and Lawrence Dutton, both freeman weavers, and active as players and theatrical entrepreneurs from the early 1570s onwards.[16] If Shank had apprenticed as a nominal weaver with John Dutton, one of the founder members of the Queen's men in 1583, he probably did not have much expert working knowledge of looms, but perhaps had had some contact with the famous clown Richard Tarlton, whose last five years of playing were spent as a Queen's man, and a colleague of Dutton.[17] Shank's later reputation was as a comedian who was skilled, like Tarlton, in jigs and rhymes, the independent comic turns that might follow the performance of a play proper. The fool's performance as an improviser and song-and-dance man, similar in some ways to the modern stand-up comedian, or the somewhat earlier music-hall and vaudeville artists like George Robey, Dan Leno, or Harry Lauder, is well attested in the stories about Tarlton, Kemp, and Armin, and in the facetious personae they assumed in print. As with the Victorian and Edwardian music-hall comics, eccentric dress and grotesque or ridiculous facial expressions characterized the Elizabethan stage clowns and their successors, and 'signature' routines, like Tarlton's peering onto the stage before making his entrance, became favourites with audiences.

In most histories of Shakespeare's company Shank is represented as the comic specialist acquired to replace Robert Armin, who died in 1615, perhaps after protracted illness, being 'weak in body' when he made his will almost a year earlier.[18] Armin had signed his own apprenticeship bond, for a term of eleven years, in 1581, so probably when he was quite young, perhaps twelve or thirteen; he was, I would guess, in his later forties at the time of his death, and hence the contemporary, rather than the elder, of John Shank, who was probably born about the year 1570. If, as I have suggested, Shank apprenticed with John Dutton and began to act as a teenager in the 1580s, his stage career lasted some fifty years, and his claim to be old in his quality was well founded. Armin certainly served out the term of his own apprenticeship, chiefly with the goldsmith John Kettlewood, and subsequently began as an actor in the first half of the 1590s. In comparison with Shank he may have been the more famous player, but his apprenticeship was not theatrical, and his entire career on the stage was a mere two decades, the second with the King's men. The legend recounted in the popular book *Tarlton's Jests* has it that while he was an apprentice goldsmith Armin met the famous comic actor in London. By composing some improvised verses Armin is supposed to have received Tarlton's blessing as his recognized successor and adopted 'son', 'to wear my clown's suit after me', a mock coronation of the fool apparent. This may be just a story (although historical circumstances would certainly have rendered it possible), but the man more likely to have had some direct contact with the tradition of Tarlton is Shank, either through apprenticeship during Tarlton's lifetime or through working with his colleagues after his death in 1588.

Several general points about training emerge from these conjoined and overlapping careers. Thomas Pollard's value to the King's men in 1613 was his early-adolescent stature and voice: his first roles with the company no doubt included some which are still played on stage; since he was evidently a talented player his early parts may have included Juliet, Hermia, Beatrice, and Viola. Shank, in other words, would not have been training him directly in his own speciality as a low comic, unless we are to suppose Pollard took on such roles as the Nurse or Mistress Quickly, in which a broader style and physical exaggeration have more scope. Pollard certainly became a comic actor as an adult, if only in the later part of his career, with some facility in verbal improvisation and facetious exaggeration, and his own skills had undoubtedly been influenced by observing his master at work on stage. Shank's role as chief supervisor of boy apprentices to the company, however, especially after 1630, proudly emphasized in his submission to the Lord Chamberlain in the sharers' dispute, was hardly to produce a series of copies of himself. Like any adult master actor in charge of an apprentice, he would have offered general supervision and guidance in action and accent, including, probably, his own approaches to such technical matters as breath control and suitable exercise to improve the grace and precision of both speech and movement on stage. Since most apprentices began with roles the adults themselves did not play, and possibly never had played in their own beginning years, any instruction was from the outside rather than the inside, so to speak. One does not have to have a flexible soprano range, however, to be able to offer useful interpretative, enunciative, and musical guidance on the singing of a part.

All the other apprentices Shank mentions in his reply to the junior actors' complaint addressed to the Lord Chamberlain – Thomas Holcombe, John Honeyman, and John Thompson – are known for having taken prominent female roles in the King's men's plays performed between 1616 and the early 1630s. Though all three died relatively young, their adult roles, as far as we know them, do not seem to have been broad comic parts; I shall have more to say about the playing of Honeyman and Thompson in Chapter 5. After Armin's death Shank was the chief specialist in clown parts within the King's company. Pollard's own skills and personal style were such that he became Shank's support and successor in waiting, but otherwise the boys under Shank's care – and he says that he was still responsible for three of them in 1635 – were being generally schooled in performance, and primarily in performance of female roles. If my guess that Shank had apprenticed with John Dutton is correct, he himself had undergone the same experience in his teens, yet like any working member of an ensemble he stood to learn a good deal by watching and listening to others of his colleagues, perhaps at least as much as from direct instruction by his master. That Richard Tarlton was among those players would suggest that a tradition of comic playing might have continued through the entire length of the Shakespearean theatre, from Tarlton himself to Shank and Armin, and from them, through instruction and observation, to Thomas Pollard and Andrew Cane, the latter following Armin's own route to the stage.

We know very little about how Armin's predecessor in Shakespeare's company, Will Kemp, arrived at his position as a leading fool, first with the Earl of Leicester's troupe and then with the Chamberlain's men. Nothing has been discovered, to date, about either his family origins or his activities before the mid 1580s, but it would hardly be surprising to find out that his comic performances were largely self-invented, or at the least were developed from his evident gifts as an athlete with an ear for rhythm: he was a renowned dancer. The careers of Tarlton, Armin, and Andrew Cane, all of whom spent their formative years doing something quite different from their later activities on stage, suggest that independent jesting and improvisatory skill were innate gifts, which one could develop on one's own account. All these men were, presumably, inherently witty, and given to an ironic view of human existence, with some individual force of personality which they translated into their stage antics. All taught themselves the skills to take part in written plays – both Tarlton and Armin wrote plays themselves – but otherwise the clown's skills were those which might be easily dismissed as trivial, but which were enormously popular: grotesque gesture and movement, including dance, and the recital and occasional improvisatory invention of comic verses and songs. The stage clown was both an original and a practitioner of unremarkable and accessible folk skills: dances, shuffles, and mocking jokes. A performer such as Tarlton was simultaneously ordinary and extraordinary, enlightening and delighting through, and in despite of, mere childish antics and puerile jokes. All the stories of his performance now tend to sound either limp or laboured, but he was very clearly an extraordinary presence on the stage, with a vivid connection with audiences, long remembered by those who had seen him; one simply had to be there, as one no longer can. So his successors, I believe, each found his own way to an individual style of animating a received set of farcical routines and gags. The specialist comic actor remained rather a figure apart within the early modern acting troupes; Tarlton, Armin, Cane, and possibly Kemp also, all apprenticed to their own wit.

Thomas Pollard quickly entered upon a prominent stage career, having been apprenticed to a chief actor within the King's men, and performing early in his life at the Globe and the Blackfriars playhouses: he experienced a smooth progression from talented youth to leading player with the most eminent troupe of the country. Michael Bowyer, who ended up as Pollard's colleague and co-administrator of the company's stock after the closing of the Globe and Blackfriars in September 1642, had a more indirect path to eventual prominence, although he too was apprenticed to a player, the rather obscure figure William Hovell, who has not left much record of his activities as they have so far been noticed and collected in standard histories of the stage. Hovell made his will in December 1615, and died shortly afterwards; he was then almost fifty-five years old, having been born in Colchester in early 1561.[19] At the time of his final sickness he was a parishioner of St Saviour Southwark, living in a house leased from Philip Henslowe, and holding various investments in leased property in the neighbourhood, the disposal of which forms the chief theme of the will. He was involved in local government and politics, as a former member of the administration of the Liberty of the Clink: a man, then, of some local standing. His bequests include two pounds 'unto my apprentice Michael Bowyer' and one pound 'to my apprentice William Wilson'. Bowyer, then sixteen, was probably the senior boy. Further indications of Hovell's theatrical activity are contained in the clause which follows: 'I give and bequeath unto Nathaniel Clay and John Podger my fifth part of my stock of apparel and other things which I have in the company wherein they play, and my horse which is with them, to be equally shared and divided between them two.'[20] Clay and Podger are similarly shadowy presences, in terms of theatre history, to Hovell, but it was among such members of the profession that a player as eventually well known as Michael Bowyer received his first training. He was indeed, like the horse, with the travelling playing company rather than in Hovell's household in late 1615, and a few weeks later his apprenticeship would probably have formally passed, as perhaps it already had in practice, to one of the other adult players in the company.

Hovell's connections with Henslowe, in financial transactions and immediate neighbourhood, are suggestive. The two men died within a few weeks of each other and were buried in the same church, now Southwark Cathedral. There is no record of Hovell's ever having been connected with the playhouses and acting companies with which Henslowe dealt, although it is not unlikely. Rather Hovell was involved in touring companies, travelling from town to town outside London, while investing his money and keeping a home in the thriving theatre district on the south bank of the metropolis, where he seems to have been an established resident. The company in which Clay and Podger were players was apparently constituted of five adults (since Hovell left them his fifth part in the stock); the other two may have been John Swinnerton and John Edmonds, both mentioned in Hovell's widow's will, made in 1620, as then owing her money, probably via inheritance from her husband.[21] Other candidates are William Perry and Nathan May, named with Hovell in a royal licence of February 1615 that was shown to the authorities in Norwich in June of the same year.[22] Perry, particularly, had a long subsequent history of managing various touring groups of players. A group of five men, two boys, and a horse sounds like a marginal enterprise, but it was probably carefully planned; Hovell's will suggests he was a man of some substance rather than someone just scraping by. That his company toured probably accounts for his acquisition of Bowyer as apprentice; Michael Bowyer had been born in Kidderminster in Worcestershire in 1599, the son of John Bowyer, a weaver.[23] The town long remained a centre of the textile industry, and as such it had strong links with London, suggesting a second possible means by which a provincial boy might have become attached to a master a hundred and twenty miles distant. Yet the hypothesis often offered for the missing part of Shakespeare's career, that he attached himself to an acting troupe touring the Midlands, seems the strong likelihood in Bowyer's case: Hovell and his colleagues, I think, ran the kind of company which was always on the lookout for talented recruits as apprentices.

A performing group of about five adults, each with two apprentices, on the model of Hovell's share, would have made up a company of fifteen, the average strength of playing troupes in the early seventeenth century. To perform a typical play of the time, with only two or three female roles, the older apprentices would have been cast in secondary or younger lead roles – the young men in a comedy, for example. The economic advantage would have been that the principal sharers were reduced and their proportional share of profits increased, the apprentices having been paid low wages, if any. The official justification for such an arrangement, in seeking patronage and licensing, may have been that it was a training company, specifically designed to prepare boys for the stage, and as such a provincial version of various similar ventures in London. Nicholas Long, also mentioned in Hovell's will as 'sometime my servant' (and thus perhaps a former playing apprentice), had been involved with the touring enterprises of the Children of the Queen's Revels in 1615, a company which by then was constituted of older youths and young men rather than boys, although it was managed by adult entrepreneurs. Nathaniel Clay and John Edmonds, with other individuals also involved in the Queen's Revels troupes, were both associated with another venture which began its life about 1615, and was recognized in letters patent of that year issued to 'John Daniel and his assigns'.[24] Like other earlier boys' troupes it appears to have had musical roots, and was variously called the Children of the Queen's Chamber of Bristol or the Youths of her Majesty's Royal Chamber of Bristol. Its base, evidently, was to be the city of Bristol, but it toured the south-west, Midlands, and East Anglia, at least, and survived for ten years or so. It was certainly not constituted solely of 'youths', nor always and everywhere on the model I have described above, and when the company presented its licence in Exeter in June 1618 it was challenged by the mayor of the city, who wrote in complaint to Sir Thomas Lake, Secretary of State: 'I perused their patent, and finding that it is only for children and youths (for so are the words), I did … restrain them from playing here, for that being fifteen of their company there are but only five youths among them, and all the rest are men, some about 30 and 40 and 50 years as they confessed unto me.'[25] The Youths of Bristol, evidently, had transformed themselves into something more closely resembling an adult troupe, perhaps as a consequence of earlier success, but the company's constitution was probably always fairly elastic in practice. The rejected adult players in Exeter in 1618 might have brought to mind the words of another older man on a different occasion: 'they hate us youth'.[26]

How the mayor counted his 'youths', of course, we do not know. Michael Bowyer, had he been a member of the group, was eighteen in the summer of 1618, and perhaps had already moved into juvenile lead roles; his apprenticeship bonds would have had another few years to run, however. By 1621 he was a married father living in London, and identified in the parish records of St Botolph Aldgate as a stage player: he had achieved his freedom, which brought with it the freedom to marry.[27] If he had spent his apprenticeship entirely in a provincial touring group, professional networks were such that entry to London careers, particularly for gifted performers, remained possible. Hovell, evidently, had moved among the theatrical fraternity of Southwark, while Edwards knew Alleyn, and was by 1619 a member of Queen Anne's men.[28] Through such linkages Bowyer became known to the actor and theatrical manager Christopher Beeston, with whose companies at the Cockpit in Drury Lane he may already have been performing as a hired actor in 1621. With the foundation of Queen Henrietta's men in 1625 Bowyer became a leading player at the Cockpit for the next ten years or so, before joining the King's men for the last part of his career. His progress, the early part of which has only recently become apparent, suggests why some performers appear as if from nowhere as adult actors in prominent troupes. The obscurity and rather changeable nature of many touring groups, which spent their entire existence moving from town to town in various parts of England and Wales, make it difficult to track many members of the profession who were either temporarily or permanently associated with them. Such companies were undoubtedly regarded by the more eminent troupes as sources of recruitment, rather as the Masters of the London choirs approached provincial cathedrals, and Bowyer's apprenticeship is likely to be quite typical of others of his colleagues, the circumstances of which, through the accidents of written records, we happen not to know. There was also, evidently, money to be made in running a troupe made up entirely or substantially of apprentices or trainees. In 1622 such a project was planned by a group of prominent London players, then performing at the Red Bull, recognized in a licence extended to 'Robert Lee, Richard Perkins, Ellis Worth, Thomas Blaney, John Cumber, and William Robins, late comedians to Queen Anne deceased, to bring up children in the quality and exercise of playing comedies, histories, interludes, morals, pastorals, and such other like . . . to be called by the name of the Children of the Revels'.[29] Quite how the six adult actors named were to administer or participate in the proposed troupe, whether it was to play at the Red Bull or was to be a distinct touring group, and so on, we cannot discover from its subsequent history, since it appears to have had none: it was a gambit never played beyond its opening move. The numerical figure of six men is intriguingly close to the five suggested by Hovell's will, and that actors of the calibre of Perkins and Worth may have been contemplating taking to the road with an apprentice troupe speaks either to the public appeal of such performances, or, perhaps more likely, their temporary desperation at conditions of the market in London. Alternatively we might read the plan as indicative of the commitment of leading professionals to a system of training, simultaneously ensuring a supply of talented younger players to support the companies in which they worked.

At least two subsequent troupes in London were formed on the model of training companies, somewhat like the modern formula of the 'youth orchestra', made up of junior professionals. The first was the joint enterprise of William Blagrave, deputy to the Master of the Revels, and Richard Gunnell, actor and playwright. They invested money in the construction of a new indoor playhouse, at Salisbury Court, south of Fleet Street, in 1629. It was to be the home of a company 'of His Majesty's Revels', which in its first incarnation, at least, was made up principally of 'boy' players under the chief supervision of Gunnell, and it was 'to train and bring up certain boys in the quality of playing not only with intent to be a supply of able actors to his majesty's servants at the Blackfriars when there should be occasion ... but the solace of his royal majesty when his majesty should please to see them, and also for the recreation of his majesty's subjects'.[30] What formal agreement with the King's men may have preceded this enterprise is hard to tell, although the involvement of Blagrave of the Revels Office was no doubt designed to give the venture the cover of official approval. It was an ambitious plan: there were fourteen boys, although we know nothing of their ages or identities.[31] The company thus appears to have been designed to perform a conventional repertory of plays commercially: Thomas Randolph's *Amyntas* and *The Muses' Looking Glass* appear to have been among the plays performed by the boy troupe in its relatively short career.

Thus the older tradition of the choirboy players, perhaps, may have been revived in a purely commercial context – there is no suggestion in the surviving records that the boys were being taught anything other than acting – under the supervision of an experienced professional player. The model would have been more like Sebastian Westcott's or William Hunnis's supervision, since no one player could give detailed attention to fourteen apprentices; even Shank seems to have had only two or three under his care at any one time. What the contractual arrangements among the boys, their parents and guardians, and Gunnell and Blagrave acting as management may have been is hard to say, although some written commitments are likely once to have existed. The model may have been that of the Queen's Revels companies of a generation earlier. In 1607 Thomas Kendall, one of the sharers in the Queen's Revels company of that date, had launched a lawsuit against Alice Cooke, the mother of the boy actor Abel Cooke, for her son's breaking the term of his bond 'to be practiced and exercised in the ... quality of playing ... for and during the term of three years now next ensuing'.[32] A three-year contract allowed for more fluidity in the troupe, and for judicious pruning of those who hadn't proved themselves: a black mark would already have been on young Cooke's record. The agreement between the adult actor Martin Slater and his partners at the Whitefriars playhouse in 1608 states that 'all the children are to be bound to the said Martin Slater for the term of three years'.[33] So, in this case, eighteen to twenty youths were indeed apprenticed to one man only. Slater was a freeman of the Ironmongers' Company, but since a three-year term of apprenticeship contravened the conditions of the Statute of Artificers, the theatrical bonds signed within the Queen's Revels company are unlikely to have been the kind of document which bound William Trigge, say, to John Heminges. The company of 1629, however, was truly a teaching company with an expected lifespan, going by earlier models, of at least three years. Its failure within the next two was no doubt partly due to the bad plague outbreak of 1630, but it may otherwise have been over-ambitious and under-capitalized. The King's Revels company that was reconstituted at the Salisbury Court playhouse in 1634 had a larger number of adult actors, and its mission as a training company had evidently been scaled down.

Yet 'training and bringing up' actors within a professional context remained a concept to which senior players were committed, beyond the common practice of individual apprenticeships. Christopher Beeston, who had himself apprenticed as a player under the principal actor Augustine Phillips,[34] turned at the end of his long and eventful career as actor, manager, and theatre owner to another model of training. The troupe sometimes called 'Beeston's Boys' was established early in 1637, and Beeston was recognized as 'Governor of the new company of the King's and Queen's boys'.[35] The Master of the Revels, Sir Henry Herbert, recorded that 'Mr. Beeston was commanded to make a company of boys', as if by royal decree; if so, it is unlikely to have happened without some groundwork on the part of the man at whom it was directed.[36] The company did not begin to function commercially until late 1637, since all playhouses were closed by a bad outbreak of plague, and a year later Beeston died, the management of the company then passing to his son, William. The players themselves continued to perform at the Cockpit playhouse for the remaining four years of theatrical activity before the outbreak of war.

Despite their initial title it seems clear that the troupe never was a boy company, either of the type attempted by Gunnell and Blagrave eight years earlier or of that of the Chapel and Paul's Boys. It was rather a group of younger actors who seem to have been hand-picked by the experienced Beeston, since they included people who were subsequently to be stars of the Restoration stage, notably Michael Mohun, aged about twenty, probably, in 1637: far from a 'boy'. By later 1639 the twenty-five-year-old John Wright had joined the company; he had completed an eight-year term of apprenticeship with Andrew Cane of Prince Charles's company, where he had played female roles: I shall return to him in a subsequent chapter. By 1639 he no doubt saw himself as an independent actor, and not in further need of primary training. Theophilus Bird, also a member of the troupe, had played female roles as an apprentice in Queen Henrietta's company in the 1620s, but was a man of thirty in 1639. The principal actors, it seems, were on the younger side, but were mostly not boys or youths. The youngest of those named in records was Ezekiel Fenn, who by 1639, at the age of nineteen, had already graduated to male roles, an event celebrated in a poem by Henry Glapthorne.[37] An initial plan to set up a training troupe, perhaps, changed its character into a company of selected rising stars, or there may indeed have been a larger proportion of younger apprentices attached to the troupe than is apparent from what now remain as its records.

That the Beestons father and son saw themselves as acting instructors as much as commercial managers is suggested, G. E. Bentley has pointed out, by the epilogue to Richard Brome's play *The Court Beggar*, probably acted by the King and Queen's Young Company, to give them their fuller title, at some time later in 1640. The character Swainwit, 'a blunt country gentleman', commends to the audience 'the man [i.e., William Beeston] by whose care and directions this stage is govern'd, who hath for many years, both in his father's days and since, directed poets to write and players to speak, till he trained up these youths here to what they are now. Ay, some of 'em from before they were able to say a grace of two lines long to have more parts in their pates than would fill so many dry-fats [barrels]'.[38] That this is not entirely facetious is suggested by the later claim of William Beeston himself, who struggled on through the civil wars and Commonwealth period to make something of his suspended playhouse business. In 1651 he was attempting to regain possession of the Cockpit playhouse, and evidently contemplating opening it for plays by preparing a playing troupe, from scratch: in a lawsuit he avers that 'he took prentices and covenant servants to instruct them in the quality of acting, and fitting them for the stage'.[39] John Rhodes, who coincidentally was living in the Cockpit lodgings in the period before Beeston's attempt at theatrical revival, evidently did something similar several years later, when times were more propitious.

The notion of a training company with its own London theatre, preparing talented young people for professional stage careers, finally came to fruition after the Restoration, although, as we have seen, it was hardly a new idea. The Nursery playhouse in the Barbican operated for a dozen years, between 1671 and 1682, and was invoked by the playwright John Dryden in his satirical poem *Mac Flecknoe*: 'Where unfledged actors learn to laugh and cry, / Where infant punks their tender voices try, / And little Maximins the gods defy'.[40] As the lines suggest, while sneering at the notion, the training of girls and young women was now as necessary to the professional stage as producing 'little Maximins', or future heroic male actors; the character Maximin was indeed one of Dryden's own inventions. The Nursery project had begun in 1667, and from soon thereafter was nominally led by the actor George Jolly, whose remarkable stage career had probably begun in the 1630s; by 1640 he was performing at the Fortune playhouse. Most of his work thereafter, before his return to England in 1660, was in exile in Germany and other parts of continental Europe, as an actor-manager running a variety of companies that by the 1650s also included actresses.[41] As a potential teacher of young performers, then, he knew both the traditions of the older stage, under which he himself had trained, and of the mixed-sex troupes which quickly became the English norm after 1660. It seems unlikely, however, that he had much close involvement with the practicalities of instruction but rather employed deputies to run the day-to-day business of the Nursery company while he was involved in other theatrical projects, including his own provincial touring troupe. Beyond these few bare circumstances we know very little about the operations, size, recruitment, and teaching procedures of the Restoration Nursery, which evidently was not successful enough to survive much longer than had earlier attempts at running troupes with a training mission.

Besides on the one hand the widely recognized path of full apprenticeship, for seven years or more, in which individual was closely connected to individual, and on the other that of the boy companies, in which a group of minors was supervised by an adult instructor for a few years, without any necessary commitment to professional continuity, there were evidently other means of training, or of taking probationary status as a player, the last presumably employed when a talented but inexperienced adult such as an Andrew Cane or perhaps a William Shakespeare happened to turn up.

Talented younger actors could be attached to masters under terms less restrictive than the seven to a dozen years many teenaged apprentices served out. David Mateer has recently discovered that the leading actor Richard Perkins, the tragic star at the Red Bull, the Cockpit, and Salisbury Court playhouses for over twenty years, was acting in his teens with the famous Edward Alleyn of the Admiral's men at the Rose, and was contractually bound to him as a 'servant' (the term Augustine Phillips also used to refer to Christopher Beeston)[42] for a term of three years from late November 1596; Perkins was seventeen when he signed the agreement, and would have been twenty when it was over. In fact he broke its terms in April 1597 and moved, probably with some inducement, to the company playing at the nearby Swan, Pembroke's men. Alleyn sued him, and was awarded damages, but Perkins possibly remained with his new troupe.

Mateer thinks that Perkins's value, either to Alleyn or his new colleagues, was as an experienced player of female parts, which any successful company would have regarded as a chief asset. This may have been so, and Alleyn's written contract may have been an attempt to hang on to Perkins's skills for the final phase of his performances in that range. He was old, relative to puberty and a broken voice, but numerous other male performers continued to play women into those years, as we shall see.[43] Alternatively we might think that Perkins, already showing the strength and power he demonstrated later in life (in, for example, Alleyn's old role of Barabas in Marlowe's *The Jew of Malta*), had already graduated to principal male parts, and that Alleyn was preparing to groom a successor. In either case, probably what determined Perkins's move was money – he was offered more by the neighbouring theatre troupe – and he was acting as an independent economic agent: as an adult, in fact. He was already a skilled and valued performer at the age of seventeen, whatever his particular roles may have been. That he was being paid was not unusual; that he thought the Admiral's men were not paying him enough was perhaps not so unusual either, but not everyone would have taken the risk of breaking a legal agreement, and he had probably ensured that his new colleagues would bail him out of any ensuing trouble. William Browne should have been paid, but was not, as a teenaged actor at the Red Bull; and the theatrical apprentice acquired by Philip Henslowe, 'my boy', James Bristow, was being paid wages of three shillings a week, more than likely for playing female roles, which Henslowe calculated as part of the income due to him.[44] The fee of eight pounds he had paid to the player William Augustine to take over the mastership of young Bristow was another of his many investments. Such an instance illustrates both that apprentices might be regarded as an asset and that in the theatre they were not necessarily being taught by their masters so much as by their colleagues, the other members of the acting troupe, both older and younger. Henslowe, so far as we can tell, never played a stage role in his life, let alone a female part. Perhaps the compensation for James Bristow was that he would eventually have been able to claim freedom of the Dyers' Company. As to whether wages were differential, that is, whether they rewarded experience and talent, paying the principal older boys more, it is difficult to tell, but one would think that Alleyn's experience with Perkins might have been instructive, if indeed wages were out of step with ablities.

The expectation of adult actors apprenticing boys at the common age of fourteen or so would have been that they would have been able to play female roles for a year or two at the least. Both of Andrew Cane's apprentices in 1631 appeared on stage in female roles during that year, in a performance I shall examine at more length in a subsequent chapter. We know most about continuous apprentice careers where cast lists have survived, so that the habit of writing down the parts as cast, which was either not always observed or not always preserved as a document, occasionally yields information for more than one isolated occasion. In *A Midsummer Night's Dream* Peter Quince knows the names of the actors he has cast, and recorded in writing, for the play of Pyramus and Thisby, so that he can hand them each the appropriate scrolls containing their parts: a handwritten roll of paper containing only their lines, with the preceding cues. In the 1620s and 1630s a series of six printed plays performed by the King's men give fairly full cast lists, and reveal that the chief players of female roles for the troupe in the late twenties and early thirties formed a group of three or four boys including John Thompson, Alexander Gough, and William Trigge; John Honeyman as their leading partner was replaced by Stephen Hammerton in the revival of Fletcher's *The Wild-Goose Chase* in late 1632.[45] Thompson and Honeyman played parts of up to five hundred lines in length: Honeyman's part in Massinger's play *The Picture*, for example, was second only to the adult Joseph Taylor's in the leading role of Mathias, and John Thompson as Honoria came third in line-number ranking, ahead of John Lowin in the role of Eubulus. Gough had only a small role in *The Roman Actor* of 1626, but within a few years had moved up to the principal female role of the witty and dynamic Lillia Bianca in *The Wild-Goose Chase*. The younger apprentices took the smaller parts: the unnamed 'Maid' in the manuscript play by John Clavell, *The Soddered Citizen*, with twenty-odd lines to speak, was played by the otherwise unidentified 'John: Shanks Boy'.[46]

All these performers, with the exception of Hammerton, appear to have been under John Shank's immediate supervision in the playhouse. Gough, who was born in 1614, may have received some early training from his father, the King's player Robert Gough (who had himself trained under the player Thomas Pope), who died when his son was eleven. Alexander Gough began in female roles the following year, at the age of twelve, in *The Roman Actor*; he was eighteen when he played Lillia Bianca. William Trigge was one of the numerous boys apprenticed to John Heminges, of whom more below; his bonds were signed on 20 December 1625, when he was thirteen, for a term of twelve years. He was, then, reasonably close in age to Gough, and about twenty when he played Rosalura in *The Wild-Goose Chase*. After Heminges's death in 1630 Trigge petitioned, successfully, for release from his formal bonds, and was granted his freedom (as a grocer) in 1632. Honeyman and Thompson were certainly Shank's boys, or so the actor himself regarded them. Honeyman was born early in 1613, and probably began his apprenticeship around 1626, when he first appeared on stage; his career in female roles was shorter than Trigge's and after the age of sixteen he appears to have taken male parts, becoming a full member of the company when he was twenty. The joint careers of Trigge and Honeyman suggest that freedom as a player, given sufficient evidence of value to the acting company, may have been attained rather faster than in the traditional trades and occupations; somewhat shorter terms of service would also have improved the cycle of training new, younger boys for the female roles.[47] Richard Perkins, at eighteen, may hence have regarded himself as past his apprentice years when he left his subordinate position to Alleyn. Of John Thompson, whose skills appear to have been the equal of his peers, we know very little beyond his roles and his connection with Shank. He seems to have begun playing about 1620, when he took the role of the Cardinal's mistress Julia (140 lines) in a revival of *The Duchess of Malfi*, and he continued in female roles until 1631, when he must have been in his early twenties and at the end of his apprenticeship. Such a long career in female parts was unusual; when it fortuitously happened it was no doubt regarded as a benefit to the acting company.

Shank, as I have suggested, was the principal working actor with responsibility for supervising the boys on the stages of the Globe and Blackfriars between 1613 and 1635, the year of his death, although, as in any theatrical enterprise, the pragmatic circumstances of casting and distribution of roles scene by scene in individual plays would have provided the boys with a range of adult models and potential supervisors. Working partners are always latent instructors. Heminges, to whom many of the boy performers, including Trigge, were formally apprenticed as grocers, gradually withdrew from playing in the second decade of the seventeenth century, and thereafter became chief business manager, in modern terms, for the King's men. Although his household probably lodged the boys to whom he was master, and though he may have given them some individual coaching there, Heminges is unlikely to have seen them regularly in rehearsal and performance; their relationship with him is more likely to have resembled that of James Bristow with Philip Henslowe. When Thompson played Julia in *The Duchess of Malfi* at some time early in the 1620s his partners in the other female roles were Richard Sharpe as the Duchess – at 550 lines the second longest role, after Bosola, played by John Lowin – and Robert Pallant as Cariola. Both these boys were apprenticed to Heminges, from 1616 and 1620 respectively. Sharpe was the eldest boy, born in late 1601; if the performance took place in the year after Pallant's apprenticeship, Sharpe would have been nineteen or twenty, with several years of stage experience, Pallant fourteen or fifteen, and John Thompson about twelve. Shank's name does not appear in the cast list; the principal adult acting partners of Sharpe in his demanding role were, apart from Lowin as Bosola, Joseph Taylor as Ferdinand, Richard Robinson as the Cardinal, and Robert Benfield as Antonio.

Between 1595 and 1628 the apprentice books of the Grocers' Company record ten boys bound at various times to John Heminges as apprentices, for terms of varying length: they include Sharpe, Trigge, and Pallant, and all of them were involved in the theatre in one way or another.[48] Heminges's direct relationship with his apprentices was undoubtedly stronger and more influential in the case of those bound in the late Elizabethan and early Jacobean years – Thomas Belt, Alexander Cook, and George Birch – with whom he appeared on stage. The names of the first two may be recorded in the 'plot', a schematic plan by scene, characters, and some actors' names of a vanished play called *The Seven Deadly Sins*, while Birch perhaps appeared as Dol Common in *The Alchemist* and as Lady Politic Would-be in *Volpone* while Heminges was still performing.[49] The older man's retirement from the stage may have been to do with advancing age, and with some progressive debility affecting his speech: he was described as 'old stuttering Heminges' in a ballad on the burning of the Globe in 1613,[50] when he was a relatively youthful forty-seven; he was to live for another seventeen active years. A stuttering master would not have been what an apprentice would have wanted: apart from the bad model, any instruction would have taken longer. If Heminges's characteristics as described in the ballad were a consciously adopted *stage* persona, however (actors' personalities frequently being confused with their stage parts), then we might well imagine him as a doddery, pedantic Sir Pol, playing opposite his apprentice in the virago role of his Lady. As we shall see, stage training certainly included the apprentice playing the dominant role to the deluded dupe part, taken by the master. In the case of *Volpone*, however, Heminges appears rather to have played Corbaccio, a senile and half-deaf schemer whose debility as a character might similarly have informed the version of the actor retailed in the ballad.[51]

Heminges was demonstrably closely involved in the preparation of John Rice for lines by Ben Jonson delivered in a show for King James in 1607, sponsored and hosted by the Company of the Merchant Taylors, who rewarded the adult actor with a fee of two pounds 'for his direction of his boy that made the speech to his Majesty'.[52] The apprentice's reward as costumed performer was one eighth of his master's sum. In what sense he was Heminges's 'boy' is difficult to tell; he certainly does not appear as an apprentice in the Grocers' records, and Heminges had another unnamed 'boy' in 1613, who performed in *The Middle Temple Masque* for the wedding of Princess Elizabeth. Rice was undoubtedly a boy actor with the King's men in the years before he joined another playing company in late 1611. In the preceding year he had accompanied Richard Burbage in performing costumed water deities in a pageant for Prince Henry; Rice's role, which involved floating in a decorated boat on the Thames, was female, the nymph Corinea. Heminges's connection to Rice appears to have been the less formal arrangement of master actor, perhaps recognized with a signed agreement, but not conforming to the full statutory requirements of apprenticeship as recognized by the city of London. Rice, as David Kathman suggests, was probably at the end of his useful career as a performer of female roles by 1610–11, and likely to have been about twenty when he left the King's men, having worked under Heminges's supervision for perhaps six or seven years.[53] He is likely to have played leading roles in the King's men's repertory for at least the second half of his career, and might be considered a likely first performer of the roles of Cleopatra, Imogen in *Cymbeline*, and Hermione in *The Winter's Tale*, among others.

Most professional careers that began in the teenage years, then (as those of numerous prominent players did *not*), typically included at least a year or two in female roles. Richard Burbage, the son of a player, is quite likely to have begun acting in wigs and female dress; Edward Alleyn, on the stage by the age of seventeen, may also have begun in the same way. Another son of a player had a protracted career in women's roles. Theophilus Bird may have begun under the tutelage of his father, the actor William Bird (or Borne), who by the end of his career was performing at the Fortune with the King and Queen of Bohemia's company. Bird the younger was fifteen when his father died in 1624, and he was then taken on by the new Queen Henrietta's company at the Cockpit playhouse, probably as an apprentice of the actor-manager Christopher Beeston. His first recorded female role, in 1625, when he was sixteen, was Paulina in Massinger's *The Renegado*. Paulina is the second-rank female role in the play, with 135 lines. Thereafter Bird's career must have delighted Beeston, as he continued to take on senior female roles into his later teens and early twenties, when he was a player of some experience and demonstrated power, of breath as well as psychological range. Although, on the decidedly limited evidence of two cast lists, he never attained to *prima donna* parts, he was still playing women in his twenty-second year, a career in the female range approaching that of John Thompson in length, assuming Bird had done some playing before joining Beeston. He then not only passed into the playing troupe as a full member but allied himself to his master's family by marrying Beeston's daughter Anne, probably at some time in his middle twenties. He thus became an heir to the Beeston fortunes, although much of their value was to dissipate after the theatres were closed.

As Bird had first learnt his art from a man who had acted at the Rose in its heyday, so he was to influence future generations of performers, appearing himself on the Restoration stage for a year or two after 1660, and, as one of the leading older actors in the Beeston's Boys company after 1637, serving as a model and possibly as instructor for such younger players as Michael Mohun, whose true prominence was to be achieved after 1660, when he too joined the extended Beeston clan, marrying Bird's daughter Anne, Christopher Beeston's granddaughter. In terms of immediate collaborative contact on the stage, then, there are many links between the Elizabethan theatre of the later sixteenth century and that of a hundred years later, even if its external habits and conventions had changed considerably.

What may be said in general terms on the basis of the various careers I have surveyed above is that theatrical apprenticeship commonly involved close bonds of affection and trust, as well as of legal obligation. Skilled apprentice players were valuable acting partners, and had, in the circumstances of performance before audiences, to be treated as respected equals in presenting the play as well as the joint efforts of the entire company could manage. Their legal status as dependent minors and their absence, usually, from official lists of members of the company did not carry over into the boys' contribution to the fictional world of the acted play, where they might, as Ophelia, Rosalind, or Viola, say, have carried a large weight of emotional and intellectual meaning, as well as sympathetic engagement on the part of the audience. We might remember Henry Jackson's comments on the moving effect of the murdered Desdemona. No special allowances of expectation, I think, were made either by audiences or the boys' adult colleagues in terms of their presentation of character within the fiction, or for being any less riveting, convincing, and moving in the performance of a part. Not all boys who could play convincing and moving young women at the beginning of their teens would have continued to have the bodies, faces, and voices to remain in such roles beyond a certain point, varying with individual physiology. Where physiological circumstance, training, and skill combined in a favourable way, female playing could be sustained for a remarkably long time. As I have said above, I do not believe that a considerably later onset of puberty accounts for such careers, but that some young men with lighter features and higher voice ranges trained themselves, with some help from the vocal and movement coaching of their masters and colleagues, to retain a convincingly 'female' range, in voice, appearance, and gesture, is apparent from the evidence reviewed above. A seventeen- or eighteen-year-old youth playing a female role would not look or sound the same as a twelve-year-old boy; male performers of such diverse ages appeared together on stage in female roles in the pre-Restoration theatre, usually with the older actors in the longer and more taxing roles. The great value of the 'long career' in female parts was that the player in his late teens had a fuller, more coloured vocal range, breath power equivalent or superior to that of an adult, and a broader sympathetic emotional experience. He also had a new kind of interest in and respect for women; marriage closely followed the end of many apprenticeships. Hence the 'youth' rather than the 'boy' actor, if one can make that distinction, would be likely to have had a good deal more subtlety and range in the portrayal of character, mental reflection, and emotional states, and would have possessed both a fuller physical confidence in movement and greater power in the projection and modulation of his voice. He would have been the player of choice for the long and demanding female parts, and his Cleopatra would have been unlikely to have squeaked. He would have looked and sounded quite different, of course, from a modern woman performing lead roles in twenty-first century performances of early modern plays, but such is the difference of conventions of representation between Shakespeare's theatre and ours. Having grappled imaginatively with that difference, there is no reason then to suppose that earlier audiences, used to their own conventions, would have found a Richard Sharpe any less moving, affecting, or memorable on the stage than modern audiences have found a Judi Dench.

A second general point is that stage apprenticeship provided on-the-job training, chiefly. One might say the same of any apprenticeship, but in

other skilled trades one is usually first put to work mastering some fundamental skills before being allowed to move on to more complex tasks. Boy
actors were expected to be working performers with the entire company
more or less from the start. They were probably auditioned in some way
before they were signed on: actors would have wanted clear signs of a talent
that might be developed, but also would have wanted any boy to be
immediately useful. The learning of a part, or a set of parts, was no doubt
the first task the new boy was given. After rehearsal of some kind, probably
individually with his master and then with his partners in his scenes, he
could expect to be on stage before audiences, day after day and week after
week throughout the playing season. Working in a playhouse would have
provided some physical continuity, but apprentices with touring groups,
like Michael Bowyer, lived a nomadic existence and performed in a considerable variety of playing spaces; the London apprentice would have had
fewer 'dark' days, but a more settled and predictable mode of life. The
contribution of all apprentices to the joint artistic effort of their colleagues
would have been expected to be the same: full partnership in the fictional
world of plays presented to a variety of audiences. The value of good
apprentices in that respect also gave them cash value: not only did
Henslowe buy James Bristow from William Augustine (a perfectly legal
transaction under the terms of statute and custom), but Robert Armin
seems to have passed on one of his own apprentices, and Stephen
Hammerton's transfer to the King's men in 1632 gave rise to a dispute
over the circumstances of his apprenticeship: he was somehow the servant of
two masters.[54]

It was evidently more likely that boys would enter the theatrical profession if they came from a theatrical family; equally, many theatre apprentices,
as far as we can now see, had no prior connection with the theatre. In wide
terms, extended families, local connections within parishes, and commercial
contacts very often were involved in establishing a boy with a master.
Andrew Cane, from the outlying area of Windsor in Berkshire, the son of
a butcher, apprenticed as a goldsmith in London with his older brother,
who had himself gained his freedom under a goldsmith called Christopher
Ledane, possibly known to the Canes' father in some way we can no longer
detect. The now largely invisible webs of affinity, affiliation, and patronage
easily elude us in looking back at the society of Shakespeare's time, but they
are sometimes clear. As we have seen, actors took on fellows' sons after their
fathers died, as Beeston appears to have done with Bird, and as Cane and
Fowler did with young Stratford. Many London apprentices, speaking in
general terms, came from outside London; once again the connections their

fathers or guardians may have had with London masters are hard to trace, although local reputation and trade links were two common determinants. Robert Armin, the fourteen-year-old son of a tailor from King's Lynn, Norfolk, was apprenticed initially to the prominent London goldsmith John Lonyson in 1581 through home-town networking. Lonyson had been born in King's Lynn, and left money to the town when he died (soon after Armin became his boy): he clearly was a famous local son who had made good in the capital, and might be approached by those who wanted their sons to follow him. Men who made their way in London often remembered their native districts, even if they did not, like William Shakespeare, invest in and retire to them. As for Armin senior, he is unlikely to have thought he was launching his son on a career as a renowned comic actor; Robert Armin discovered performance for himself, and entered the profession after he had served out his years as an apprentice goldsmith. His older colleague John Heminges had followed a similar path, although it is impossible to tell how his father George Heminges, of Droitwich, Worcestershire, some considerable distance from London, selected the master James Collins, to whom young Heminges was apprenticed in 1578, at the age of eleven, for nine years. Heminges served his term successfully, becoming a freeman of the Grocers' Company before his twenty-first birthday, in technical contravention of the statute. He was, however, still a relatively young man, and his marriage in the following year to the widow of another actor is a sign that he was already moving in theatrical circles.

If the fathers of Heminges, Armin, and Cane had been aiming their sons at conventional bourgeois careers, which were deflected by personal talents, interests, and opportunities, other parents and guardians must have been quite aware that apprenticeship with such masters as John Shank, weaver, or Richard Tarlton, vintner, would have included at least some sort of career on the stage for their sons, even if it were no longer than a year or two: the peak period of suitability to female roles. Within London, the social position of actors as neighbours and fellow parishioners no doubt testified, mostly, to their individual reliability and soundness of character, whatever the general reputation of playing. Apprenticeship was quasi-familial: the boy or youth entered a household, to the head of which he owed an essentially filial duty. Where it was possible, then, we might gather that concerned parents would have taken a careful look at potential masters and their establishments. Quite why the fourteen-year-old John Wright was apprenticed as goldsmith to Andrew Cane in 1629 we can't fully explain, but his father, John Wright senior, a baker resident in the parish of St Giles Cripplegate, undoubtedly knew Cane as a neighbour and fellow parishioner, and as a man prominently involved in playing at the local theatre, the Fortune, although Cane also certainly ran a goldsmith's shop, producing jewellery and domestic silverware. Although Cane was possibly taking a break from the stage in the year of Wright's binding, within a couple of years master and apprentice were on stage together at the fashionable Salisbury Court playhouse, Wright playing female roles, as was to be expected.

Not every parent would have wanted to see teenage sons put on wigs and dresses, and commit themselves to fictional pretence, the more so when many of the godly fulminated against the moral abhorrence of crossdressing. However skilled their sons' performances may have been, playing was also an uncertain trade; bakers were in constant demand, where players served quite other appetites, with very variable rewards. It seems unlikely that stage fathers or mothers would have pushed their sons in the direction of the stage; far more likely is that boys like the young John Wright had shown some enthusiasm and aptitude for performing, and that fathers – *some* fathers – might be persuaded to give such talent a chance to develop. The advantage of an apprenticeship with a man like Cane, acknowledged in a written agreement preserved in the hall of a leading livery company of the city, was that it resulted, after full and satisfactory performance of the term, in freedom as citizen and goldsmith. Wright, in the event, continued to make his way as an actor; his contemporary as apprentice to Cane, Arthur Saville, apparently did not, but was freed as a goldsmith.

The social world of actors in London was that of the middling sort. Edward Alleyn and John Heminges both came from reasonably well-off families, it appears, and both built on their social position during their lifetimes. The actor Ellis Worth was a son of a freeman of the Merchant Taylors, and hence could claim, as eventually he did, his own freedom by patrimony. The eldest son of the actor Robert Browne was apprenticed and freed as a haberdasher, possibly in recognition of some family history in that trade. Andrew Cane seems not to have encouraged any theatrical ambitions in his own son, rather founding a dynasty of goldsmiths that continued into the eighteenth century. Despite the terms of many stage comedies about London life, in which the money-making activities of the city are set in opposition to the courtly and gentlemanly circles of wit and culture, actors themselves were intimately involved, socially and economically, in the institutions and practices of the city of London, which included the formal machinery of apprenticeship.

Young men freed by the livery companies after working their term of years under a master were recognized as having qualified in their trades 'by service'. Such was the model, I believe, in the theatre. Whether or not one's master as a player was also, like Heminges, the freeman of a London company, under the regulations of which one was formally bound to him, the chief contract was to offer one's services as a performer within the joint membership of an acting troupe, some fifteen to twenty individuals or so, for a set term of years, which might well be shorter than the minimum of seven stipulated in the Statute of Artificers. One would have been expected to begin playing, in smaller roles, more or less immediately, and without spending very much time in preliminary training off the stage itself. As Thomas Havers promised John Risley to 'teach and instruct' him 'by the best means he can . . . in the same art which he useth', so acting apprentices would have expected coaching and direction in developing their skills as performers. Any master player taking on a talented apprentice would have looked to bringing him to the point of tackling longer and more complex roles – *female* roles – while he was physically suited to such parts. The leading female specialist in any troupe was one of its major assets, and the assured supply of replacements for a player whose years in such a position were normally three or four demanded a continuing search for new apprentices. Shank, one would think, did a certain amount of scouting.

That older supervisory actors were years removed from playing female roles themselves – and neither Heminges nor Cane, given their histories, had ever done so at all – would have meant that the senior boys, immediately involved in the pragmatic business of playing the major parts, also became instructors of their younger colleagues, if only through careful observation and listening on the part of the latter. Instruction in the art of playing was, and is, collaborative. Apprentices must have learnt as much from watching their partners within their scenes on the stage as they did from individual coaching from masters. The entire playing company, potentially, constituted their teachers.

CHAPTER 4

Playing many parts

> ... I, your servant, who have labour'd here
> In buskins and in socks, this thirty year ...
>
> William Davenant, *The Platonic Lovers*, 1635

The speaker of the above lines from the epilogue to Davenant's comedy for the King's men was undoubtedly John Lowin, by late 1635 the longest-serving member of the troupe. Although the 'here' of the first performance of the play was the stage of the Blackfriars playhouse, Lowin had begun playing before that space was in the possession of the company; he had spent his thirty years or so acting in both of their playhouses, and had played at the Globe before its destruction and subsequent rebuilding in 1613 – indeed he was probably playing the title part in Shakespeare and Fletcher's play *Henry VIII* when the fire began. In his 1927 book *The Organization and Personnel of the Shakespearean Company*, T. W. Baldwin attempted to argue that each actor had a particular 'line' or speciality in types of character, although Davenant's verses make it clear that Lowin acted in both tragedy and comedy, indicated by the conventional footwear of actors on the classical stage, standing as signs for the ancient genres. (In the poem 'L'Allegro', published in 1645, Milton writes of 'Jonson's learnèd sock', for example.) Furthermore, most modern commentators would agree that actors playing in a wide variety of kinds of drama within a repertory company of a fixed core size could not have maintained an essentially narrow specialism in stage characters.[1] The practical function of leading actors within a troupe was to take the larger roles in plays chosen or commissioned for performance, and since a generically varied repertory appears to have been the choice of any company with ambition, lead actors had to be able to compass comic as well as heroic and tragic parts.

Edward Alleyn, whose career we tend to define through the title roles in *Tamburlaine* and *Doctor Faustus*, was undoubtedly also seen in principal comic parts, although his range, given the patchy survival of texts from the

Admiral's men in Alleyn's heyday, is now difficult to judge in any detail. One part with which he is unarguably associated, however, is that of Barabas in Marlowe's *The Jew of Malta*, on the testimony of a prologue likely to have been written by Thomas Heywood, for a revival of the play at the Cockpit playhouse in the early 1630s, and printed in its first surviving text (1633):

> We know not how our play may pass this stage;
> But by the best of poets in that age
> The *Malta-Jew* had being, and was made,
> And he then by the best of actors played.
> In *Hero and Leander*, one did gain
> A lasting memory; in *Tamburlaine*,
> This *Jew*, with others many, th'other wan
> The attribute of peerless, being a man
> Whom we may rank with (doing no one wrong)
> Proteus for shapes, and Roscius for a tongue,
> So could he speak, so vary . . . [2]

Alleyn's 'varying' in his complete repertory of roles ('others many') remains largely irrecoverable, but the contrast between what is required of the actor in the two roles Heywood names is instructive. Tamburlaine is a bravura part in an unrelievedly heroic style, composed almost entirely in blank verse of a verbal richness and syntactic flow never heard on the stage before, the characteristic expansive incantation Ben Jonson dubbed 'Marlowe's mighty line'.[3] Tamburlaine, in both of the two plays covering his career, is a long part,[4] and while far from being monotonous – the shepherd king is variously tender, rhapsodic, defiant, grim, and triumphant – all the speaker's skill is needed to prevent the long set speeches typical of the play from losing their magical effect (since part of Tamburlaine's power is a kind of verbal enchantment), and from slipping into rhythmic noise to which the audience ceases to pay attention in terms of verbal detail, and hence of dramatic development. The part is at once sensationally histrionic and fiendishly demanding.

Although the role itself, and the two-part play which contains it, are not without some ironic humour, both are very different from *The Jew of Malta* and its title role. A sardonic satire of the aspiration to and exercise of power, the play might even be seen as Marlowe's own parody of his earlier success in the heroic style. Barabas, the central character, is an ironist and a schemer, a confider in the audience, and an amused observer of his own and of others' duplicity. The plotting and counterplotting of the play, in spite of repeated fatal consequences, have all the exaggerations and detachment of farce, so that the tone of playing is a good deal more tongue-in-cheek than that invited by the prevailing manner of the *Tamburlaine* plays. Barabas provided one model for Shakespeare's confidential monsters – Richard of Gloucester, Edmund, and Iago – as he also did for Jonson's witty deceivers, Volpone and Face. Barabas is quicksilver and knowing where Tamburlaine is dignified and sustained: Tamburlaine is a heroic part, and Barabas predominantly a comic one, if in a distinctly black vein. There seems no reason to doubt that if Alleyn was a success as Barabas he could have moved easily into conventional comic roles. In the spring of 1596 Alleyn was playing in *The Jew* and *Doctor Faustus* at the Rose playhouse, but he is likely also to have had chief roles in the other plays of that season's repertory, including *A Toy to Please Chaste Ladies* and *Crack Me This Nut*, both now no more than titles and which were, perhaps, froth, but the second of which seems to have been particularly popular, and was revived at the Fortune after 1600.[5]

The clearest evidence of Alleyn's range in the 1590s is provided by the surviving text of George Chapman's comedy *The Blind Beggar of Alexandria*, first acted in 1595, when the leading actor of the Admiral's men was almost thirty.[6] The title page of the play as published in 1598 promises an entertainment, regarding the title character, 'most pleasantly discoursing his variable humours in disguised shapes full of conceit and pleasure'.[7] By birth Cleanthes is 'but a shepherd's son at *Memphis* born' (line 117), perhaps an allusion to one of Alleyn's other roles, as the Scythian shepherd Tamburlaine, and like Tamburlaine is a natural commander; he is banished from Egypt but remains in the country in a series of alternating disguises: his shapes are Irus the beggar, a seer and fortune-teller, Leon the wealthy usurer, and Count Hermes, 'a wild and frantic man' (line 332). The rather harum-scarum plot is a vehicle for virtuoso quick changes, of costume and personality, or 'variable humours', by the central performer, who confides in the audience as he rapidly shifts identities to confound his enemies and emerge triumphant as King of Egypt. A lively performance of the play would do a good deal to cover the implausibility and arbitrariness apparent in the text as we have it; it appears to have been particularly popular in the theatre in the year following its first performance. In its narrative Alleyn finally emerged as the energetic hero, but along the way he played the parts, suitably changing action and accent with his costume, of the old and rather feeble beggar, Irus, the Barabas-like moneylender Leon, and the fiery and choleric Count, who makes Hotspur look well-adjusted. In the last two roles he woos and marries different women, alternately cuckolding himself by wooing each of them in the person of the other's husband, and *in propria persona* as Cleanthes in the fifth act of the play, disposing of them once they have been 'widowed'. The shifts from one appearance to another are often farcically rapid – six lines serve for Alleyn to have transformed himself from the Count, between his exit in that role at line 804 and re-entry as the aged beggar Irus at line 811. Unlike Alec Guinness in the multiple-role film comedy *Kind Hearts and Coronets* (1949), Alleyn was not assisted by a make-up department, distinct takes, and editing: the changes in his costuming must have been few, and the burden of the change in 'humour' have been laid on modification of physical manner, pace, and movement (muscular rapidity to stiffness and weakness, in the above shift), of facial mask, and of vocal tone and manner. The actor transformed himself, and that beneath the surface change he was recognizably the same man (Cleanthes *and* Edward Alleyn) provided part of the audience's pleasure.

The outward accoutrements of disguise the play itself tells us something about. The Count wears a 'velvet gown' (line 322) and a 'pistol' stuck in his girdle, so similarly characteristic gowns – furred for the usurer, and a tattered religious gown for the beggar-hermit – were probably enough for a quick change, capable of being easily slipped off and on in the tiring-house behind the stage. A similar dramatic piece played by the Admiral's company, the anonymous *Look About You*, printed in 1600 and recently identified as the otherwise unknown play *The Disguises*, acted in 1595, tells us a little more about such quick-fire disguising.[8] Although a number of characters in the play assume other identities, the first to alert the audience to the tricks of changeability is Skink, banished from the court for his role as political hitman, and now appearing, as the stage direction for his first entry puts it, *'like an Hermit'* (line 14).[9] At the end of the first scene, alone, he removes his 'hermit's weed', remarking as he does so, like the disrobing Prospero in *The Tempest*, 'Lie there religion' (line 45). Later in the play we discover he must also have removed a 'false hair and beard', subsequently found by other characters and taken over by the fugitive nobleman Gloster in an overlapping series of shifts of identity which give the play its central energy: *'Enter Gloster in the Hermit's gown, putting on the beard'* reads the stage direction at the start of the fourteenth scene of the play; his accompanying speech keeps the audience informed about a further twist of concealment and confusion. There must in fact be two identical disguises, since Skink later reappears in his first disguise, and the two rival 'hermits' contest about their identity; arrested, Skink insists 'Lay hold upon that other hermit. / He is a counterfeit as well as I' (lines 2655–6). Such language about the disguises in the play thus coincides with some of that used about acting, discussed in Chapter 1, and with that of the praise of notably versatile performers like Alleyn. Gloster promises to be 'a Proteus every hour' (line 1514), and 'changes himself to sundry shapes' (line 2121), phrases used in Heywood's prologue quoted above.

Such mechanical change of identity, an engine of farce, may not have called for particularly developed mimetic skill, but none the less Edward Alleyn took a principal part in putting such plays on the stage. *Look About You*, unlike *The Blind Beggar*, calls for more than one tricky disguiser, so the company did not rely on a single actor in mounting such plays. (One might compare the two pairs of doubled parts, masters and servants, in Shakespeare's *The Comedy of Errors*, a play from a year or two earlier, but in the Chamberlain's men's repertory by 1594.) Between 1597 and 1600, indeed, the Admiral's men had to do without Alleyn entirely; temporarily retired from the stage, he must have passed his parts, in plays that remained in the continuing repertory, to other men. The opening of the company's new playhouse, the Fortune, in 1600, brought Alleyn back to the stage for several seasons, and his probable roles in that period, when he was in his late thirties, come from a remarkable range of material. Alleyn appears to have retired from playing entirely before he was forty, and thus never had a career playing senior roles – or rather playing senior roles *only*. It is a modern assumption that career actors should play Romeo and Hamlet before a certain age, and King Lear only after a further limit of years. The first Hamlet, however, played the part when he was about thirty-one, and Lear only four years later. Lead players took lead parts, and Burbage, who remained on the stage until his death at the age of fifty, did not have a remarkably longer career than his famous colleague and rival; probably their range of parts was comparable.

Alleyn's 1600 return to the stage at the new playhouse, designed to rival the Globe, was marked by revivals of earlier successes, including his multiple disguised roles in *The Blind Beggar of Alexandria*, Hercules in at least one of a pair of plays by that title first acted in 1595, Hieronimo in *The Spanish Tragedy*, and Barabas in *The Jew of Malta*. The new additions to the repertory in the first few years at the Fortune suggest that Alleyn also took the title roles in biblical plays of *Samson*, *Jephthah*, *Joshua*, and *Pontius Pilate*, as well as the great cardinal in two plays on the rise and fall of Wolsey. These last plays, which do not survive beyond the records in Henslowe's *Diary*,[10] are among the first in a series of plays on earlier Tudor history staged by a variety of companies, and form part of a popular examination of national identity, as defined by a century of political and religious history. Playing Wolsey, a crucial figure in the 'great matter' of King Henry's divorce and the break with Rome, was to become a performance tradition, which

Alleyn initiated; his successors included Burbage (probably), the Restoration actor Henry Harris, recorded in costume for the part in a surviving portrait, the Victorian Sir Henry Irving, and Orson Welles, the last in the film version of Robert Bolt's play *A Man for All Seasons*. It was Shakespeare and Fletcher's play of 1613, *Henry VIII*, or *All is True*, and not the lost Fortune plays by Chettle, Munday, and Drayton, which was to establish the continuing theatrical line across subsequent generations of performance, although at its first showings more than a few members of the audience might have seen Alleyn as Wolsey at the Fortune a decade earlier. He himself, indeed, freed from the demands of daily repertory performance in 1613, might have gone to take a look at what the Globe writers and actors had made of material he knew well.

Rival playing was evidently of some interest to early audiences. I have referred in the Introduction to the acting contest undertaken by Prince Hal and Falstaff, successively in the roles of prince and king, son and father, Falstaff's performance enthusiastically endorsed by Mistress Quickly: 'O Jesu, he doth it as like one of these harlotry players as ever I see!' (*1 Henry IV*, 2.4.395–6), a remark which rather tars Falstaff with hammy overacting. To play notably like a player is to introduce one layer too many between actor and role. The apprentice Ralph, enthusiastically volunteered for performance by his master in *The Knight of the Burning Pestle*, 'should have played Jeronimo with a shoemaker for a wager'.[11] These amateur games had some corresponding life in the playhouses, perhaps. Verses by William Fennor, dating from 1614, make the following claim:

> I challenged Kendall on the Fortune stage;
> And he did promise 'fore an audience
> For to oppose me; note the accidence:
> I set up bills, the people thronged apace,
> With full intention to disgrace, or grace.
> The house was full, the trumpets twice had sounded,
> And though he came not, I was not confounded,
> But stepped upon the stage, and told them this:
> My adverse would not come. Not one did hiss,
> But flung me themes. I then extempore
> Did blot his name from out their memory,
> And pleased them all, in spite of one to brave me,
> Witness the ringing plaudits that they gave me.[12]

Fennor, as far as we know, was never a player, but William Kendall was certainly an actor at the Fortune. The proposed contest sounds like a variation on the old solo routine of providing versified jokes in response to suggestions called out from the audience, a routine still practised – in prose, typically – by comedians, as it was by the legendary performer Richard Tarlton in the 1580s. We have no other evidence to suggest that Kendall was renowned for this kind of act, though Fennor seems to claim he had a 'name' with the Fortune audience, obliterated in his absence by Fennor's own success. 'Challenges' at playhouses were more often fencing bouts, when the players rented out their stages for that purpose, but if Fennor is to be believed they could also accommodate wit contests.

More thoroughly theatrical were those moments when one could compare professional players in the same role, a common enough experience for devoted Shakespearean playgoers today, but which in the early theatre did not arrive too often, since plays belonged to specific companies and parts to specific actors. When players left a given company, as Will Kemp did the Chamberlain's men in 1599, regular playgoers could have assessed what his successor in his parts, generally taken to be Robert Armin, made of, say, Dogberry in *Much Ado About Nothing*, a play which continued in the repertory of the company following its first year of performance. Death or sickness called for replacements, rather than rivals, although once again frequent playgoers no doubt made their own comparisons. The King's men had to weather the crisis caused by Richard Burbage's death early in 1619; he perhaps died unexpectedly, since he left no written, signed will, a document frequently drawn up during final sickness, and he appears to have been performing until the end. His successor, Joseph Taylor, inevitably would have had to weather some comparative comment when he first played the older roles from the repertory of a generation earlier, the famous and long-lived Shakespearean parts. When a leading actor was temporarily incapacitated, other challenges arose in a company of a fixed size, in which each man had his own set of roles. Somehow it was contrived, as we learn in a 1593 letter from Philip Henslowe, in London, to Edward Alleyn, who was on tour: 'we heard that you were very sick at Bath, and that one of your fellows were fain to play your part for you'.[13] The audience at Bath did not have Alleyn's own performance to serve as a standard, but such accidents must also occasionally have happened during London seasons, as they still do, but usually with a pre-emptive understudy system in place. Two things are incidentally indicated by the Bath anecdote, first that experienced actors could perhaps learn even a long part in a day or so, and second that 'parts', the manuscript scrolls containing all the lines of a given role, must have been taken along by actors on the road. If Alleyn was sick enough not to perform, he would not have wanted to spend hours reciting his part for a colleague to learn by repetition.

The unusual circumstances surrounding John Marston's play *The Malcontent* would have given London playgoers some chance to see two quite different troupes of players tackling the same piece within a relatively short space of time. The first performance of the play was given by the Queen's Revels boys in 1604, and not much time later it was played in a somewhat amended version, with a theatrical 'Induction', or prologue, at the Globe by the King's men. The reasons for this appropriation are hard to understand. The Induction itself explains matters as theatrical tit for tat: the young company is supposed to have taken over a King's men's play called, loosely, *Jeronimo*, of which nothing at all is now known in connection with either company. What seems certain, at the least, is that both companies played *The Malcontent*, and at the Globe Burbage took the central role of Malevole, the dispossessed Duke of Milan who has taken to disguise to plan his return to power. The Globe Induction puts on stage two company actors by their proper names, Lowin and Condell, and they 'play' themselves, justifying the circumstances of the show. Two other performers, also identified by their own names in the speech prefixes (Will) Sly and (John) Sincler, actually play naïve members of the assembling audience, looking for seats, and for the famous actors. Sly, in character, judges that the play will not be 'as well acted as it hath been' (a line that demonstrates the order of the performances, and characterizes him as a comparative playgoer), while Lowin and Condell respond with sardonic rebuttal of such an unlikely verdict. Yet their superior amusement might in fact have been somewhat defensive; the performance of the play at the Blackfriars, a playhouse still in the tenancy of the young Queen's Revels company in 1604, had featured Nathan Field, a rising star then aged seventeen, in the role of Malevole. Burbage would certainly have played the part differently, yet the superiority of one performance over the other would not have been exactly the foregone conclusion assumed by the dramatized Lowin and Condell. Field's subsequent career brought him to the King's men, and he was sharing the stage with Burbage in roles of equal weight a decade after the *Malcontent* affair. He might well have become leading player of the troupe after Burbage's death, but he himself died in the following year, 1620, at the age of only thirty-three, yet still having achieved a prominent twenty-year career on the stage.

Field began as a boy player when the old tradition of boy playing was breaking up: chorister groups did not survive very long in the new reign of King James, and the professionalization of the Chapel troupe saw it severed from the traditional musical training, and transformed into an independent group of young adults rather than treble singers who occasionally gave dramatic performances. Field did not, as far as we know, spend his earlier years on the stage playing female roles, the selection for which in the boy troupes must always have been made on the bases of physique and facial characteristics: 'prettier' boys made better girls and women, in costume; vocal ranges among the choristers as a group evidently would not have varied much. Ben Jonson's famous elegy on the Chapel player Salomon Pavy, who died aged thirteen in 1602, claims that he was skilled at playing old men. This may be a poetic conceit rather than the literal truth (the Fates were tragically deceived into marking him for death by a convincing portrayal of advanced years, the poem claims), yet some members of boy troupes must have taken on the *senex* roles in classical or classically inspired comedy, for example.

Thirteen-year-olds attached as apprentices and trainees to adult professional troupes would have been expected to wear the skirts on stage; in the next chapter I will discuss some specific instances of such performance. How soon they might have left them behind would have depended on individual skills and physical characteristics, as I have described in Chapter 3. Actors whom we know to have had professional careers beginning in their youth, then, we might expect to have experienced playing female roles as their entrée to the stage, giving them some sympathetic insight when they came to be master actors training their own apprentices in such parts. John Heminges, who looked after many of the King's men's apprentices, was not in such a position: he had spent his youth in a conventional city apprenticeship, turning to acting as an adult and beginning in male parts. The two most famous actors of the age began young, but we know very little about the circumstances of their doing so. Edward Alleyn was on the stage by the time he was sixteen (in 1583), and thus is quite likely to have begun in female roles. Richard Burbage, on his brother's testimony, began playing at the age of fifteen, so also probably played female roles first. Among the earliest indications of the parts he took are two theatrical 'plots' – outlines, by scene divisions and character entries, of plays for use in the playhouse. Burbage's name appears in the plot of the lost play *The Dead Man's Fortune* and again in *The Second Part of the Seven Deadly Sins*, where he is assigned two parts in the episodes contained in the play: King Gorboduc in the Envy playlet and Tereus in that illustrating Lechery. Both parts are male leads; there is some controversy about the date of the manuscript, but it is clear that Burbage was an established adult actor at the time of the show.[14]

The manuscript of *The Dead Man's Fortune* is rather different. It supplies only a few actors' names, largely in supernumerary roles, although the development of the two plots – the play has a comic subplot which seems to be based on a scenario from the Italian *commedia dell'arte* – can be followed reasonably clearly from its skeleton plan. Read in one way, it might seem that Burbage played the humble role of a Messenger (and hence probably other unindicated smaller roles). In his commentary on the plot W. W. Greg argued that it was more likely that the name 'Burbage', in the one place it appears, was a slip for the character he was playing, Urganda. In his reconstruction of the events of the plot, Greg calls Burbage's part 'the magician Urganda', but in fact the name and character, borrowed from the Amadis and Palmerin romances, are those of an enchantress, 'Urganda the Unknown' in Anthony Munday's translation (1618).[15] While undoubtedly a central part in the play, then, as Greg recognized, Urganda was a female role, a magical ally of the lovers, rather like Friar Bacon in Greene's *Friar Bacon and Friar Bungay*, but, rather remarkably, a female figure of supernatural power. The conventional dating of the plot, on no very compelling grounds, is about 1590, in which year Burbage was twenty-one. We know from later evidence that it was not impossible for young men to continue in female roles until their early twenties, although it was the exception rather than the rule. Hardly anything can be said with certainty about the circumstances which gave rise to the plot of *The Dead Man's Fortune*, but if Greg's guess about the casting is right, the play itself is more likely to have seen the stage at some time nearer the mid 1580s, when Burbage was still in his teens.

David Mateer's recent discovery of a lawsuit revealed that the prominent actor Richard Perkins, lead performer at the Red Bull, Cockpit, and Salisbury Court playhouses in the first decades of the seventeenth century, began, perhaps, with Edward Alleyn, when Perkins was about seventeen.[16] The agreement binding Perkins as a 'servant' for the term of three years from November 1596 – to Alleyn individually, and hence to the Admiral's men collectively – was broken when Perkins was poached by the management of the Swan playhouse. Mateer thinks that Perkins's value was as a specialist in female roles; that may have been so, but Perkins was of an age when the transition to male roles was commonly made. His value, I think, was simply that he was a very good young actor, like Nathan Field at the same age, some years later. The circumstances of the law case do not tell us whether the agreement signed in 1596 was the first of its kind between the principal parties, or the renewal of a similar earlier term. In the latter case Perkins might have been with Alleyn since he was fourteen or so, and hence would have been more likely to have played female roles directly opposite his master, including one of the young women in *The Blind Beggar of*

Alexandria, for example. Perkins's career on stage, in the event, was twice as long as his master's, and he played many parts over the course of forty-odd years in the theatre, only a few of which we now know.

Another prominent figure in the seventeenth-century theatre and a colleague of Perkins for many years, Christopher Beeston, perhaps retired from appearing on stage when he opened his new playhouse, the Cockpit in Drury Lane, in 1616, opting for a managerial role in the companies with which he was subsequently associated. His beginnings as a player were with the Chamberlain's company: he is named in the casts of the printed versions of Jonson's two *Humour* plays (1598 and 1599), performed when he was in his late teens, at a time when he is likely to have taken secondary male roles rather than female parts. Some years afterwards he was remembered in the will of the senior player Augustine Phillips, who called him 'my servant'.[17] Beeston was by then an independent performer in another company, so the phrase refers to a past relationship, and it was likely to have been a rather happier version of Perkins's with Alleyn (Beeston named a son after his master, for example); once again, it may have begun when Beeston was younger, and thus he may have figured in female roles in the Chamberlain's men's plays of the mid 1590s, the period of the first performances of Shakespeare's *A Midsummer Night's Dream*, *Love's Labour's Lost*, *The Merchant of Venice*, *Romeo and Juliet*, and the histories *King John*, *Richard II*, and the two parts of *Henry IV*.

An exception to the general observation made at the start of this chapter, that players over their careers would have been expected to take on a range of parts, we might think could be made in the case of 'those that play your clowns', as Hamlet puts it to the players visiting Elsinore (*Hamlet*, 3.2.38–9). The plural form is significant. While we tend to think of a single performer specializing in broad comic parts as a member of leading companies, and particular of the prominent trio, successively, of Richard Tarlton, Will Kemp, and Robert Armin, repertory frequently demanded more than one 'clown', whatever we might mean by that rather variable term. Ridding ourselves of any thoughts of post-Grimaldi circus grotesques, we should remember that 'clown' in early modern English tended to convey the meaning of a rustic, and hence, from an urban point of view, something of an unpolished simpleton: Costard in *Love's Labour's Lost*, for example, or William in *As You Like It*. *Hamlet* contains two clowns, so called in the early texts, who dig Ophelia's grave:[18] not rustics, perhaps, but at the bottom of the social ladder, a traditional clown status. Their opening discussion (5.1) of the ethics of suicide is full of 'mistaking words', a common generic characteristic of clown scenes,[19] written into the parts learnt by the actors.

The First Clown's subsequent bantering with Hamlet himself is also a well established generic trope: the wisdom of the fool, expressed obliquely in teasing play with words and their logic, tests the limits of human reason and knowledge, and teaches the great humility. The chief practitioner of that art in *Hamlet* is an absent presence, so to speak, and is called a jester rather than a clown: Yorick, whose skull the gravedigger presents to the prince.

To think of the practicalities of casting *Hamlet* within the Chamberlain's company, in 1601 or thereabouts, we naturally assume that Burbage took the title role. The principal clown actor of that period, Robert Armin, would presumably have played the First Clown, a crucial role, though a short one, appearing only in one scene of a long play (one might compare, in *Macbeth*, the role of the Porter). Armin was a sharer, an important member of the company, and one of its younger full members: he was in his early thirties in 1601. Thus we might think he would have been more fully employed in staging *Hamlet*, and the structure of the play allows for him also to have played, for example, Polonius, a role which ends with the character's death in act three, or Osric, an extravagant fop who appears in the scene following the burial, but probably with enough intervening lines for Armin to have made the shift from earthy rags to showy silks and velvets. We might further speculate that Armin took all three roles, as a bravura trio of variations on folly an audience might well have appreciated.[20] My general point is that as a sharer in a company playing a varied repertory the fool specialist was undoubtedly involved in taking other parts than those of recognizable clowns when plays did not give such characters much if any stage time.

The corollary is that in plays calling for more than one designated fool (Feste in *Twelfth Night*, called '*Clown*' in the stage directions and speech prefixes of the first text of the play, Touchstone in *As You Like It*, the Fool in *King Lear*, etc.) other members of the company were required and presumably able to take on such roles when the play demanded them. The 1601 *Hamlet* called on a second actor to play a double act with Armin, and in earlier years if Will Kemp played Nick Bottom, Dogberry, and Falstaff, who accompanied him in playing Francis Flute, Snug, Verges, George Seacoal, Ancient Pistol, Silence, and their companions? Groups of 'irregular humorists', as the Shakespeare Folio of 1623 describes them,[21] or 'a crew of patches' in Puck's phrase (*A Midsummer Night's Dream*, 3.2.9), demanded that a number of actors work together in the fool's genre, and players must have been used to adjusting the register of their performance style to suit the changing repertory. Although renowned comic performers such as Tarlton, Kemp, and Armin were very good at virtuoso solo acts, it was not all they did, and their work in plays was not isolated. One should not make too much of a fetish of the leading comic performer within early modern playing companies; comic grotesquerie was a style within the reach of many actors, and required of much of the company in certain plays: Jonson's *Every Man Out of His Humour*, for example. To put the matter another way, how would the company have cast Will Kemp in *A Midsummer Night's Dream*, or what part would he have claimed for himself? Bottom is its leading clown, but Puck is its jester, a 'merry wanderer of the night', a shape-changer, a 'shrewd and knavish sprite' (see 2.1.32–57), and something of an athlete. Both roles are crucial to a successful performance of the play, but Kemp could have taken only one of them.

What concerns Hamlet is what the clown might do outside the discipline of the play text: 'And let those that play your clowns speak no more than is set down for them; for there be of them that will themselves laugh, to set on some quality of barren spectators to laugh too, though in the meantime some necessary question of the play be then to be considered' (*Hamlet*, 3.2.38–43.) Two issues are raised here, in fact. Speaking more than is set down suggests some verbal improvisation or riffing, which is certainly what Kendall was challenged to do at the Fortune, what Tarlton was renowned for, and what he is supposed to have admired in the young Armin. Laughter at the inappropriate moment is simply upstaging, which can also be practised by subtler means; more largely, any performance of a play is necessarily a good deal more than the words set down on paper. Once the words are sounded from live bodies they are shaped by the varying contexts of physical presence, and by particular qualities of vocal colour, volume, pitch, and rhythm, and as the fool is frequently a subverter of language and sense, a 'corrupter of words' in Feste's phrase (*Twelfth Night*, 3.1.35–6), he can subvert by gesture and tone. Speaking what is set down is a fundamentally unstable matter, especially in comedy.

The matter of comic improvisation might be broken down further. All leading actors with a reputation for comic performance, from Tarlton on, practised some kinds of perfomative routine outside the frame of the fiction of the play: jigs, themes, ballads, rhymes, songs, and dances, entertainment offered to a theatre crowd in addition to a play, like the cartoons preceding the main feature in cinema of a generation ago. Such things in early theatre seem, as far as we can tell on the basis of very limited material (there is pitifully little hard evidence concerning jigs, for example), to have followed plays rather than preceded them, but at such moments the clown appeared as himself, even if he adopted a comedian's persona. He was thus one of the best known personalities of the playing troupe, and so he was celebrated, in

Tarlton's case particularly. If we think of comic actors of our own period, widely familiar to many through the popular media of film and television – John Cleese or Rowan Atkinson, for example – we know that when we see them in new films or television comedies they are instantly recognizable, and bring with them a whole constellation of comic expectation. It needs only a certain movement of the face or intonation of the voice for us to begin to laugh: we know the sorts of characters the actor plays, how he or she exposes the ridiculous, and we pleasurably anticipate what is likely to unfold. Such familiarity invested the comic performers of the early modern theatre, and would have hovered about the reception of roles the actor might be playing within a fiction which were not primarily 'clown' parts. Once one had made the audience laugh in a stand-up act, one was hardly a neutral figure on the stage. The liberty given clowns as extra-textual entertainers, then, might infect their presence in dramatic fictions, worrying Prince Hamlet.

We might also ask whether improvisation was entirely excluded from the performance of plays; that is, was absolutely eveything that was spoken, by design and intent, 'set down'? Technically, all plays had to receive the approval of the Master of the Revels, who read and passed for performance the texts presented to him before production. He was free to demand cuts and changes if he judged the play not to meet the standards he was charged to uphold.[22] None the less, several printed dramatic texts demonstrate curious lacunae when it comes to comic performance that we might expect to have been more fully developed and extended, while another, rather oddly, claims to have excluded material 'unmeet for the matter' in a pair of plays where we would hardly expect, judging by what we now have, 'such conceits as clownage keeps in pay': this is the edition of the two *Tamburlaine* plays, published together in 1590.[23] There was once, it seems, *written* material, presumably emanating from the playhouse if not directly from Marlowe's hand, which added some accompanying comic material to the story of Tamburlaine's epic conquests.

The comedy *A Knack to Know a Knave*, acted at the Rose in 1592 by Lord Strange's men, was published in 1594 as 'Newly set forth, as it hath sundry / times been played by ED. ALLEYN / and his company. / *With KEMP'S applauded Merriments* / of the men of Gotham, in receiving / the King into Gotham'.[24] Two famous actors were involved in the first performances of the play, although by 1594 they had moved on in separate directions, Alleyn to the Admiral's company and Kemp to the rival Chamberlain's company. The *'applauded merriments'* touted on the title page as an evident success in the theatre one awaits, as a modern reader, with some expectation. In the

printed text the episode takes up roughly a page and a half in length – three
or four minutes of playing time in the theatre – and there is no obviously
prominent role for Kemp. The 'mad men of Gotham' are a trio, with lines
fairly evenly distributed among them. The Cobbler is chosen to address the
King, briefly, and without any extravagant display of wit. Surely such a brief
and simple moment could not have been very much 'applauded' at the
Rose, and either the text does not fully reveal what was done in the theatre,
or Kemp had more roles in the play, perhaps taking one of the 'knave' parts,
for example. (The play is a rather old-fashioned quasi-morality, on the
theme of good government; the chief *raisonneur* is called Honesty.) While
Kemp took named parts, he had other accomplishments, and one of his
chief performances was to morris-dance from London to Norwich, in daily
stages spread over the course of a month. Earlier in his career, while still a
member of the Earl of Leicester's household players, he received a reward for
'leaping into a ditch', the kind of athletic clown stunt which hardly depends
on verbal wit, although it may have been accompanied by some kind of
absurd rhetorical flourish.[25]

Kemp made intermittent visits to mainland Europe, and may have come
into contact with foreign actors there. His reputation, at least, was that he
was known to the *commedia dell'arte* actors, and adopted some of their style.
At the time of his ditch-ducking gag one of his identities was 'Don
Gulihelmo', and in 1590 Thomas Nashe, writing of his own travels, recounts
this anecdote:

coming from Venice the last summer, and taking Bergamo in my way homeward
to England, it was my hap, sojourning there some four or five days, to light into
fellowship with that famous Francatrip Harlequin, who perceiving me to be an
Englishman asked me many particulars of the order and manner of our plays,
which he termed by the name of representations; amongst other talk he enquired of
me if I knew any *parabolano* [mountebank, spieler] here in London as Signor
Chiarlatano Kempino. Very well, quoth I, and have been oft in his company. He,
hearing me say so, began to embrace me anew, and offered me all the courtesy he
could for his sake, saying although he knew him not, yet for the reports he had
heard of his pleasure he could not but be in love with his perfections being
absent.[26]

Quite how Kemp's style might have corresponded to that of contemporary
Italian *zanni* is impossible to say, but the actor's adoption of Italianate stage
names indicates that he knew something about the *commedia all'improvviso*,
and hence that he perhaps was able to practise the art of rhetorical improvisation from a *scenario* or *soggetto*, a sketch outline of the development of a
scene.[27]

For such performers comic episodes within a play that was otherwise scripted need not have been fully written down. Their general lines were defined by the rest of the fiction – receiving the King into Gotham, for example – and the precise contents of such an episode might have varied somewhat from performance to performance; the more the merriments were applauded, the more elaborated or extended they might have become. A similar phenomenon may be observed in the printed text of *The Fair Maid of Bristow*, a comedy acted by the King's men at about the same time as *Measure for Measure*, in 1603–4.[28] In *Measure for Measure* Robert Armin perhaps had the role of Pompey – the most obvious part for him to have taken in that play, which is again identified as 'Clown' in the Folio text – while in *The Fair Maid of Bristow* the part suited to his talents would appear to have been that of the comic servant, Frog, who has a female counterpart, and lover, Douce. The difference in length of the two parts, Pompey and Frog, however, is quite considerable (Pompey has 165 lines, and appears in a good number of scenes), and while actor-sharers might have welcomed smaller roles in certain repertory pieces, to give them some relief, the text of *The Fair Maid* gives the impression that at least some and possibly a fair amount of Frog's part has not survived in print. He has, in the play as published in 1605, two scenes, the first a fairly brief messenger episode, and the second a comic dialogue with Douce, in which they resolve to get married. A few scenes later there appears the cryptic marginal direction 'The drunken mirth' (C3^r). This evidently once was a theatrical episode, probably involving some music, singing, and dancing, and presumably celebrating the marriage of Frog and Douce. Perhaps part of the original manuscript book belonging to the Globe has been cut in printing, although hardly for the same reasons that Richard Jones cut 'fond and frivolous gestures' from *Tamburlaine*; drunken mirth is the stuff of comedy. Equally, we might consider that there never *was* a written text for whatever happened during 'The drunken mirth', consisting as it probably did of absurd singing, dancing, and sight gags; it was rehearsed by the actors involved (one of them a boy), but it was a routine which did not involve much in the way of spoken dialogue – perhaps not quite nothing but roaring, but tending in that direction.

Comic action, in short, might substitute for speech, as in silent cinema, which produced many classics of comedy. In the sixteenth and seventeenth centuries the success of foreign actors outside the districts of their native languages – the *commedia* actors in France, or English actors in Germany, Sweden, and Denmark – depended not a little on the eloquence of action, and with German audiences one of the favourite English types was the fool or clown, soon spawning German versions of the character named Hanswurst or Hans Stockfisch, memorializing the clown's typical fixation on bodily appetites, as in the episodes quoted immediately below. In England the clown's extra-textual vitality is noted in the first of the Cambridge *Parnassus* plays, discussed in Chapter 2; in *The Pilgrimage to Parnassus* the character Dromo, pulling 'a clown' onto the stage with a rope, gives his reasons: 'Clowns have been thrust into plays by head and shoulders ever since Kemp could make a scurvy face … Why, if thou can but draw thy mouth awry, lay thy leg over thy staff, saw a piece of cheese asunder with thy dagger, lap up drink on the earth, I warrant thee they'll laugh mightily.'[29] All these physical actions are *lazzi*, or set comic routines; that of laying the leg over the staff sounds remarkably like a running gag practised by Harpo Marx, the silent fool of the Marx Brothers' film comedies.

To return to the general question of doubling, invoked in connection with the Clown-Gravedigger's part in *Hamlet*, the practice had a long tradition. Early plays and interludes frequently had more parts than players in the troupe, and some plays were printed with doubling schemes laid out. The early Elizabethan play *The Longer Thou Livest, the More Fool Thou Art*, by William Wager, has fifteen dramatic characters, but the printed text includes a plan to perform it with four actors, the first taking five parts. Evidently for such schemes to work the dramaturgy had to be fairly simple, and there can never be more than four figures on the stage. The evidently popular *Cambises*, published in 1584, breaks down a wide range of dramatic characters among ten performers, the first taking six widely varied roles. The long title role is played by one actor without any doubling (save delivering the epilogue, following Cambises' death); the vice Ambidexter also plays Trial, and 'one man' – presumably a boy or youth – plays *all* the female roles save Venus, which is a part tacked on to the load of the fourth actor, already playing five male parts. One need not believe that actors working things out for themselves would have followed such schemes religiously, but the lists themselves demonstrate that large-cast plays were something of a challenge to playing troupes of a fixed size. A popular romance comedy we know to have come into the repertory of the King's men by the early Jacobean period, *Mucedorus*, continued to include a casting scheme in the many editions of the play published between 1598 and the Restoration. The edition of 1610 breaks the parts between ten actors, six taking a single role, including Amadine, the King of Aragon's daughter, and Mouse, the clown: two specialist performers. (No actor is assigned the role of the bear, which has a brief appearance in the second scene, but has, unsurprisingly, no part written. The costume for the part evidently had a detachable head, which subsequently figures as a prop, once Mucedorus has slain the bear, off stage.) The other actors have at least two roles each; the younger actor who plays Comedy, a personified female figure, in the Induction and at the end, also subsequently plays a boy, the young woman Ariena, Amadine's maid, and a comic old woman, who quarrels with Mouse. The sequence involves a relaxed change of costume, following the Induction, for the mute part of the Boy, who carries the bear's head in the seventh scene, but then a fairly rapid shift into the dress and wig of Ariena, who appears, briefly, in the following scene. (The character hardly seems necessary, in fact, and might be cut entirely without much loss.) Roughly 160 lines later the performer must re-enter as the Old Woman, who fights with Mouse over an unpaid bill and a stolen pot of drink, in a knockabout scene of clowning. There is then a considerable break for the actor to resume the costume of Comedy and be ready to play the epilogue. The middle two roles are simply walk-ons, the first entirely mute, but Comedy has the important opening and closing moments, with speech of some rhetorical elaboration, and a spirited antag-onistic debate with Envy, who has come to sow discord: the epilogue endorses Comedy's triumph. Dressed, one might guess, something like the figure of Comedy shown on the right-hand side of the title page to Ben Jonson's folio *Works* in 1616, the character is a dignified daughter of Apollo, and interestingly different, for the performer, from the comic-grotesque and belligerent Old Woman, another face of comedy he plays between his two appearances as the personified ideal, at least according to the printed scheme.

Actual doubling practice in the theatre, of which the following chapter demonstrates some concrete instances, was governed partly by status, but also by specialization. The doubling favoured by some modern commenta-tors on *King Lear*, and occasionally practised on the modern stage, of Cordelia with the Fool (two truth-telling loyalists), while certainly feasible in terms of stage time is not at all historical. The Fool, in the first perform-ances, would have been played by the adult Armin, and Cordelia by one of the three talented boys required to play the three daughters, possibly by the youngest of that group. *King Lear* is a play that assembles most of its major speaking roles on stage together at the beginning, and subsequently keeps most of them in view for an extended period. Cordelia has a prolonged absence, from 1.1 to 4.6 (and a relatively modest total of lines: 89), and the Fool a presence contained entirely within those limits, from 1.4 to 3.6, a coincidence which has led to modern speculation about doubling, but which would have been out of the question for the actors of the King's men. Otherwise the only major roles not to appear in the first scene of the play – that is, they are not named in entry directions or given any lines – are Edgar and Oswald. Since the important roles of the rival suitors, Burgundy and France, do not have further appearances after the opening scene, it seems fairly certain that the two actors playing them doubled other parts. The Edgar actor would have had 160 lines after France leaves the stage to change for his main part – a moral pairing which might have been matched by having the Burgundy actor change for Oswald, who finally dies at Edgar's hands. As with the Cordelia–Fool pairing, this is a speculation based on thematic considerations rather than theatrical practice: the King's men would have followed the easiest practicable route to matching performers with parts: certainly they would have needed to call on a group of hired actors to take on the mutiple soldiers, attendants, servants, knights, and gentlemen called for in the texts of the play; the total cast might have numbered in the low twenties.[30]

Documents surviving from the Shakespearean period that connect named actors with parts constitute a number of distinct kinds. Printed lists in published plays usually give only partial information, and only rarely a completely full cast which we might connect with a specific date of production: two of the most informative of these will provide the central focus of the following chapter. Manuscript plays and printed texts marked up for production occasionally include actors' names, but not consistently, and usually only for minor parts: to fix, at the date of the notation, the specific details of the kind of multiple-part playing referred to above. Philip Massinger's play *Believe As You List*, a King's men's piece from 1631, survived its immediate moment in the theatre only as a theatrically annotated manuscript; it was never printed in the early modern period. It incidentally indicates, from property and warning directions added to the basic text of the play, that Joseph Taylor played the leading role of Antiochus (680 lines), John Lowin that of Flaminius (597 lines), Thomas Pollard Berecinthius (237 lines), Robert Benfield Marcellus (166 lines), Eilert Swanston Chrysalus (71 lines), and Richard Robinson Lentulus (36 lines). As T. J. King has suggested, some of the principal actors with smaller roles – Swanston and Robinson, notably – could have doubled other medium-length parts, given the dramaturgy of the play, but there is no direct evidence that they did so. Otherwise the annotations keep track of a number of actors in minor roles, not altogether consistently. The hired man Rowland Dowle had four parts spread across the play, only one of them a speaking role. Freelance actors in the Shakespearean period were minor actors, and they could have expected to be employed exactly as was Dowle when temporarily hired by a company, whether in *King Lear* or *Believe as You List*.

Fairly full information about casting is given in four of the five surviving manuscript plots of plays, but in only one case do we have a roughly matching play text to connect to assigned roles and thus to calculate the length and significance of actors' parts. This is *The Battle of Alcazar*, written by George Peele and probably first acted in 1589. It was evidently something of a favourite with the popular theatre crowds in its heyday; Pistol quotes one of Alleyn's lines from the play in his playhouse-infected rodomontade in *2 Henry IV*. The plot of *Alcazar* was made for a revival, possibly at the Fortune in or after 1600, in a version of the play somewhat different from the printed text of 1594, and yet substantially related to it.[31] Analysis of the now damaged manuscript moves into speculation in some areas, but we can be confident that Edward Alleyn played the leading role of Muly Mahamet, his colleagues in the Admiral's men taking the other parts. Twenty-six distinct performers are named in the plot – the play includes some spectacular scenes – but only ten of these are sharer-actors, and there are eight boys, an unusually high number; there are only three female speaking roles, however, a more typical average in plays of the period (the other boys played children and pages). The plot represents a production with all the stops out, concerned to fill the stage with impressive numbers, Moorish costumes (to match the exotic setting of the play, Morocco), and impressive visual effects in the dumb shows that precede each act. Alleyn was no doubt made up in Othello-like face paint, some years before Burbage appeared as the 'black' general. In the printed text of the play no particular single part dominates: Alleyn had the longest, but it is merely two hundred-odd lines; one other actor had roughly the same number, but only three other roles are more than a hundred lines in length. Numerous actors, including some of the sharers, doubled roles, Charles Massey having taken three parts, and the hired men up to four apiece. A crowd of characters, then, people the play, and its particular narrative and form drive the casting. It would have been an expensive play to mount, and its production was no doubt calculated on the ratio of profit it was likely to generate from audience receipts.

One further plot, possibly from around 1590, and briefly mentioned above, casts Richard Burbage in two distinct roles, but in what appears to have been a rather unusually organized play, in that it is not one continuous fiction (no text survives): *The Second Part of the Seven Deadly Sins*, perhaps written by Richard Tarlton and revived by Lord Strange's men at the date given above, when the named actors were members of that company (many of them passing, with Burbage, to the Chamberlain's men in 1594). The play had a three-part structure, the plot reveals, each with a story illustrating a sin; presumably the entirely lost first part covered the other four. The scheme, then, is a series of moralized episodes, each perhaps with a playing time of thirty to forty minutes. The three episodes of the *Second Part*, separated by a choric framework, are (1) the King Gorboduc story (the subject of the 1562 play by Sackville and Norton), illustrating Envy, (2) the story of the emperor Sardanapalus (Sloth), and (3) the Ovidian myth of Tereus and Philomela (Lechery). Burbage is cast for Gorboduc in the first episode, and Tereus in the third. His companions included Augustine Phillips, playing Sardanapulus (2), George Bryan, with three distinct parts (2 and 3), Thomas Pope as Arbactus (2), Henry Condell as Ferrex (1) and a Lord (3), and Will Sly as Porrex (1) and a Lord (3). The future Chamberlain's actors John Duke, John Holland, and Richard Cowley, with other men, took as many as six parts apiece, distributed across the three episodes. Four boys played seven female roles; 'Saunder' (not Alexander Cook, if the 1590 date is correct) took the roles of the Queen in the first playlet and Procne in the third; Robert Gough, probably, played Aspatia in the second and Philomela, to Burbage's Tereus, in the third.

In all, twenty distinct people are named in the plot, by surname, Christian name, or abbreviated forms, and a number of the parts are not assigned to players, including the choric role of the poet John Lydgate (perhaps somewhat in the fashion of Gower in *Pericles*), and the framing figure of King Henry VI. It has been suggested that Edward Alleyn, a member of Strange's company in the early 1590s, took one of these parts, and hence that the performance brought together, early in their careers, the two legendary players of the age; once more, such casting is speculative, if possible.

Burbage's life-long career cannot be filled out in much detail: Gorboduc and Tereus are two of his documented roles, Malevole is another, as is Ferdinand in *The Duchess of Malfi*, and the funeral elegies allude to his having played Hamlet, Hieronimo, Lear, and Othello. Hieronimo is something of a puzzle, as is the reference to the same character-title in *The Malcontent*; Hieronimo in *The Spanish Tragedy* was a famous Alleyn role. What seems to be an early seventeenth-century annotation in a copy of Jonson's plays assigns Burbage the title role of *Volpone*, and the role of Subtle in *The Alchemist*.[32] Other references suggest he played, as we might guess, the title role in *Richard III*, and given his position as leading actor we can reasonably infer he took the major roles in plays with a dominant central character: Henry V, Macbeth, Coriolanus, Antony, and so on. That Shakespeare wrote for him, as has often been asserted, we can believe, if we take that to mean that Shakespeare would have been quite aware of and familiar with Burbage's kinds of power on the stage, but that parts were precisely calculated to match

Burbage's characteristics is not credible to me; dramatic character was not conceived with such particular individuality.

What parts Burbage may have played in such repertory items as *The Fair Maid of Bristow*, *The Merry Devil of Edmonton*, and *Mucedorus* is impossible to guess; in comedies generally, typically constructed with a spread of more evenly balanced roles, the 'Burbage part' is not often plainly evident. By modern standards he was not so old at his death that he could not have continued playing younger roles without too much apology. Playgoers who had grown up with his Romeo, a part we might reasonably guess he premiered, may not have been willing to see him pass it to a younger successor, like the tenacious fans of opera singers today. In the Christmas season of 1612–13, for example, when Burbage was in his early forties, the King's men revived, among other plays, Jonson's *The Alchemist*, Shakespeare's *Much Ado About Nothing*, the *Henry IV* plays, *Julius Caesar*, and the anonymous comedy *The Merry Devil of Edmonton*. Taking it that Burbage was then playing Subtle in the Jonson play, as he was a year or two later after Nathan Field had joined the company and was playing Face opposite him, he had also presumably been the original Benedick, the leading male role, in *Much Ado*, and probably was still playing it fifteen years later. (In later 2007 the no longer youthful Simon Russell Beale, then forty-six, played the part in a National Theatre production, and the middle-aged and somewhat portly Benedick gave the comedy a particularly poignant flavour.)

Burbage probably also hung on to other roles he had first played as a younger man: Prince Hal in the *Henry IV* plays (he had played in *Henry V* in 1604–5), by 1612–13, it is likely, against John Lowin as Falstaff, and Brutus, the noblest Roman of them all, in *Julius Caesar*. Burbage had presumably been in the first cast of *The Merry Devil* also (*c.* 1602?), but it would be a desperate guess to nominate his role. The play is a very middle-of-the-road piece of work, popular though it seems to have been; it seems to owe something of its style, and the framing of its title, to *The Merry Wives of Windsor* (it also has a voluble, extravagant Host, a romantic abduction, and a deer-hunting episode), but has neither outstanding individual parts nor a series of brilliant eccentric vignettes, like Jonson at his best. Burbage, like Alleyn, must have done his best in sustaining his colleagues in showing such indifferent material to the best advantage, and the presence of such plays as *The Merry Devil of Edmonton* in company repertories reminds us of the importance of ensemble playing within acting troupes of Shakespeare's day. If such comedies were to work on stage they needed strong and convincing playing, evenly distributed through the cast. The material may seem rather thin and implausible when read, like many an indifferent play, but in watching performance one can be carried by vivacity and energy, and even by actors' knowing triumph over the insubstantiality of the fictions to which they have given life, a kind of delight in the ridiculous, particularly appropriate to comedy. Burbage's stardom was one aspect of his stage success; another was his membership of a strong and balanced collective, in which the combined energies and talents of the entire troupe were directed to bringing every piece in their repertory to full and entertaining life before their audiences.

John Lowin, with whom this chapter began, spent roughly the first third of his long career with Burbage as a companion on stage. They partnered, I have suggested, as Hal and Falstaff, and possibly as Wolsey and his King in Shakespeare and Fletcher's *Henry VIII* in 1613 (Henry has thirty more lines than Wolsey, but they are both substantial roles, over 400 lines in length). Lowin's career was long enough for him to be remembered, and to be the subject of reminiscences, after the Restoration: one of these has to do with *Henry VIII*, retailed by John Downes. Thomas Betterton, acting the part of Henry after 1660, had, Downes claimed, been trained by Sir William Davenant, 'who had it from old Mr. Lowin, that had his indications from Mr. Shakespeare himself'.[33] The pedigree is not impossible – Davenant and Lowin were active at the same time, as the epigraph to this chapter demonstrates – but somewhat improbable as regards Shakespeare, largely retired from day-to-day theatre business by 1613, supervising Lowin's performance. Another hint of Lowin's partnership with Burbage is provided by a further post-Restoration memory, that 'before the wars Lowin used to act with mighty applause Falstaff, Morose, Volpone ... Mammon in *The Alchemist*, Melantius in *The Maid's Tragedy*'.[34] The first three parts Lowin picked up after their first performances, Volpone after Burbage's death; Lowin was in the first production of the play (1605), and is assigned the part of Sir Pol in the manuscript cast list for *Volpone* relating to the period 1615–19, that for *The Alchemist* confirming that he played Mammon at the same time (after Field had joined the King's men) and probably had done so since the first production in 1610.[35] Sir Epicure Mammon, the slow-moving and self-centred sybarite, the 'fat knight' (5.3.41), and one of the chief gulls in the con trick, is a considerably different role from that of Volpone. Lowin's personal bulk, visible in his portrait, and no doubt used to advantage in playing Falstaff, would have added a suitably ludicrous underlining of Sir Epicure's fleshliness.

In *The Alchemist* of the late 1610s, Lowin played the role with Henry Condell as Mammon's sceptical companion Surly, Nathan Field as Face, initially in disguise as the humble lab assistant Lungs, and Burbage as Subtle, in the two scenes he played with Lowin in the guise of the learned and pious old alchemist. The hilarious scene of the collapse of Mammon's hopes for wealth and power (4.5), as the 'great lady' he has been wooing descends into her mad fit of garrulous babble drawn from biblical commentary, is one of Jonson's masterpieces of accelerating noise and chaos, including the off stage explosion of the alchemical equipment; Subtle plays mock despair at his 'son's' moral failure, and the naïve Mammon is overcome with fearful guilt. It is, simply, a gift to actors, and the sheer fun of the play's games of deceit must have bound the players together in performance with a particular bond of affection. The player of the crucial role of Dol Common, disguised in 4.5 as the noble madwoman, was probably George Birch, an apprentice of John Heminges in his late teens by 1615–19; it was another thoroughly enjoyable part, energetic, tough, and absurdly inventive, and played throughout in the company of the leading adult actors of the King's men. The part must have passed from one senior boy to another, over the thirty years the play remained in the repertory, and Lowin as Mammon have paid his breathy, greasy court to a number of fellow actors over the course of his career in the role.

The final part mentioned in *Historia Histrionica* suggests a further pairing of Lowin and Burbage on the stage. *The Maid's Tragedy*, one of a series of plays written for the King's company by Francis Beaumont and John Fletcher at the time Shakespeare was disengaging himself from his position as chief house dramatist, and first staged at about the same time as the premiere of *The Alchemist*, must have been initially cast with the same actors who appeared in the first staging of the Jonson play (Burbage, Lowin, Condell, Cook, Armin, Heminges, Ostler, Underwood, Tooley, and Eccleston). If Lowin's fame extended back to having been the first Melantius in *The Maid's Tragedy*, the bluff soldier brother of Evadne, Burbage is likely to have taken the other major male role, Amintor, colleague and friend of Melantius, and the victim of a plot of enforced marriage to Evadne, revealed on their wedding night to be mistress of the King, who has commanded the wedding to provide a complaisant husband of convenience. (The part of Amintor was certainly subsequently played by Burbage's replacement after 1619, Joseph Taylor.) Though Amintor is the younger of the two fictional friends and Burbage was the older actor, by seven years, his skills may have been better matched to the heroic pathos of the role – Amintor is torn between ideal loyalty to the monarch and the desire to right his wrong; Burbage played the suffering Othello, for example, rather than the longer role of Iago. In *The Maid's Tragedy* Amintor is sworn

to silence by the King, but his efforts at concealment do not convince his old
friend and new brother-in-law, who in a famous scene in the third act
alternately challenges him first with false friendship, in not revealing the
cause of his apparent grief, and then, once Amintor confides in him, with
dishonour, in calumniating his family. Melantius then shifts to a vow of
vengeance against the King, arousing Amintor's resistance as a loyal subject;
eventually they are reconciled. The scene can seem to be a rather mechanical
seesaw of overreactions, but it was a great favourite with audiences into the
Restoration period, and clearly calls on subtle performance to make it work.
After the civil wars the famous partnership in the play was between Michael
Mohun (Melantius) and Charles Hart (Amintor); that the first audiences
saw Lowin and Burbage in the parts is an intriguing possibility.

The cast list published with the first printed text of John Webster's *The
Duchess of Malfi* in 1623 shows that Lowin played Bosola at the premiere of
the play (*c.* 1613) and kept the part in the revival ten or so years later, which
might give us more confidence in tracing the Restoration identifications
of his roles back to the initial productions, where otherwise likely. (At
the opening of the Whitehall Cockpit playhouse at court in 1630, Lowin
played three of his famous roles before the King and Queen: *The Duchess of
Malfi*, *Volpone*, and *The Maid's Tragedy* were all played by the King's men
on the stage of the new theatre, designed by Inigo Jones.) Like most similar
lists, the *Duchess* casting information is fleeting and partial. Lowin's principal adult stage partners in the first production were Burbage as Ferdinand,
Henry Condell as the Cardinal, and Will Ostler as Antonio; the first
perfomers of the Duchess herself, and of Cariola and Julia, are not identified. The speaking parts of Castruchio, Roderigo, Grisolan, and the Old
Lady are not listed among the dramatis personae. The roles of Ferdinand,
the Cardinal, and Antonio also list actors for the post-1620 staging of the
play (Taylor, Robinson, and Benfield), and it is this later production to
which the names attached to the female roles pertain: Richard Sharpe as the
Duchess, Robert Pallant as Cariola, and John Thompson as Julia.

The 1623 list is arranged, conventionally, with the male roles first, the
female roles below, and it gives them in order, almost, of length: Bosola, the
longest part by some measure in the published text of the play (824 lines),
comes first. The Duchess is the second-ranking role (556 lines), but the
second male role, Ferdinand (476 lines), follows Bosola. Antonio, with 448
lines, has a larger part than that of the Cardinal (273 lines), but he is listed
fourth, probably because the brothers have been paired, as they are in the
play. The *Duchess* cast list, lacunae aside, is clear testimony that by
Burbage's last decade on stage Lowin was taking principal parts, and their

partnership on stage in numerous plays can be safely assumed. In *The Duchess of Malfi* they played a number of scenes together, including the frantic last scene of the play (5.5), in which each kills the other, Ferdinand emerging as he dies from the madness into which he has descended, or taken refuge, to acknowledge the fatal obsession which has shaped the progress of the action: 'My sister! O! my sister! There's the cause on't' (5.5.71).[36]

The Duchess of Malfi might be characterized as a play of passionate and wilful action accompanied by obscure motivation, as if Webster had been inspired by Shakespeare's Iago, say, to play variations on the strongly marked character whose deepest rationale remains 'in a mist', to use one of Bosola's phrases from the final scene. Ferdinand's savage jealousy of his sister has been psychoanalysed in the modern period, but Burbage is likely to have thought of his part as primarily a portrayal of unbalanced aristocratic pride. The ominous scene in which he appears in the Duchess's chamber, presenting her with 'a poniard' and refusing to countenance her remarriage (3.2), would have presumably reminded the first actor of the part of another strong scene in *Hamlet*, on which it draws, at a remove. Revulsion against sexuality is an element in both scenes, but hardly needs labouring; I take it that an early seventeenth-century audience would have understood the grim bawdy of the proffered dagger at least as readily as a modern audience might.

Bosola's puzzling position and status in the play are central to its peculiar design. Introduced as a 'court-gall' or disaffected satirist (like Malevole in the earlier *Malcontent*), he is an inconvenient cast-off of the powerful men in the play, until he is rehired as spy or 'intelligencer' placed in the Duchess's household. He pursues this role with assiduity, as subsequently he does those of the Duchess's jailer, torturer, and executioner. Simultaneously he is by way of being a philosopher, described in act three as 'a fantastical scholar' from Padua, 'like such who study to know how many knots was in Hercules' club' (3.3.41–3): both deep and futile. Bosola's lack of moral compass, his misdirected intelligence, and his belated attempt to get his bearings and right the wrongs in which he has been complicit together create a perhaps surprisingly modern character, who would not be out of place in certain recent films, for example. (The play in the modern theatre tends to attract distinguished actresses to the title part as the casting priority, but players as different as Bob Hoskins (1980) and Ian McKellen (1986) have performed Bosola on the stage.) Bosola's approach to the situations in which he finds himself might be described as a mixture of time-tested toughness (he has worked as an operator on the shady side of the law before the play begins) and experiment, on others and himself. James Agate called Bosola a 'mixture of Enobarbus and Thersites', a suggestive phrase, if not entirely capturing all of the character's moods and sympathies.[37] The part, in short, is challenging, if Bosola is not to be reduced to a rather confused thug. Lowin, remembered for the role, must have mastered the interplay of humour, bitterness, detachment, and sympathy that an actor must maintain to animate this complex and mysterious character.

Of Lowin's other colleagues in the first production of the play, Henry Condell as the Cardinal had partnered Lowin in the relatively recent *Alchemist*. Condell is famous, if he is famous at all today, for being jointly responsible with John Heminges for the oversight of the Folio Shakespeare, *Mr. William Shakespeare's Comedies, Histories, & Tragedies* (1623), and for the prefatory matter to that book. Condell was probably a contemporary of Burbage, taking parts in the principal Jonson plays from 1598 onwards as well as being listed among the chief actors of Shakespeare's plays, and he seems to have retired from the stage about the time of the death of his eminent colleague; he himself lived for almost another nine years. The first Cardinal and the first Ferdinand, then, would have appeared as roughly the same age. In the play Ferdinand is supposedly the twin brother of the Duchess, 'a young widow' (1.1.225), so that he is still technically a young man. I think that the actors would not have worried much about the evident mismatch between the forty-four-year-old Burbage and the teenaged apprentice playing the Duchess, nor, probably, would the audience, and in any case Webster enters a disclaimer within the text of the play about the resemblances to be expected from mere genetic relationships: 'You never fix'd your eye on three fair medals, / Cast in one figure, of so different temper' (1.1.188–9). The first speaker of these lines was William Ostler as Antonio, the man the Duchess chooses as her husband. He was a distinctly younger player than Condell, Burbage, and Lowin, and his casting is indicative of how the actors thought about the roles. If seniority alone had counted in assigning parts then we might expect to see a rather different distribution: Antonio's part is more or less equal to Ferdinand's in line-count; the Cardinal's is rather more than half the length of theirs. Ostler had begun as a boy performer with the Chapel troupe: he may have been thirteen or fourteen in 1601 when he acted in Jonson's *Poetaster*; he married John Heminges's daughter Thomasine ten years later. At the time of the first performance of *The Duchess of Malfi* he had not been with the King's men for more than a year or two, and was very likely in his middle twenties – notably younger than the performers of his male antagonists in the play. The Duchess and her secret husband as embodied in the first productions, then, were a young couple preyed upon by envious and destructive middle-aged men. Though we know very little about him, Ostler was clearly a rising star, called 'the Roscius of these times' in a poem by John Davies written shortly before Webster's play, and like Nathan Field after him was eclipsed by an early death. Had he not died in 1614, soon after first production of *The Duchess*, he might well have been marked out as Burbage's successor. He is listed in the Folio Shakespeare as a principal actor, although his status as first performer of any Shakespearean parts must relate to the latest plays in the canon.

Also appearing in the same list is Joseph Taylor, the principal younger actor of the King's men for the final two decades of their existence: Burbage's successor in the part of Ferdinand in *The Duchess of Malfi*, as well as, it is reckoned, in most of the other roles Burbage had initiated, in such repertory as remained in the company's stock for occasional revival: most of Shakespeare's plays were in that category. There were some changes in casting, however; where Burbage had played Othello, Taylor was known for his Iago, and perhaps he played Mosca to Lowin's Volpone. Taylor moved to the company, it seems, in the year 1619, acting as a replacement equally for Burbage and for the lost hopes Ostler and Field. He had been acting with other companies for some years, and was in the first cast, with Field, of Jonson's *Bartholomew Fair* in 1614. When Taylor played Ferdinand at some time in the early 1620s he was probably then in his early thirties: Lowin, his chief stage partner and co-leader of the company for the next twenty years, was by then in his mid forties: the age balance between Bosola and Ferdinand had been reversed since the first stagings of the play.[38] Richard Sharpe, who played the Duchess, had been apprenticed to Heminges in 1616, and was probably in his late teens at the start of the 1620s; we have no clues about his appearance, but an older youth in the part of the Duchess would have lessened the apparent difference between the twins. Robert Benfield was the new Antonio; he too had begun with other companies, but moved to the King's men a few years before Taylor. It seems likely he was roughly Taylor's age, so that the distinct position of the visibly younger Antonio in the first production would not have been a characteristic of the revival.

Taylor evidently did not initiate any Shakespearean parts; his Hamlet must have been subject to the comparative discriminations of older play-goers who had known Burbage's playing, and similarly so in the Jonson comedies, the older Fletcher plays, including *The Maid's Tragedy*, as well as *The Duchess of Malfi*. Taylor premiered the role of Paris, the title role in Massinger's *The Roman Actor* (1626), playing against Lowin as the tyrannical emperor Domitian; this production will be the subject of more detailed attention in the following chapter. He also took lead roles in two further

Massinger plays, as Mathias in *The Picture* (1629), and as Antiochus in *Believe as You List* (1631), addressed above. That about the same time Taylor is entirely absent from the cast of the comedy *The Soddered Citizen*, a play which survives only in manuscript,[39] is perhaps merely accident, but may serve as an indication that leading actors might occasionally be given a break from the constant pressures of repertory playing; Taylor averaged roughly 500 lines in the Massinger parts. Otherwise Taylor premiered the leading parts in the later Fletcher plays (roughly twenty in number), among the most successful of which on stage was the lively comedy *The Wild-Goose Chase* (1621), published, finally, in 1652, with a full cast list which includes the following notes on the character, and on its first actor: 'MIRABELL, the Wild Goose, a travelled monsieur, and great defier of all ladies in the way of marriage, otherwise their much loose servant, at last caught by the despised *Oriana*. Incomparably acted by Mr. *Joseph Taylor*'.[40] Taylor first played this dynamic, light-hearted part at roughly the same time he did the morbid, violent Duke Ferdinand: his brilliance as a performer shone equally in a range of roles.

Although he continued to act until the theatres were closed, Taylor established himself as a financial sharer in the King's men's two theatres, the Globe and the Blackfriars, as did his older colleague Lowin. Like Burbage before him Taylor became well known at court, brought in to instruct the Queen, Henrietta Maria, and her ladies in their amateur theatricals,[41] and evidently profiting from his connections to secure the post of Yeoman of the Revels in 1639, then serving as deputy of Sir Henry Herbert for the final year or two of pre-war activity. Coming when it did the appointment could not have made him a lot richer: the Yeoman was paid sixpence a day from the royal purse (the wealth dreamed of for Bottom the player in *A Midsummer Night's Dream*), but the royal purse was in trouble by 1639. In normal times the Yeoman, like the Master of the Revels, probably made a good deal more money in fees paid to the Revels officials by the players. Whether Taylor intended to continue to act, at least for some of the year, while also serving as a royal officer we do not know; perhaps it was a step to retirement from the stage – he was probably in his early fifties in 1639 – but retirement was soon afterwards enforced by national politics. Taylor, with Lowin, appears to have attempted to revive some theatrical activity in the lull between the King's arrest by the Parliamentary army and his eventual execution. Taylor was apparently playing the title part in Fletcher's old play *Rollo* at the Cockpit playhouse in 1648 when the performance was raided by the militia. Thereafter, in the few years left to him, he seems to have retired for good: his name does not appear in agreements which some of the younger actors of the King's men made to further pursue attempts at public performances.[42]

The King's men had become the elite London troupe by the time of Burbage's death, and both maintained and strengthened that position. They continued either to produce from within their ranks or to recruit leading players, giving the company as a whole a depth of talent and technique as impressive as it had been during Shakespeare's years with them. Apart from their acquisition of John Shank and his apprentice Thomas Pollard (1613), and of Eilert Swanston (1624), they may briefly have enlisted the leading player Richard Perkins, star of the Red Bull and the Cockpit, the last theatre being the closest rival to the Blackfriars. He did not stay, but his younger colleague Michael Bowyer, his chief stage partner for a decade in performances by Queen Henrietta's men at the Cockpit, joined the King's men in 1636 or so, when he was in his middle thirties, and at the height of his powers. Unlike Perkins, who had apprenticed with Alleyn and was clearly a hot commodity by the time of his later teens, Bowyer had a life in the theatre that started more obscurely, and the flower of his talent blushed unseen until rather later in his life.

The circumstances of his apprenticeship have been described in the previous chapter. His master, at least until he was sixteen, William Hovell, has very little profile in the annals of seventeenth-century theatre, and the other actors certainly or possibly associated with the touring troupe of which Bowyer was a junior member – Nathaniel Clay, John Podger, Nicholas Long, and William Wilson – never entered the major leagues, as their young colleague did. Bowyer's start in his professional life is a salutary reminder that not all playing in Shakespeare's time was based in London playhouses, and there may have been a good deal more provincial activity by such touring groups as Hovell's than has been, or ever will be, caught in a historically authenticating documentary net. It seems fairly likely that Bowyer began in female roles, although in what parts and what plays it is impossible to tell. Perhaps such provincial troupes concentrated on older plays, copies of which were in print, and might have been regarded as 'out of copyright', to use an anachronistic term; when played in Kidderminster, at least, a performance of *Doctor Faustus*, say, offered no direct competition to the Admiral's men, whose major market was in London. If, as I suspect, Hovell's troupe had a rather larger component of younger players than did mainstream adult companies in London, Bowyer may have passed to adult male roles fairly early in his career.

Like Perkins, we might guess, his evident talent gave him a fairly rapid rise once he came to London, which he appears to have done as soon as he reached his majority; by the age of twenty-five he was at the Cockpit playhouse playing the role of Vitelli in Massinger's comedy *The Renegado*, the largest role in the play, with somewhat more than 500 lines. The following year he took the role of Beauford (578 lines) in James Shirley's comedy *The Wedding*; Perkins was also cast in the play, as Sir John Belfare, only the fifth-ranked part by line-count (203 lines). In about 1630 Bowyer and Perkins partnered as Spencer and Goodlack in Thomas Heywood's two sequenced romantic comedies *1* and *2 The Fair Maid of the West*, with equally balanced roles in the first play; Spencer becomes more prominent in the second play. Bowyer, evidently, shone in comedy; he also played the title male role in Robert Davenport's *King John and Matilda* (*c.* 1630), called a tragedy but truly a mixture of history and pathetic romance. Bowyer's role was again the longest (448 lines); Perkins, playing Fitzwater (369 lines), took the older role of the father of Matilda, the victim of John's adulterous desire. 'The Names of the Persons in the Play', published in the first edition of 1655, notes alongside Perkins's name that his 'action gave grace to the play'.[43] A modern reader might be inclined to think it was much needed. In 1635, just before his move to the King's company, Bowyer played the second title role in Thomas Nabbes's *Hannibal and Scipio*, a 'historical tragedy' – actually a classical chronicle based on the Punic wars. The tragedy is that of the defeated Hannibal, the rather larger role (564 lines to Scipio's 459), first played by William Allen. Perkins was not cast in the play, possibly further indicating that occasional breathing room was afforded to leading players.

By his middle thirties, then, Bowyer had demonstrated his command of leading parts in a variety of genres and styles. He must, of course, have acted in numerous plays over a career, by 1636, of over twenty years on the stage; as usual we are reliant on a very slim representation of that activity preserved in surviving documents. His all-round ability, as well as the outstanding quality of his acting, would have constituted his appeal to the King's men: a younger actor able to take leading parts in a varied repertory, and perhaps with especial strength in leading romantic-comic roles, available as Taylor was getting older and perhaps already looking to lessen his commitment to full-time playing. It would have been expected that Bowyer had another two decades of outstanding theatrical productivity to contribute to his new company; as it was he played as a King's actor for a mere seven or eight years, and then died young, before his forty-sixth birthday. What roles he played during his time at Blackfriars and the Globe we do not know, but at least some of them must have been in the reliable older repertory of the company, constantly revived, the plays of Jonson, Shakespeare, and Fletcher.

Bowyer's career demonstrates the sheer force of talent, as well as the hard work and determination required of any player. He was not born into a theatrical family, perhaps never saw a playhouse until he was a young man, and did not train with eminent or influential members of the profession. He was, clearly, very good at the art to which he was apprenticed, and became the colleague and equal partner of some of the greatest players of the earlier seventeenth century. It is the communal partnership of the actors in the work of preparing and presenting their plays to which I turn in the following chapter.

CHAPTER 5

Players at work

Have you the lion's part written? Pray you, if it be, give it me, for I am
slow of study.

> Snug, *A Midsummer Night's Dream*, 1.2.66–7

To prove his best, and if none here gainsay it,
The part he hath studied, and intends to play it.

> Thomas Heywood, 'The Prologue to the Stage,
> at the Cockpit', *The Jew of Malta* (1633)

Studying one's part preceded meeting for the full rehearsal of a given play,
limited as the latter activity may have been in the English theatre of the
sixteenth and seventeenth centuries.[1] Extended rehearsal periods under the
supervision of a director developed only in the later nineteeth-century theatre,
and even then they were something of a luxury. Up to the middle of the last
century actors in 'weekly rep', or even at the Stratford Memorial Theatre, did
not see much rehearsal time: they were hired to play a range of parts in existing
plays, and were expected to know the main framework into which they were
to fit.[2] Searching and original work on text and character simultaneously with
attention to an ensemble style, overseen by one guiding artistic intelligence, the
kind of approach practised at the Royal Shakespeare Company, for example,
from about 1960 onwards, stems from such experimental nineteenth-century
practice as that pioneered by the Duke of Saxe-Meiningen, and, notably,
Konstantin Stanislavski. In establishing his Moscow Art Theatre and its acting
studios, jointly with Nemirovich-Danchenko, and particularly in writing
about his principles, Stanislavski became a modern master of theatrical practice, his teachings spreading especially to the United States as 'the Method'.

Stanislavski's writings about acting, it is as well to point out, do not say
anything particularly new about the art, but rather describe what actors
do, with certain kinds of attention to technique: the relationship between
the player's personal experience and the imagined experience of dramatic
characters (Aeneas, or Hecuba, say), the invocation of emotion, and the

discipline and control of the entire body, among other matters. Stanislavski himself was born to reasonable wealth and leisure, and cultivated a lively interest in amateur theatricals. His self-examination in his own acting – his dissatisfaction at failure, and will to improve – led him ever deeper into the theatre, both in practice and theory.

'Study', then, a common term for the individual preparation of players in Shakespeare's day, is of some interest in the light of modern attitudes to rehearsal and to the ways in which an actor prepares. To study a part meant at its simplest to learn it, and its cues, by heart; Snug's anxiety is that he will not have time to do this thoroughly enough to be a 'perfect' lion. To be perfect, at its simplest, meant that one said all one's lines correctly and accurately ('Ninus' rather than 'Ninny'), at the appropriate dramatic cues and in the right order: giving a cue was as important as receiving one. Bottom urges his companion actors to 'Take pains, be perfit' (*A Midsummer Night's Dream*, 1.2.108–9); Costard in *Love's Labour's Lost*, giving a speech in the character of Pompey the Great, hopes after he has delivered it that he 'was perfect', but realizes he made 'a little fault' in getting a word wrong (5.2.558–9). Even experienced actors occasionally get words wrong, as most playgoers can witness; being 'perfect' is a high bar.

Yet if study was, at one level, to make one word- and line-perfect, it surely involved a good deal more for actors of some ability and experience. The entire development and emotional contour of a role was contained within a written part. Speeches of any length would have been weighed for their rhythms and their structures of thought and feeling; experimental patterns of delivery, subject to careful self-criticism, would have been tried out, like a pianist listening to his or her own playing concurrently with working out the intricacies of the written notes in the score. Imagining oneself into a character and a fictional dramatic experience began with and was continued in the process of learning a part; as an actor one studied more than a sequence of words, unreflectingly, parrot-like, but necessarily one absorbed the entire fiction of which they were to be, on stage, the audible determinant. Study for early actors, as much as for those of the post-Stanislavski generations, necessarily meant the assumption of character and emotional temperature as they proceeded, rereading and checking back to the scrolls of paper which gave a map to compelling vocalization and embodiment, accent and action, the life of the stage characters they committed themselves to play. Study is a term which subsumes the actor's personal thought, imagination, experimentation, and self-censorship in bringing a part 'off the pages' and into realized presence; in the Shakespearean period actors would have done a good deal of this work on their own, before the necessarily limited group rehearsal period began.

How deeply actors might have studied their parts would have depended partly on individual character and approach (every actor has his or her own combination of disciplines, or apparent lack of them, in modern rehearsal work), and on the demands of the part itself. Burbage and his colleagues would have thought more searchingly about characters with more profound, complex, and anguished fictional lives, and to that extent Hamlet, Othello, Lear, and Macbeth, evidently, called then and call now for more effort and technical resource than do such parts as Orsino or Malvolio, whose kinds of character are more contained by the deliberately artificial world of comedy. Individual preparation of whatever complexity and care, however, was inevitably subject to adjustment once the entire play came together on stage, with the whole company giving it energy and movement. In that respect also the demands of individual dramatic fictions varied. Some plays include numerous ensemble scenes where others alternate smaller groupings of characters, scene by scene, and are hence easier to break down for the purposes of rehearsal. I take it that however limited full-cast rehearsals and stage runthroughs may have been before the initial performance of the play before an audience, once Burbage began to study Othello, for example, he would have wanted at least to read with his Iago and his Desdemona, for each of them to develop his part in response to his principal partners' work. Such small-group work on scenes did not need to take place on the stage, but could have been done in any reasonably private convenient room. Actors' houses and lodgings probably were frequently called on for such professional preparation.

In this chapter I examine two distinct instances in which the common work of actors on a play can be approached rather more precisely than by informed guesswork, our only possible means for understanding the casting and rehearsal of the first performances of Shakespeare's plays. Largely as a result of historical accident, our detailed knowledge of the casting of certain plays is fuller in the later rather than the earlier part of the sixty years between 1580 and 1640; generically comedy is rather better represented than tragedy in this fairly limited body of evidence. Within such constraints I shall attempt to suggest the range of work to which actors in different companies and at different times committed themselves in putting on entertainments for the London playgoing public, as also for the court, although my two particular examples do not seem to have been played for the King and Queen. All theatrical productions are governed by the pragmatic matters of the performers taking part, the space of performance, and the text (if any) of the show. In the Shakespearean period 'a play', in the playhouse or elsewhere, unfailingly derived from a written text, but even when such texts survive (sometimes in differing versions) we cannot be too confident that the first actors performed exactly what we can now read. Printed texts occasionally show signs of omissions and cuts, as I have noted above, and these may have been made in the printing house rather than the theatre. Correspondingly a long text, like that of Q2 *Hamlet*, which had passed the approval of the Master of the Revels, need not always have been played in its entirety. To add speeches to a play, as Hamlet does, was to court trouble, but to cut them from a licensed text was a pragmatic theatrical issue. 'This is too long' is a simple and telling criticism that would not have been confined to Polonius. In the following instances, then, I am assuming that surviving play texts were *more or less* what the actors brought to life on stage, in the full knowledge that the working theatre is always changing and developing the material of written scripts.

HOLLAND'S LEAGUER (1631)

Shakerly Marmion's comedy *Holland's Leaguer*, a play little read today, was performed in December 1631 at the relatively recently established Salisbury Court playhouse, south of Fleet Street, not far from the surviving site of St Bride's Church. Like the playhouse, the playing company also was new, under the nominal patronage of the infant Prince Charles, who was to mature into King Charles II. The playhouse was a small indoor venue, lit by candles, on the model of its predecessors the Blackfriars and Cockpit theatres. Though the company was newly minted its senior players had considerable prior experience, and partnership, in other companies. The prologue in the text of the play published early in 1632 alludes to the company's recent arrival at the playhouse ('*the Muses' colony / New planted in this soil*'),[3] to their geographical position between the Phoenix (or Cockpit) to the north-west and the Globe to the south-east, and to the players' aspiration to the standards of Perkins, Bowyer, Lowin, and Taylor, so that the venue might be renamed, and '*Phoebus shall not disdain to style't his Court*' (A4ᵛ). (In the event the players, no doubt calculating their advantages, soon moved to the Red Bull playhouse, so Salisbury Court never did become Phoebus, or Apollo, Court.) The title page proclaims the play's success on stage, 'often acted with great applause'. The cast list which precedes the prologue in print names an unusually full complement of sixteen performers and identifies their parts; eight of the nine men who were certainly or probably over the age of twenty-one at the time of the show are also named in the subsequent royal warrant formally establishing the company. Nearly half the performers in *Holland's Leaguer*, however, were demonstrably or probably in their minority; three of this younger group, we know for certain, were formally apprenticed, and others probably were. The play text thus provides an opportunity to explore something of the relationships between master actors and apprentices in a specific practical context.

We might further think that the balance of the newly formed company may have reflected artistic policy: it was designed for playing erotic comedy as a principal genre, with a matching number of specialists in male and female roles. Such a policy may have reflected the anticipated market at a smaller indoor theatre in a fashionable district during the early 1630s, or, perhaps, indicates that the role of the playhouse as a 'nursery' or training studio for younger players was being in some respects continued.[4] Otherwise, for this particular production, as in most modern professional casting, the number of actors matched the number of dramatic characters, with the possible exception of the unassigned bit parts listed at the end of the dramatis personae, which can be doubled, as I shall suggest. The signs are that the company had come to an agreement with Shakerly Marmion, the author of the play, to write for their repertory for the first couple of seasons. A lost play by Marmion called *The Country Gentleman* was 'allowed to be acted' by Sir Henry Herbert in 1632, probably by Prince Charles's company;[5] it was followed by *A Fine Companion*, entered in the Stationers' Register in June 1633, and published as 'Acted before the King and Queen at Whitehall, / And sundry times with great applause at the private house in Salisbury Court / By the Prince his servants'.[6] The court performance is likely to have been at Christmas 1632–3, undoubtedly at the Whitehall Cockpit theatre completed in 1630.

The oldest members of the Prince's troupe were its leading managerial figures and principal players: Andrew Cane, forty-two in 1631, and Ellis Worth, forty-four.[7] Both men had considerable prior experience at the Cockpit, Fortune, and Red Bull playhouses, at the least, as members of a variety of companies. Cane had been a leading player for a decade, following an apprenticeship that had no connection with the theatre, and Worth's career had begun by 1612. Other adult members of Prince Charles's troupe in 1631 had earlier been their colleagues in other professional companies. Richard Fowler had been at the Fortune from 1618, probably then as a young man, and had played with Cane there; most immediately before *Holland's Leaguer* he had been a fellow player of Matthew Smith, in the King and Queen of Bohemia's company. Both Fowler and Smith were probably in their middle thirties in 1631. William Browne and Thomas Bond, two further recruits to Prince Charles's men, had previous associations with the Red Bull, and with its management: Browne, whose father was the player Robert Browne and stepfather the famous clown Thomas Greene, was the son of Susan Baskerville, and Bond, married to Browne's sister, her son-in-law. Six years before 1631 Browne and Ellis Worth had been on opposite sides of a legal dispute over theatre business at the Bull, which must have resolved itself sufficiently for them to have become working colleagues. Browne was twenty-nine in late 1631, and Bond probably the same age.[8] The remaining three adult players named in the *Holland's Leaguer* list, James Sneller, Henry Gradwell, and Edward May, are fairly obscure figures, of whom we know little. We might guess that May and Sneller were older, playing parts comparable in length to that of Fowler, and that Gradwell, playing the role of '*Capritio, a young novice*', eighty-odd lines in length, was a beginner in his early twenties.

We know the ages of three of the junior performers, and also know the legal status of two of those people, and of one other whose age is unknown, in terms of apprenticeship. John Wright, playing Millicent, was seventeen, and had been formally apprenticed to Andrew Cane as a goldsmith since September 1629. (Unusually, Cane actually practised the trade of which he was a freeman, concurrently with his prominent stage career: he specialized in making jewellery and domestic silverware.) Arthur Saville, in the role of Quartilla, was fourteen, and was similarly apprenticed to Cane, for eight years dating from the August preceding the performance. Robert Stratford, playing Triphoena, was thirteen, and the son of the actor William Stratford, a former colleague of Cane and Fowler at the Fortune, who had died in the bad plague epidemic of 1625. Stratford's colleagues, it seems, had taken over the paternal role of training, or at least trying out, his son for the stage; he was being brought up to earn his living as his father had. The charitable protection London trade companies extended to the orphaned or distressed dependants of 'brothers' was also observed among the community of players.

David Kathman has discovered that Samuel Mannery, playing the Bawd, was apprenticed to Thomas Goodwin, as a farrier, for a nine-year term running from August 1629.[9] Despite his company affiliation Goodwin was in fact a musician, and Kathman suggests he may have been attached to the Salisbury Court playhouse in that capacity. Mannery's situation – his father was dead at the time of his apprenticeship binding – and the length of his term of service invite comparison with the situation of Arthur Saville, also orphaned of his father when he began with Cane. If they had begun at similar ages Mannery would have been fifteen or sixteen in late 1631, and twenty-two or twenty-three when he married in 1638: such a profile seems quite likely. The possible presence of Thomas Goodwin as an adult member of the extended theatrical company at Salisbury Court further suggests that Robert 'Godwin', so spelt, playing Faustina, the longest female role, and otherwise unknown to theatrical history, may have been his son, training as a musician as well as, perhaps incidentally, an actor.[10]

Of the adult actors of Prince Charles's troupe only Cane was, in 1631, a freeman of a London company, as Heminges and Shank, principally, were in the King's men.[11] All three men bound apprentices for the stage through the statutes of the City of London, which allowed freemen (like Thomas Goodwin) to practise trades other than those in which they held their membership: Goldsmiths, Grocers, and Weavers in the case of the three actors named above, although Cane was perhaps unique in continuing to practise the craft in which he was trained. Among Cane's companions, Ellis Worth was the son of a merchant taylor, and he might have claimed membership in that company by patrimony, but he did not eventually do so until 1638, and did not take any apprentices until after the theatres were closed. Thomas Bond may have been the son of a freeman of the Founders' Company, and possibly the same Thomas Bond who took freedom of that company by patrimony in 1631–2.[12] He did not, according to the limited records of the Founders, bind apprentices around the time of *Holland's Leaguer*. After William Browne's early death in 1634 a dispute over the administration of his will revealed that *he* had a theatrical apprentice, possibly Robert Stratford or Richard Fouch, the two boys from the cast list of whose formal attachments to adult members of the troupe we otherwise know nothing. Not all such attachments were statutory apprenticeships, as we have seen. The name of the player Robert Huyt (Hewitt?), with the role of Jeffrey, a servant, occurs at the mid-point of the list, below the adults and before the boys. I think that he was probably a younger hired actor; his part, at sixty-one lines, is fairly short, and his name does not reappear in subsequent records of the company.[13]

The list of parts and actors' names in the published text (Figure 4) shows the usual division between male and female roles, conventionally in first and second position. When rearranged in rank of the line-length of parts, the list looks like this:

1.	Cane/Trimalchio	433
2.	Smith/Agurtes	401
3.	Worth/Ardelio	239
4.	Browne/Philautus	229
5.	Bond/Miscellanio	187
6.	Sneller/Autolycus	168
7.	May/Fidelio	165
8.	Fowler/Snarl	163
9.	Godwin/Faustina	115
10.	Mannery/Bawd	87
11.	Gradwell/Capritio	83
12.	Wright/Millicent	82
13.	Huyt/Jeffrey	61
14.	Saville/Quartilla	61
15.	Stratford/Triphoena	60
16.	Fouch/Margery	30[14]

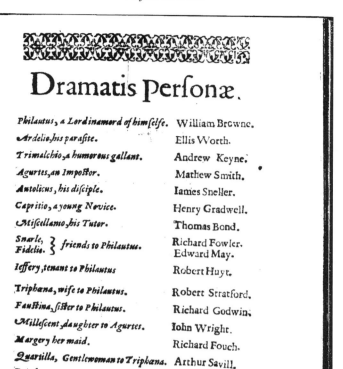

Dramatis Perſonæ.

Philautus, a Lord inamord of himſelfe.	William Browne.
Ardelio, his paraſite.	Ellis Worth.
Trimalchio, a humorous gallant.	Andrew Keyne.
Agurtes, an Impoſtor.	Mathew Smith.
Autolicus, his diſciple.	Iames Sneller.
Capritio, a young Novice.	Henry Gradwell.
Miſcellanio, his Tutor.	Thomas Bond.
Snarle, ⎫ *friends to Philautus.*	Richard Fowler.
Fidelio. ⎭	Edward May.
Ieffery, tenant to Philautus	Robert Huyt.
Triphana, wife to Philautus.	Robert Stratford.
Fauſtina, ſiſter to Philautus.	Richard Godwin.
Milleſcent, daughter to Agurtes.	Iohn Wright.
Margery her maid.	Richard Fouch.
Quartilla, Gentlewoman to Triphana.	Arthur Savill.
Bawd.	Samuell Mannery.
2 Whores. Pander. Officers.	

4 Dramatis Personae, *Holland's Leaguer*, 1632

Adult roles generally involved longer parts, then, but the leading female and minor male roles overlapped considerably. Worth and Browne have the 'average' length of part among the senior players, although there are really three levels of part, with more men in the lowest category. Sixty-nine lines is a more representative average for the boys playing female roles, given the lesser degrees of variation. Evidently the demands on any of the boy performers were modest, in a system where major female roles could run to around seven hundred lines (e.g., Rosalind, Cleopatra). The play itself, at 2,615 lines, is of average length.

Line-count is a fairly bald indicator of a part's significance (although it is usually calculated by actors); what also needs to be figured are the number and type of scenes in which individual characters are involved, at the simplest level by sheer presence on stage. A smallish part in line numbers might have the lines concentrated in one significant episode (the actor's preference, perhaps) or spread out in a number of supporting functions. Alternatively a part short on dialogue might be long on other performative potential: in comedy, notably, physical expression through gesture and movement. In this instance Henry Gradwell did not get to say a great deal, but the slow-burning dopiness of the character Capritio, whose eighty-three lines are distributed over appearances in eight of the play's seventeen scene units, could be very amusing to an audience, since repeated sight gags, well handled, are funny, and Gradwell spent much of his time trailing behind the chief comic actor of the troupe, like a pathetic shadow;[15] one might compare the presence of the egregious Fungoso, gaping at the style of those who are always a few steps ahead of him, in Jonson's *Every Man Out of His Humour*. Marmion is decidedly a son of Ben, even if he inherited the weaker genes. Gradwell's line-count, at any rate, is not an index of a skilful performance of his part. To qualify what I say above, he may have been a younger player, but the production would have been strengthened if he was a good one. (A player in his early twenties, evidently, might already have had a decade of experience in stage performance.)

The play itself is a reasonably competent humours comedy, conventionally constructed, with a certain amount of clumsiness, which one might say is also conventional enough. Some characters appear fairly tangential to the action: Triphoena, nominally the wife of Philautus, disappears entirely after the end of the second act; husband and wife do not exchange a single line, and she has nothing at all to do with the plot to redeem him from self-love (his 'humour' being announced in the Greek sense of his name). She is not there to celebrate his new integrity at the end of the play, and in terms of the practicalities of the first production one would guess that Robert Stratford, suitably freed up, subsequently played one of the whores who feature in three scenes of the fourth act. Triphoena's feisty companion Quartilla, all of whose lines occur in one scene, would similarly be free of fictional duty after the close of 2.5, were it not that she is suddenly remembered in 5.4, with airy casualness, as a suitable wife for Miscellanio,[16] and she subsequently appears, silently, among the newly married people at the end of the play. Meanwhile in the first performances, I suspect, Arthur Saville had changed into and back out of draggle-tail finery to accompany Stratford as companion whore in act four. Other characters disappear from view for long periods, challenging either audience or reader to remember them when they resurface. Thus Snarl, Fowler's role, dominates the opening of the play as a sardonic *raisonneur*, but then does not reappear until the end of act three, and by then he has lost the dramatic initiative to Agurtes and Fidelio, becoming a relatively minor supporting figure. All the weight of the part comes early, and an audience's expectations of the character's significance are not fulfilled. Ellis Worth, playing the parasite Ardelio, was also allowed a showpiece opening (1.2/1.3), but then had a long absence from the stage, until 3.1, when the actor would have had to start again, as it were, in establishing his presence with the audience. There are several textual references to the *physical* presence of Ardelio, as a fat man, which Worth himself may or may not have been. Other actors, certainly including John Lowin and possibly William Rowley, took parts – or had parts written – matched to a naturally large physique. Other players padded up, as needed.

The play is decidedly actor-friendly in regard to Trimalchio, the rich and foolish man of fashion, played by Andrew Cane: he is never off the stage for long, and he has the most appearances of all the roles, in ten of seventeen scenes, as well as the most lines. His first appearance in the play, in fact, looks almost like a promenade turn for a popular star, to bring him out in costume, to display a characteristic gait and posture, and to wink at the cheers, briefly upstaging Browne as Philautus, whose first entry he accompanies (1.4). After twelve lines of vapouring from Ardelio and Philautus, Trimalchio, at Triphoena's invitation – '*aside*', presumably – leaves the stage again:

> Mr. *Trimalchio*, I am sick to hear him.
> I can't abide these repetitions
> And tedious encomiums of himself;
> Let you and I walk a turn in the garden … (C1^r)

Dramatically this brief appearance sets up marital tension and possible adulterous trouble ahead (of which the play makes very little) but is otherwise superfluous, were it not serving something of the purpose I suggest above. Cane's first lines (and exit lines) were played to the thirteen-year-old Robert Stratford: 'You are the only garden of my delight, / And I your dear *Adonis*, honour'd lady' (*ibid.*). This parody of courtly *préciosité* characterizes Trimalchio throughout; as a would-be man of fashion, 'compliment', and style he naturally addresses himself to the company of ladies. Thus the chief comic actor of the troupe spent much of his time with the apprentices, in rehearsal and performance.

The roles of the boys actually vary considerably in regard to their interaction with other players. Faustina, the sentimental romantic lead, played by Godwin, is in fact a pretty isolated part, having nothing at all to do with the rather ramshackle collection of comic plots that comprise the rest of the action. She is more of a Beaumont-and-Fletcher figure than a Jonsonian one, set up by her lover Fidelio as a honey-trap to cure her estranged brother Philautus of his self-conceit: a typically Fletcherian situation, simultaneously prurient and stretching the limits of credibility. More disbelief than the average has to be willingly signed off in the face of such material, although seventeenth-century audiences seem to have been happy to do so. Her rejection of Philautus' lecherous wooing (he is unaware of who she truly is) prompts in him a road-to-Damascus moment, and he leaves to seek honour in the wars, blessing the marriage of Fidelio and Faustina on his return: they do not, however, appear with the other couples at the end of the play, possibly an authorial oversight which the actors might well have put right in production. Godwin, at least to judge by the play text, was in effect not involved in any ensemble scenes. He had a total of three appearances, the first a two-hander with May (2.2); the second, after a brief introduction by Fidelio, a two-hander with Browne as Philautus, in which Faustina stands up for Virtue (3.4);[17] and the third a three-hander with May and Browne, in which Philautus is brought to recognize his long-lost sister, and all is forgiven (5.1). The part is perhaps not very interesting – she is more of a principle than a character – but it requires a strong presence and good, clear delivery; it can, evidently, be rehearsed very economically, without the need of much time on the stage itself. In the first production we might reasonably think that William Browne, a sharer in the company as Edward May, on the evidence, was not, would have taken principal responsibility for ensuring that Godwin's performance was at least acceptable.

All the other female roles are livelier, and involve more complex interactions on the stage. There are two sets of paired characters: the witty Millicent (Wright) and her sparky maid Margery (Fouch), and the rather moony and disaffected Triphoena (Stratford) and her animated companion Quartilla (Saville). The latter pair play an extended episode together at the start of 2.4, Triphoena lamenting her abandonment, and dreaming of a cure, and Quartilla playing the worldly *soubrette*, in the style of Despina from *Così fan tutte*:

>   This chastity
> Is quite out of date, a mere obsolete thing,
> Clean out of use since I was first a maid.
> Why do I say a maid? Let *Juno* plague me
> If I remember it, for I began

> Betimes, and so progressed from less to bigger,
> From boys to lads, and as I grew in years
> I writ my venery in larger volume. (E3ʳ)

The scene expands (and becomes 2.5) with the arrival of Triphoena's awkward brother Capritio (Gradwell) and his ebullient 'tutor' Miscellanio (Bond) – a master of etiquette rather than learning. Miscellanio gives a demonstration of the proper salutation of ladies, with Quartilla as model, and Capritio follows with his own lumpish performance of a similar routine. Trimalchio's arrival complicates the dynamics: the men engage in flurries of mutual compliment, which the women watch with admiration, Quartilla eventually stepping in to prevent injury from excess of polite flourishes. It is an entirely stageworthy comic scene, quite the equal of Shirley and Brome at comparable moments, but these characters do not come together again in the play. Trimalchio, having agreed to take on Capritio as an apprentice wit, leaves with his charge, and Triphoena closes the scene: 'Let's in, for I shall mourn / And be melancholy till his return' (F2ᵛ). He never does, and she never reappears, nor is mentioned again in the play. Whatever development Marmion may have first been thinking of in the Trimalchio–Triphoena relationship became buried under other material, and derailed: Quartilla, as noted, is arbitrarily resurrected for a marriage of convenience.

Rehearsal of this scene would evidently have required ensemble work. The two women need to be in close contact throughout; both have a proprietary and rather pitying interest in the hapless Capritio; Quartilla has her eye (and more) on Miscellanio ('a rare man, / One that hath poison'd me with eloquence; / I fear he will make my belly swell with it', E3ʳ), and Triphoena watches Trimalchio admiringly. Both the dominant men are more interested in themselves than anyone else, so that the flourishes of courtesy are merely display, ostentatious but enclosed. If, in rehearsal, Cane's primary responsibility was to his apprentice Saville, both boys would have required the guidance and co-operation of all three senior performers in the scene, particularly of Thomas Bond. The pace and internal cross-currents of the episode call on careful preparation to make them work to full effect. Cane may have been the star comic performer of the company, but his success in 2.5 of *Holland's Leaguer* depended on his four fellow players, and both Stratford and Saville were required to lead as much as to follow in the footwork of the scene.

The female characters played by John Wright and Richard Fouch are decided leaders: Millicent and Margery are in the camp of the true wits, and their intelligence and irony are far superior to the mental armaments of the men they gull into marriage, Trimalchio and Capritio. The clever apprentice bests the slow-witted master, a situational joke for those in the original audiences who knew something of the constitution of the playing company, and probably fun for Wright himself. Wright's first scene (2.3) was played principally with Matthew Smith as Agurtes, Millicent's con-man father, who sets her up as a supposed orphaned heir to a fortune, a bait for Trimalchio, whose own money they are after. To catch him she must 'act it handsomely' (E1ᵛ): the performer must engage in a double performance. Her spirited assurance that she is up to the role even contains a joke about apprenticeship, and the merely trivial skills that are the reward of the submissive. If she cannot succeed in the assignment, she says:

> Let me serve
> Seven years' apprenticeship, and learn nothing else
> But to preserve and candy.   (E2ʳ)

The lively apprentice speaks out about the tediousness of apprenticeship: another local jest, perhaps. After two years and some months of his own bonds, Wright's casting in the role suggests he had learnt rather more.

Wright played directly with his principal teacher as partner in his next scene, the expected introduction of Trimalchio to the young 'heiress' (3.3). This takes place as part of an ensemble: Agurtes and his companion Autolycus (Sneller) bring Trimalchio and the trailing Capritio to meet Millicent and Margery. In matching stage groups Agurtes manages Trimalchio and his partner while Autolycus eases Capritio in the direction of Margery, a harder assignment. Trimalchio's preposterous wooing, in character – he calls Millicent 'most luculent lady' (F4ᵛ), a borrowing from a similarly egregious Jonsonian moment – is matched by Millicent's assumption of elegant dignity, signifying good breeding and the money to go with it. The actors are required to sustain their encounter silently while the matching group is given the focus, via dialogue, for some sixty-odd lines. When they resume, Trimalchio's clumsy confusion over a proffered gift triggers the 'lady's' haughty withdrawal from the stage; Agurtes, on cue, steps forward to see what he can do to mollify her – Trimalchio had better be prepared to spend some money. Capritio, having finally got the idea about wooing, dispenses it freely. This scene also needs ensemble rehearsal, though the farcical wooing sequences between Cane and Wright (roughly 40 per cent of the whole) could have been worked through together privately; Wright most likely lived with Cane as a member of his family, as did Saville. The scene is a strong, amusing episode in a style its first audiences would have immediately recognized, continuing the comedy of ineptitude, now played within the ironic framework of gulling comedy: the fools are marked for plucking. Once again the strength of the boys' performance was essential to the comic effect.

Wright and Fouch had some rest time after playing their second scene. There intervenes the episode of the visit to the brothel which gives the play its title (after a well-known establishment in Southwark), and the subsequent stage-managed arrests and arraignments, run by the disguised Agurtes and Autolycus, as Trimalchio, Capritio, Miscellanio, and Ardelio are made to undergo humiliation and shaming. They are released by a letter supposedly sent by Millicent, leading the wandering plot back to the marriage trick, now complicated by competition from Miscellanio, who imagines that he has been laid under obligations of honour to Millicent, eventually leading him to the brink of a comic duel with Trimalchio.

The boys played a witty duet at the start of 5.2, matching the earlier twosome of Stratford and Saville, on the theme of 'What shall I do with him when I am married' (K2^v), Fouch given the chance at a clever satirical riff on marriage *à la mode*, his longest continuous speech. The arrival of the pretentious Miscellanio (Bond) defines the threesome of the remaining part of the scene. Jointly the women demolish his delusion that Millicent favours him, and generally rough him up, leaving him to a few lines of peevish resentment to close the scene. Once again, women are on top; the senior performer plays the weaker, stupid character, a foil for their scorn. If Bond supervised rehearsal of this scene his concerns would have been to manage the balance as his vacuous confidence ran up against their contempt, to ensure his partners' playing of assurance, and to emphasize the comedy of mutual bafflement following his abrupt arrival in what the opening defines as their private, confidential, female space. There remain two further appearances of Millicent and Margery (the latter of whom has no lines in either) in scenes which wind up the plot: they arrive in 5.4 to stop the impending duel, and for Millicent to declare her forgiveness of Trimalchio and her readiness to marry him; Capritio is pushed into taking Margery off to the same church. This forms a fairly brief episode within an ensemble scene (of seven), and a few lines later the couples re-enter, within a larger ensemble (of ten, the largest grouping in the play), to play the revelation of Trimalchio's gulling, in which Snarl resumes something of his initial prominence. Such traditional final scenes, it may be presumed, would have been worked out by the entire company; no unusual demands are placed on the boy performers. To her last line the attractive Millicent insists that she is 'honest', and her value is endorsed by Philautus in comforting the deceived Trimalchio: 'The gentlewoman is not to be despised; / Her wit and virtues are dowry sufficient' (L4^v). If Wright had been as good as the part demanded, Cane may have reflected as he received the lines on the virtues of his apprentice as a performer, and on his value to the company, and to Cane himself as sharer, in terms of profitable receipts.

It remains to look at the low-life parts of act four, and specifically the series of scenes in which the fops and would-be wits enter and leave the brothel (4.1–4.4). The running joke is that the brothel is something of an armed camp, and its clients valiant assailants or besiegers;[18] there is even an episode 'on the walls', as the militant sex-workers hurl abuse at the effete gentry slinking away below. The play was exploiting contemporary news; some kind of riotous incident had recently taken place, in late 1631, at a notorious brothel on the Bankside run by one Mrs Holland, and known ironically by the title given to the play (a 'leaguer', derived from the Dutch *leger*, was a contemporary term for a fortified camp). One could therefore ask whether the '*Bawd*' of the play might have been costumed and played to resemble a real-life original. Sir Henry Herbert had censored parts of the text, but parody in performance is a slippery eel. Did the company encourage Samuel Mannery to imitate what they may have known about the voice and characteristics of the notorious Mrs Holland? Was he charged, even subsidized, perhaps, to undertake some field research?

Another way to approach the question is to consider how generic a part simply called '*Bawd*' might be. One general assumption, reaching back to classical comedy, is that bawds were older women, like Mistress Overdone, and were traditionally broad comic characters; the differing demands of older female lower-class roles (the Nurse in *Romeo and Juliet*, teasingly called a bawd by Mercutio in 2.4, Mistress Quickly, and Ursula in *Bartholomew Fair*, for example), have led to the suggestion that they were played by male clown specialists, as some of them certainly were by the early eighteenth century, and possibly somewhat earlier.[19] Mannery, evidently, was at the furthest an adolescent youth – it seems likeliest he was around fifteen or sixteen at the time of *Holland's Leaguer*; his physique could not have been notably different from that of the other boys in the troupe, though his vocal characteristics may have been suited to the brassy aggression the part requires: a voice to fill a football field.[20] Bawds of one kind or another are conventional personnel in the drama of the period, in city comedy particularly, but the characteristics of the figure in *Holland's Leaguer* seem especially individualized. She is a stickler for the 'reverence' due to her office, and the 'credit' of her 'house' (used in the sense of pedigree as well as physical structure), and a strident proto-Conservative champion of property rights:

Did I not purchase it?
And am I not the lady of the manor? [Another local theatrical joke?]
And who shall dare to question me? (H2ᵛ)

The role, then, demands a noisy, aggressive eccentricity, quite unlike what
was required of the other boys, and it gave Mannery the opportunity to
create a striking character vignette, dominating the stage for the length of
4.2, and raucously exploding from the acting area 'above' in 4.3, outfacing
the complaints of Trimalchio and Capritio that they have been robbed
in the brothel. (Once more bested by apprentice actors, Cane's character
can think only of the legendary rough stuff of holiday apprentices to
get his own back: 'let's think of some revenge, call up / The gentlemen
prentices, and make a Shrove Tuesday', 11ᵛ].) In general terms Mannery's
role and age constitute a reminder that not all younger male actors were
cast because they could be made to look and sound like young women. As
the Bawd, Mannery was acting outside his own gender, age, and class,
as the son of Nicholas Mannery, gentleman. Apprentice actors played
female roles of a variety of fictional ages, social positions, and characteristics, although no doubt individual performers may have been suited to
certain types, and have changed or expanded their repertory as they grew
older.

The carnival violence of the fourth act of the play is something of a
surprise. It certainly succeeds in adding variety to the play, if at the expense
of general cohesion. Mannery's performance of a distinct style of grotesque,
whether or not it was an *ad feminam* caricature, was supported by three
other actors, in the parts of the '*Pander*' – a male role, later called 'Captain'
by the Bawd – who opens the gate to Trimalchio and Capritio in 4.1, as they
approach the brothel, and also the two Whores, who accompany the
bawd in all her appearances. The structure of the play is such that Robert
Stratford would have been entirely free to appear as one of these latter two,
and Arthur Saville would have had plenty of time to switch the Quartilla
costume and play the other, resuming Quartilla's clothes after 4.4.[21] The
shift from elegant lady and lady's maid to loud-mouthed tarts would have
offered good performative fun, particularly in the shouting match from the
balcony, and the episode of hilarious mutual congratulation which follows
it (4.4); professionally the young actors could have demonstrated, or have
attempted to demonstrate, their command of a range of physical and vocal
styles.

The short gap between the beginning of Arthur Saville's term of
apprenticeship to Andrew Cane and his performance in *Holland's Leaguer*

indicates, I think, that he had been carefully chosen, since he was expected to operate as an independent actor – and there is no other kind, on stage before an expectant audience – as part of a professional company at a prominent playhouse within four months of beginning his training. One might practise for a stage career privately, on one's own account – Armin is said to have done so during his apprenticeship, not to an actor in his case. If one apprenticed to a working actor like Cane, however, one was soon thrown in the deep end, and became a working actor oneself, in a tough system where plays were prepared for production under considerable pressure, learning not just from one's master but from all one's stage partners, as show succeeded show. The published text of *Holland's Leaguer* enables us to approach some of the pragmatics of a particular moment of theatrical production in the earlier seventeenth century. One would not want to claim too much in general terms for what it seems to demonstrate, but it tells us a certain amount about the balance between senior and apprentice roles in comedy, where female parts are so important, and it might thus shed some retrospective light on the Chamberlain's company's work on such plays as *A Midsummer Night's Dream, Love's Labour's Lost, The Merchant of Venice, Much Ado About Nothing, Twelfth Night,* and *As You Like It,* first acted thirty and more years earlier.

THE ROMAN ACTOR (1626)

My second instance is chosen for its difference, in several respects, from the production of *Holland's Leaguer*. First, it was played by the leading company of the Stuart period, the King's men, at the Blackfriars theatre, some five years before Marmion's play. The cast, given fairly fully in the published text of 1629 (Figure 5),[22] contains some rather better-known names than those of the actors in Prince Charles's men, although we do not necessarily know a great deal more about the actors, nor about their relationships with one another. Second, the play is a tragedy, by a mainstream dramatic author who succeeded Shakespeare and Fletcher as the chief contributing dramatist to the King's men. If Philip Massinger's plays are not much read or produced today, *The Roman Actor* has found its way into at least two modern anthologies of Renaissance drama, and a somewhat cut version of the play was revived by the Royal Shakespeare Company in 2002, with Antony Sher taking the part first played by John Lowin. As the title suggests, the setting of the play is imperial Rome, under the tyrannical rule of Domitian. In 1626 it was presumably costumed in Roman style, not necessarily historically correctly: one of the women in the play is reported to wear a 'smock', for

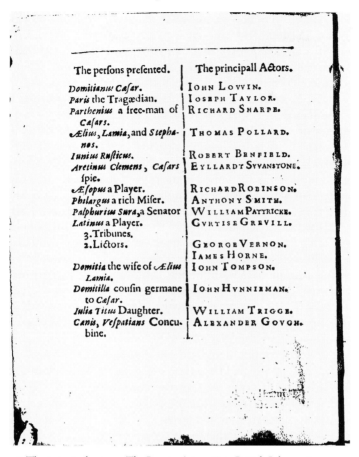

The perfons prefented.	The principall Actors.
Domitianus Cæfar.	IOHN LOVVIN.
Paris the Tragædian.	IOSEPH TAYLOR.
Parthenius a free-man of *Cæfars.*	RICHARD SHARPE.
Ælius, Lamia, and *Stephanos.*	THOMAS POLLARD.
Iunius Rufticus.	ROBERT BENFIELD.
Aretinus Clemens, Cæfars fpie.	EYLLARDT SVVANSTONE.
Æfopus a Player.	RICHARD ROBINSON.
Philargus a rich Mifer.	ANTHONY SMITH.
Palphurius Sura, a Senator	WILLIAM PATTRICKE.
Latinus a Player.	CVRTISE GREVILL.
3. Tribunes.	
2. Lictors.	GEORGE VERNON.
	IAMES HORNE.
Domitia the wife of *Ælius Lamia.*	IOHN TOMPSON.
Domitilla coufin germane to *Cæfar.*	IOHN HVNNIEMAN.
Iulia Titus Daughter.	WILLIAM TRIGGE.
Canis, Vefpatians Concubine.	ALEXANDER GOVGH.

5 The principal actors, *The Roman Actor*, 1629. British Library 644.e.74

example, a decidedly seventeenth-century item of underwear. The company would have had a stock of classical costumes in storage, as required by the reasonably frequent repertory items with a Roman setting. Shakespeare's *Julius Caesar*, for example, seems to have maintained its popularity: it is mentioned in the prefatory verses to the Folio of 1623, and was played at court twice in the 1630s.[23] In terms of repertory fashion, *The Roman Actor* also had a theme audiences would have readily recognized: the breakdown of Roman order under the influence of sexual desire characterizes plays as different as *Titus Andronicus* and *Antony and Cleopatra*; Massinger's play also draws directly on Jonson's *Sejanus*. The passionate and jealous tyrant

Domitian is in the debt of such various Shakespearean characters as Richard III, Othello, Macbeth, and Antony.

The politics of *The Roman Actor* are of some interest, and had it been written ten years later it might have been suspected, like the plays of the Roman actors within the fiction, of glancing rather too much at arbitrary tyranny in the contemporary world.[24] As it was, Sir Henry Herbert licensed it for performance on 11 October 1626, and it was probably performed not long afterwards. A further point concerning comparison with *Holland's Leaguer* is that the play has prominent parts for four boys playing female roles, all of whom took similar parts in other plays for which we have cast lists; twelve adult actors are named in the printed list, but another four to six supernumeraries would have been required to cast the play as it appears in its printed form, making for a total cast of around twenty. There are a number of spectacular scenes calling for the total complement of players on stage, including a triumphal entry with the emperor drawn in a chariot (1.4), perhaps a deliberate invocation of one of the most famous Elizabethan stage pictures, the triumph of the conquering Tamburlaine. Three distinct scenes involve the staging of a play or dramatic scene before an on stage audience (as in *Hamlet*, whose theatrical language Massinger's play partly echoes), and in the last of them the emperor takes a role as jealous revenger, fatal to the title character of the play, Paris the actor. This motif also draws on earlier dramatic tropes, deriving from another Elizabethan classic, *The Spanish Tragedy*, in which Hieronimo's revenge is finally brought about under cover of a play performed for the court. *The Roman Actor* is thus reflexive at a number of levels, bringing debate about theatrical art onto the stage, and reminding experienced playgoers of the 1620s of some of the most famous achievements of the theatre of the preceding decades.

The play is of average length, at roughly 2,500 lines, and contains eleven scenes, conventionally divided into acts; act two is constituted of a single scene, and the first act has four scenes. Its cast had some significant overlaps with that of the revival of *The Duchess of Malfi* by the same company a few years earlier. We can note the transition of Richard Sharpe, following the completion of his apprenticeship to John Heminges in February 1624, to male roles, and full membership in the company. Having played the title role in *The Duchess of Malfi* in his late teens, or even early twenties, Sharpe, probably twenty-three or twenty-four in 1626, played Parthenius in *The Roman Actor*, the third adult role in rank by line length (205 lines). The other leading adult roles are those of Domitian, the emperor, played by John Lowin, aged fifty at the time of the production (703 lines), and of the Roman actor Paris (442 lines), taken by Joseph Taylor, ten years younger;

respectively the two men had been Bosola and Ferdinand in *The Duchess*. In the prefatory matter to the 1629 edition of *The Roman Actor* a dedicatory poem by Taylor reveals him to have been the 'long known and loved friend' of the author of the play.[25] A new recruit to the company in the interim between the production of *The Duchess of Malfi* and Massinger's play, Eilert Swanston, probably then in his late twenties, took the significant role of the malignant Aretinus, Domitian's spy, and the accuser of Paris before the Senate (145 lines). Thomas Pollard, Silvio in *The Duchess*, doubled the roles of Aelius Lamia, a victim of Domitian's arbitrary power, robbed of his wife, then executed, and, appropriately, Stephanos, a chief agent in the plot leading to the culminating assassination of the emperor. His lines in the two parts totalled 137. As Lucy Munro has pointed out, there is not much sign in the earlier part of Pollard's career of his later renown in witty, eccentric characters, in which he seems to have specialized during the 1630s and early 1640s.[26] Pollard was approaching twenty-nine in late 1626, and had been with the King's men for a decade. Richard Robinson, who had probably been Burbage's apprentice and had been a celebrated performer of female roles before 1616, had played the Cardinal in *The Duchess* (273 lines), yet in *The Roman Actor* had the notably smaller part of Aesopus (46 lines), one of the other two actors in the small troupe, or *grex*, of Paris.[27] The other sharer among the adult actors was Anthony Smith, playing Philargus (49 lines), a cameo role appearing in only one scene. Smith was also a relatively recent recruit to the company, of whose career we know very little. Three hired actors, named in the list, took some of the minor parts: Curtis Greville, then perhaps in his early thirties, doubling Latinus, the third Roman actor, and the leading member of the Tribunes (115 lines in all); George Vernon and James Horne also played Tribunes and Lictors.

We know a good deal more about the boys in the cast than we do of minor actors such as Greville, Vernon, and Horne. John Thompson took the crucial role of Domitia, the *femme fatale* who is the fulcrum of the tragedy; married to Lamia at the beginning of the play, she not unwillingly becomes the mistress, then the empress, of Domitian, only to become erotically obsessed with Paris, the actor, bringing on the final catastrophe. Domitia is beautiful, sexy, and wilful, and hers is both a strong part and third in overall rank, at 251 lines, appearing in seven of the play's eleven scenes, and partnering, alternately, Domitian and Paris in some of the most charged episodes of the play. Thompson was evidently a gifted actor in female roles, with a long career – possibly eleven years – in his speciality. He played Julia in the revival of *The Duchess of Malfi*, possibly as early as 1620, and he was still being cast in female roles in 1631. He must have been at least sixteen in 1626, and may have been rather older; his colleagues among the boys we know rather more about in terms of age and situation.

John Honeyman, playing Domitilla (113 lines), the displaced mistress and Domitia's chief female antagonist, was thirteen in 1626; he had not been among the cast of *The Duchess of Malfi*, and his career in female roles was considerably shorter than Thompson's: by 1630, when he was seventeen, he had moved to minor male parts, presumably not having weathered puberty lightly. There are a couple of references in Domitilla's lines to her relatively small size, including her resentful recall of Domitia's addressing her as 'Dwarf' (4.1.16, 5.2.5–6).[28] Honeyman is quite likely to have been shorter than Thompson at the time of the first production, but it seems unlikely that Massinger wrote the lines with individual performers in mind, any more than did Shakespeare for the first Helena and Hermia in *A Midsummer Night's Dream*. The performers of female roles in a play that continued in repertory changed more frequently than any others, as anyone in the contemporary theatre would have known.

William Trigge, fifteen at the time of Massinger's play, played Julia, another victim of Domitian's lechery (46 lines). Trigge too had an extended career in female roles, playing Rosalura in a revival of *The Wild-Goose Chase* in 1632, when he was twenty-one. Alexander Gough played Caenis, another resentful cast-off of the imperial family (37 lines), completing the trio of women who plot against both Domitia and Domitian; they appear together in almost all their stage appearances (seven scenes), making up something of a revengers' chorus. Gough was the youngest member of the entire cast, aged twelve in 1626; he was subsequently to rise to leading female roles, playing Lillia-Bianca in *The Wild-Goose Chase* (357 lines) when he was eighteen, in 1632. He and Trigge were colleagues in similar parts for six years.

A considerable difference in the operations of the King's men when compared to Prince Charles's company of 1631–2 is that as far as we can tell none of the adult actors in the cast of *The Roman Actor* had a direct formal relationship – mastership – with any of the junior performers. Two members of the company not in the cast of the play, in fact, seem to have had principal charge of apprentice actors: John Heminges and John Shank. Shank later claimed that he had been responsible for bringing both Thompson and Honeyman into the company, and they were no doubt attached to him in some way, but he certainly did not share any stage time with either of them in *The Roman Actor*, as Cane did with both Saville and Wright. Another absent presence was John Heminges, no longer acting in 1626, but still binding apprentices for stage careers: Trigge was his apprentice, for a twelve-year term beginning in December 1625. Trigge had been with the company for less than a year at the time of *The Roman Actor*, and Julia must have been among his first roles. The influence of Shank and Heminges on the 1626 troupe was pervasive: Thomas Pollard had been Shank's apprentice until six or seven years previously, and Richard Sharpe had been Heminges's apprentice – his bonds had been served two and a half years earlier. At least three of the adult players, then, had had experience playing female roles during the teenage years of their careers (the third was Richard Robinson), and Sharpe was probably only a few years older than John Thompson, playing Domitia. If Heminges and Shank were not directly involved in the production, then, their training was present at a remove, in the example and advice of their trainees. Continuity in practice was an unrivalled strength of the King's men in 1626; the situation of Prince Charles's troupe five years later was notably different in that respect, even if their casting seems to have integrated the off stage and on stage training of young actors more closely.

In preparing the play for production the actors would have recognized a number of divisions in the development of the action. The main focus at the start of the play was taken by Taylor as Paris the actor. He entered to begin the first scene in the company of his fellows, in life and in character, Robinson as Aesopus, who speaks the first, metatheatrical, line ('What do we act to-day?'), and Greville as Latinus. This threesome would have formed one nucleus for rehearsal preparation: after 1.1 they subsequently appear together in the performances given in 2.1 (*The Cure of Avarice*), 3.1 (*Iphis and Anaxarete*), and 4.2 (*The False Servant*). The first scene prepares for the third, Paris' bravura defence of theatrical art before the Senate, confuting the accusations of Aretinus. The actors are summoned by the Lictors at the mid-point of the opening scene, briefly overlapping with the patricians Lamia, Junius, and Sura (Pollard, Benfield, and Patrick), who together play a choric episode on the decay of Roman civic virtue under Domitian, at whose hands they are all fated to die, Junius and Sura returning as revenging ghosts in Domitian's dream in the penultimate scene of the play (an episode owing something to Shakespeare's *Richard III*). Lamia's revenge, in the first production, was embodied in Pollard's reappearance, following Lamia's execution in 2.1, as the character Stephanos, introduced in the immediately following scene, 3.1, who is a chief energizer of the developing plot to overthrow the emperor, and who takes part in the climactic assassination.

The second scene, 1.2, involves three actors, with some mute super-numeraries appearing as an intimidating group of military enforcers. John Thompson first spoke its opening line, in the leading character of

Domitia, addressed to the kneeling Parthenius (Richard Sharpe), who presents her with a love letter from Domitian. Parthenius' flattering persuasion that her inconvenient marriage to Lamia can be easily circumvented was interrupted by Pollard's entry, now as outraged husband, and first-hand victim of tyranny. Thompson's difficult role was initiated in the company of two experienced senior colleagues, who played antagonists in the contest between virtue and sinful decadence: Parthenius shifts from slippery insinuation to brutality, once he is opposed. Sharpe's role as a whole, it might be said, demonstrates something of the confusion and moral dawning of Webster's Bosola, a part he had watched Lowin play, in *The Duchess of Malfi*. A compliant tool of Caesarean will at the beginning of the play, he slowly moves over to the opposition, and wields a knife in the final murder of Domitian.

Thompson's role in 1.2 is subtly written, and demanded corresponding skill in playing. Though outwardly she poses as the virtuous wife, Domitia's vanity, ambition, and selfishness show through early; once Parthenius shows the stark hand of power, her commitment to her husband dissolves: ''Twould argue a base mind / To live a servant, when I may command' (1.2.95–6). Her ambition for 'command' and her ease at changing affections foretell the tragic crisis of the play, although her infatuation with Paris persists beyond his death at Domitian's hands, finally aligning her with the assassins and giving her some commitment beyond herself ('This for my Paris' is her cry, and final line, as she stabs the dying emperor), which lends some edge of ambiguity to the death sentence imposed on her, as 'a monster', at the end of the play (5.2.80–5). In 1.2 the actors could have worked in a small group in refining the shape of the scene. The next scene, 1.3, involving at least nine players, reverts to the accusation against Paris, and introduces his accuser, Aretinus, played by Swanston. The fictional setting is the *curia*, or courtroom, and the staging calls for some elaboration, with the 'Fathers conscript' addressed in Aretinus' opening line probably seated, like an empanelled jury. Although technically a large scene, in fact it resolves into a rhetorical competition between two figures, accuser and defendant, interrupted only by asides from the observing assembly. Aretinus' introduction to his accusation of Paris takes some thirty lines, followed by some verbal duelling between them, Paris then taking the initiative with a peroration which approaches a hundred lines in length, an eloquent defence of the stage in which the ancient connection between acting and oratory is underlined by Latinus' comment at its conclusion: 'Well pleaded, on my life! I never saw him / Act an orator's part before' (1.3.143–4). The first audiences saw and heard a leading player of the day defend the moral value of the stage and its function in a civilized culture; those who had read Heywood's *Apology for Actors* might have recognized some similarities in argument.[29] The scene turns into a solo triumph for Paris, who swamps the antagonistic Aretinus, although the formal verdict is deferred by news of Domitian's triumphant return from the wars.

This return, a deliberate deferral of the appearance of the chief agent of the action, and for a Blackfriars audience their first view and hearing of the familiar figure and voice of John Lowin, forms the business of the following scene, 1.4. Domitian's stagey arrival *'in his triumphant chariot'* is prefaced by a brief comic cat-fight between all the female characters, three of whom are new to an observing audience, as they contend for precedence in the welcoming crowd, Domitia warning the others that they had better not get in the way of her rising fortunes. The boys of the company briefly play together as a group, without any adult actor on stage. The triumphal procession (1.4.13) brings a large group onto the stage, Domitian at its centre; Paris and his colleagues enter with the emperor, but Paris speaks only five words, towards the end of the scene. Lowin's part demanded a larger-than-life style, full of shrewdly calculated dangerous arrogance, played to defy challenge. Domitian, like Paris, is a performer, another Roman actor, self-consciously playing the role of the all-powerful tyrant. His opening lines, like his appearance in the chariot, reach back to Alleyn's rhetoric as the aspiring Tamburlaine: 'As we now touch the height of human glory, / Riding in triumph to the Capitol ...' (1.4.14–15). Theatricality invested the play's first performances, as it invests the text. Edward Alleyn died soon after its first staging, and it is tempting to think of Lowin's performance as a homage to a legendary master of charismatic and commanding roles; Lowin was old enough to have seen Alleyn in his heyday.

Having secured the nominally grateful submission of most of his male subjects, Domitian turns to the group of women, and as expected singles out Domitia as his newly chosen empress. Having dismounted from his chariot to kiss her (1.4.72), and to take Paris' hand, Domitian commands him 'To entertain the time', and the scene closes with a resumption of the procession to the Capitol, presumably in a rearranged grouping with Caesar and Domitia as a paired group, walking, the chariot having been either discreetly wheeled off or else included as part of the march off stage. Domitian's moment between Domitia and Paris, at any rate, brings together the fateful triangle of the play, and John Thompson might well have made something of it. Following her embrace by the emperor, Domitia's roving eye is immediately presented with another object, metal more attractive than the ageing Lowin, and an audience could have caught the flicker of unusual attention to it.

The fifth scene, 2.1, constitutes the entire second act; it is the longest scene unit in the play, at 447 lines, but is constructed as a series of successive episodes; the continuity is provided by a failure in experimental dramatic therapy, the attempt to cure Parthenius' miserly father, Philargus, played by Anthony Smith, of his avarice through the performance of a didactic play, an instance which rather disproves Paris' claims in 1.3 about the suasive and morally healthful force of theatre. At its centre, however, is an instance of Domitian's taunting and vindictive cruelty, also involving performance. The scene opened with successive partnerships: first Smith and Sharpe, as father and son, and then (2.1.64) Taylor and Sharpe as actor seeking guidance from a court official about appropriate entertainment for the emperor, a situation Taylor is likely to have experienced at first hand in his professional life (Paris addresses Parthenius as 'my good patron', as Taylor might have addressed Philip Herbert, Earl of Pembroke, Lord Chamberlain of the court of Charles I). Together they concoct a plan to show *The Cure of Avarice* to the assembled court, with Philargus present; Paris leaves as the scene changes tone with the entry of Domitian and Aretinus (2.1.111), the latter acting as informer about the covert resistance of Lamia, Junius, and Sura. Domitian takes firm charge of the scene at line 168, as he unfolds his intention to torment the arrested Lamia, who is brought in by the guard ten lines later. The tense scene which follows is a showpiece for strong actors, as were both Lowin and Pollard, as Domitian, outwardly silky, commends, with increasing lubriciousness, Lamia's 'gift' to him of his abducted wife, Lamia biting his tongue, inwardly boiling, yet rising to a dignified reply:

> Your compassion
> To me, in your forbearing to insult
> On my calamity, which you make your sport,
> Would more appease those gods you have provok'd
> Than all the blasphemous comparisons
> You sing unto her praise.   (2.1.209–14)

Domitian swallows this, and rises to the 'singing' cue, signalling for Domitia to sing: '*Music above and a song*', the stage direction reads (2.1.217); its lyrics are not printed in the text. We could conclude that Thompson had a good singing voice, as many contemporary actors must have had, but in fact there is no reference to the *appearance* of Domitia above; so long as the company had a good singer to hand – perhaps a younger boy, as was Gough, to sing in the treble register – the performer of the dramatic role need not have been the source of the voice heard from the music room, a lightly curtained area facing the audience on the second storey of the tiring-house.

Curtly refusing to fall in with Domitian's extravagant praise of the music, Lamia ends the sadistic game of cat and mouse, and he is dragged from the stage to his death, gagged to prevent any chance of his having the last word. This brutal exit is grotesquely followed by Domitia's triumphant entrance – she has been summoned by the emperor – '*usher'd in by Aretinus, her train with all state borne up by* Julia, Caenis, *and* Domitilla' (2.1.246). This expanded stage group initiates the court play sequence, and Domitian's welcome indicates the presence of some stage furniture, presumably in place since the start of the entire scene, and the actors' disposition on and around it:

> Thus I seat you
> By Caesar's side, commanding these, that once
> Were the adored glories of the time,
> (To witness to the world they are your vassals)
> At your feet to attend you. (2.1.255–9)

As in *Hamlet*, the court is assembled to watch a play; Philargus is reluctantly seated in the audience, and the players are called for. Latinus, playing the obssessed miser, is '*brought forth asleep in a chair, a key in his mouth*' (2.1.287). Like other contemporary scenes in which a stage audience watches a performance (e.g., *Love's Labour's Lost*, *A Midsummer Night's Dream*, *Bartholomew Fair*), the players observed a double focus, outward to the playhouse audience and inward to their fictional audience. The actors of the King's men in 1626 would have calculated how this might have been disposed on the stage of the Blackfriars playhouse. If the imperial thrones were placed centre, somewhat upstage (the evident position of symbolic hierarchical power), Latinus' chair would have been set further downstage, right or left, allowing playing which might be angled to take in both groups of observers; the playhouse audience, of course, observes the stage audience, crucially so in *Hamlet*. The little playlet in *The Roman Actor*, in which Aesopus (Robinson) has the part of son to the lunatic miser and Paris (Taylor) that of the doctor who cures him, by means of a staged dream (the action briefly entering a further level of theatrical recession), has two naïve observers. Philargus, carried away by the fiction, cries out for help when the miser's chests are opened, then dismisses the play, once it is over, as untrue to life. Domitia also dismisses the subject of the play, 'filch'd out of Horace', but during its course an aside alerts us to her peculiar attention to Paris: the performer rather than the part he plays.

> – 'Tis a cunning fellow;
> If he were indeed a doctor, as the play says,
> He should be sworn my servant, govern my slumbers,
> And minister to me waking.   (2.1.327–30)

She is, therefore, changed by the play, as Philargus is not. She calls for a further performance, to see Paris play a lover; Philargus, unwilling to reform his ways at the prompting of a mere play, is condemned to death by Domitian. Theatre becomes tyranny, as tyranny is a kind of theatre. The boundaries between genuine (unfeigned) action and language, and those which are assumed, disguised, and pretended become increasingly blurred.

Following his abrupt and violent exit at about the mid-point of 2.1, Thomas Pollard would have set about changing costume – he would have had plenty of playing time to do so – and contemplating a somewhat changed physical and vocal manner to characterize the part of Stephanos, a freed bondman of Domitilla, in which role he opened the following scene (3.1) in the company of Honeyman and Trigge as Domitilla and Julia, joined at line 78 by Gough as Caenis. The scene marks a turning of the tide, as Stephanos urges them to act against Domitian's rule. As at a number of points in the play, the scene is not without some comedy; Julia begins by conceding that Domitilla has suffered, but that compared with her own experiences Domitilla's are 'like molehills to Olympus', prompting an elaborate lament ('poor I') from her companion. Vain self-regard is not restricted to Domitia; Stephanos steps in to urge them to give up 'childish lamentations' (3.1.21). Caenis' account of Domitia's pride and new obsession with the theatre is similarly animated by catty spite. The high purpose of freeing Rome from tyranny is tempered by the comic focus on erotic competition and jealousy; Domitilla, particularly, might in performance have hovered somewhere between the noble Roman and the jilted teenager.

This short and relatively intimate scene is followed by a longer one including large stage groups: 3.2 once again brings torture and theatre together. Ignoring Parthenius' advice, Domitian has Junius and Sura, '*bound back to back*', dragged onto the stage and tormented by executioners, as described in the full stage directions in the printed text. The result is, as Parthenius calls it, 'a spectacle' (3.2.83), a theatre of suffering which does not have the effect Domitian required of it, as the victims remain stoically silent, until they speak to threaten the emperor with retribution. Having enforced a change in the style of their own drama, its principal observer, Domitian, notices unanticipated reactions in himself:

> By my shaking
> I am the guilty man, and not the judge.
> Drag from my sight these cursed ominous wizards,
> That, as they are now, like to double-fac'd Janus,
> Which way soe'er I look, are Furies to me ...   (3.2.116–20)

Lowin's part, hitherto confident, steely, and mocking, begins to become infected with self-doubt, and correspondingly to deepen. The 'fever', as he calls it (recalling the language of *Macbeth*), is dispelled by the entry of Domitia, through whom he imagines himself renewing his youth (3.2.124–7). The visible difference in age between the first performers must have given emphasis to these lines particularly. Their meeting is passionate: '*Embracing and kissing mutually*', reads the stage direction. Domitia promises to 'banish melancholy' through, unusually, the performance of a tragedy, an adaptation of Ovid's story, told by Vertumnus to Pomona, of Iphis, the low-born lover, and Anaxerete, the scornful princess with whom he is in love, a fairly thinly disguised projection of Domitia's fantasies.[30] The actors resume the arrangement of 2.1: Domitian's 'Prithee let's take our places' (3.2.147) was perhaps preceded by some setting of the stage, as the paired thrones were once more placed in position. The short play begins with a solo lament from Paris as Iphis of some fifty lines, interrupted only by admiring asides from Domitia, interesting in themselves as observations on the acting of emotion and its arousal of sympathetic feeling in an audience: 'Observe with what a feeling he delivers / His orisons to Cupid; I am rapt with't' (3.2.176–7); 'By Caesar's life he weeps! And I forbear / Hardly to keep him company' (3.2.196–7). Domitia is hardly a disinterested spectator, however, and she progressively overplays her hand, confusing the fictional with the real; as audience or readers we have to extend some licence regarding Domitian's normally keen sense of subtext: conventionally, we are to believe, his judgement is clouded with indulgence. Domitia actually rushes onto the performance area at the end of the play to prevent Iphis' suicide, a distinctly comic moment, underlined by Domitian's impercipient bafflement: 'Why are you / Transported thus, Domitia? 'tis a play' (3.2.283–4). Domitilla, by Domitia's arrangement, has been cast as Anaxarete (Honeyman the boy actor playing a woman compelled to act in a play), a double humiliation in that the great lady has to appear on the stage in the company of common players, and in a role denied union with the idealized lover Iphis-Paris. John Honeyman was free to suggest a double layer of disgust, in character as the icy Anaxarete, and as Domitilla, barely tolerating the game imposed on her, a literal theatrical torture. He was also free to convey, perhaps, that Domitilla is not a very good actor, in contrast to the polished Paris; a rather wooden and awkward performance as Anaxarete would have signalled the difference between false and true acting (his own, as Domitilla).

The conclusions that are quite apparent to the playhouse audience during the course of 3.2 are belatedly made plain to the characters in the play at the opening of 4.1, the following scene. Parthenius is initially incredulous, where Julia, Domitilla, and Caenis are in no doubt about the import of what they observed during the play and what they have gleaned since. The developing plan to inform Domitian enlists Aretinus (4.1.51), who takes the initiative in delivering a petition to the emperor (4.1.112), chorically supported by Julia, Caenis, and Domitilla in a bidding war of good reasons for the emperor's attention – another moment strongly invested with comedy. Domitian's reaction begins 'I stand doubtful', and he examines the doubts rhetorically in two long speeches, a rather external device, in which he concedes only that 'if' Domitia should be untrue then his own end is at hand. Generally the speeches keep personal feeling at a distance; 'toughness' has returned to him by the end of the scene. Lowin no doubt made what he could of this scene, but it does not seem to offer the player of Domitian much flexibility. The scene that immediately follows (4.2) is perhaps the most charged in the play, in the course of which Domitia makes gradually plain to Paris her true interest in him. 'Playing with lightning' is a phrase used early in the scene, as Paris is warned not to boast inappropriately of a private interview with the empress, and it is an appropriate phrase to describe the increasingly passionate love-play encouraged by Domitia, and the theatrical irony of the scene itself, observed by the expected audience of Domitian and the petitioners from line 101, as Domitia invites Paris to 'play' his Trojan namesake to her Helen, or Jupiter to her Alcmena.

The episode is thus remarkable for its rising tension, and its reversal of the expected: the desiring woman courts the bashful man, the empress petitions the servant, and the active apprentice leads the reactive adult actor. The demands on Thompson to play increasingly heated sexual advances are quite plain. Having induced Paris to kiss her, 'again', and to 'kiss closer', Domitia dismisses mere kisses as 'but salads / To sharpen appetite'. 'Let us to the feast', she demands, '*Courting* Paris *wantonly*' (4.2.106–8). Thompson and Taylor's big scene was interrupted by Lowin's appearance, following his descent from his watching post above the stage, with some theatrical

panache, from the curtained discovery area at the rear of the stage, throwing
back its hangings on cue:

Domitia [*to Paris*] ... I shall wish that thou wert Jupiter
   And I Alcmena, and that I had power
   To lengthen out one short night into three,
   And so beget a Hercules.
Caesar [*entering*] While Amphitrio
   Stands by, and draws the curtains.   (4.2.109–13)

Paris immediately collapses ('*Falls on his face*') but the fiery Domitia with-
stands the accusations hurled at her, offering no 'sign of sorrow', and
boldly proclaiming that 'her intent and will' was to exercise her lust as
freely as Domitian did his. Her defiance works, and Domitian wavers, his
destructive instinct falling instead on Aretinus, who misjudges Domitian's
'calm mood' to ask for his reward. There followed a subtle partnership
between the two leading actors in the first cast as Domitian laments the
necessary loss of his much loved actor, and Paris, fatally submissive in
his own person, acquiesces in the impossibility of finding pardon for what
he has done. Domitian's 'grief and unwillingness' at pronouncing Paris'
doom rather dissipate as he initiates the plan to have the actors stage, for
his own private viewing, one more play, the indicatively titled *The False
Servant*. The game Domitian embarks on is transparent: Lowin's lines to
Taylor pretty openly signalled what is to happen; Taylor's in reply, and
the exchange of regard between them, might well have conveyed Paris'
understanding and acceptance of his forthcoming death on stage. He is to
play the seducer, and Domitian takes over from Aesopus as the avenging
husband.

The other players this time include, in addition to Aesopus and Latinus,
'*a Boy dress'd for a* Lady', who has some twenty-four lines to speak in the
ensuing drama. This part does not appear in the dramatis personae of the
printed text, and hence is unassigned to a named player. It would have been
thematically appropriate, of course, if John Thompson had doubled this
role, the parallel part in the matching triangles of betrayal. He would have
had seventy lines of playing time to have shifted costume beforehand – a not
altogether impossible timing – but a mere twenty-odd lines between the end
of 4.2 and Domitia's reappearance in 5.1, which seems a considerably less
plausible gap. It is more likely that Gough, say, who had almost as long
beforehand as did Thompson but a whole scene's absence from the stage
after 4.2, shifted costume and character to play another metatheatrical
role: boy actor playing boy actor playing Lady. The expected outcome of

The False Servant – Domitian forgets his lines, but knows the crucial action – is followed by an elegy over the dying Paris, which can sound rather smug, but admits of genuine grief.

> . . . as thou didst live
> Rome's bravest actor, 'twas my plot that thou
> Shouldst die in action, and to crown it die
> With an applause enduring to all times
> By our imperial hand . . .   (4.2.296–300)

The scene closes with a kind of funeral triumph: '*A sad music, the Players bearing off* Paris' *body,* Caesar *and the rest following*'.

The plot of the Roman actor having been completed, the remaining two scenes of the play concern Domitian's doom, and Lowin's performance of the increasingly anguished emperor provided the focus of attention for the play's first audiences. Scene 5.1 begins with Parthenius and Stephanos together, comparing notes. Domitia has been freed from arrest and her 'power o'er doting Caesar' has reached new heights, immediately demonstrated at the entry of the emperor and Domitia (5.1.27). He cheers her, but she rejects him, with a pitiless analysis of what he has become: 'a weak, feeble man, a bondman / To his violent passions, and in that my slave' (5.1.48–9). Fierily, Domitia proclaims her superior power, and her determination to scorn and torment him. In soliloquy (although Parthenius and Stephanos have remained on stage as observers) Domitian, in a speech which owes a good deal to Shakespeare's Antony, examines himself honestly for the first time in the play:

> I am lost;
> Nor am I Caesar. When I first betray'd
> The freedom of my faculties and will
> To this imperious siren, I laid down
> The empire of the world, and of myself
> At her proud feet.   (5.1.81–6)

His confidence revives as he rejects the prophecy of the 'wizard' Ascletario concerning his violent death, condemning the prophet to execution, and strengthening his resolve to condemn Domitia, investing himself in something of Macbeth's defiance (see 5.1.131–55). Also like Macbeth he puts his trust in the seeming impossibility of paradoxical prophecies. Self-comforted, he calls for his 'couch' and music, and falls asleep. Domitia, prompted by Parthenius, retrieves the book of condemnation in which the emperor has marked her name; she is now committed to joining the plot against him. There follows an elaborate dream vision, to '*dreadful music*', as the avenging ghosts of Junius and Sura threaten Domitian, and remove the image of Minerva, his tutelary goddess, prompting a desperate and fearful speech as he returns to consciousness, or quasi-consciousness: the dream of condemnation continues as Jove appears to speak in thunder against him (5.1.209). Edgy and shaken, he takes the newly entering tribunes for his assassins. Reassured, he listens to their rather impossibly long report of the end of Ascletario, which has happened exactly as he foretold it. Considerably more long-winded than the news of the moving wood, it has the same effect: Domitian recognizes that his own death is at hand, and that his last card is played. Unlike Macbeth, Domitian submits, if blasphemously:

> The offended gods
> That now sit judges on me, from their envy
> Of my power and greatness here, conspire against me.   (5.1.282–4)

It is the tribunes, rather, who rouse him to continued action.

The relatively brief final scene assembles all the conspirators: the four women, Parthenius, Stephanos, and two newly introduced characters, Sejeius and Entellus, who do not appear among the dramatis personae; they were perhaps played by Benfield and Patrick, changed from their costume as ghosts in the preceding scene; Taylor was also free to appear as a revenger. They all 'stand close' – concealed, or conventionally out of view – as Domitian and his supporting tribunes enter, Parthenius only leaving the stage in preparation for the trick which finally ensnares Domitian. The emperor has been told that he will die by the hour of five; as he waits for his fate he is given a speech deliberately reminiscent of the final moments of Faustus, also counting the clock, in Marlowe's famous play, once again memorably played by Alleyn:

> How slow-pac'd are these minutes! in extremes,
> How miserable is the least delay!
> Could I imp feathers to the wings of time,
> Or with as little ease command the sun
> To scourge his coursers up heaven's eastern hill,
> Making the hour I tremble at, past recalling,
> As I can move this dial's tongue to six,
> My veins and arteries, emptied with fear,
> Would fill and swell again.   (5.2.20–8)

Parthenius enters with the false news that it is now 'past six', and that a messenger announcing new victories has arrived. In a piece of conventional location-shifting, Parthenius and Domitian leave, to re-enter only four lines later, once the dismissed tribunes, doubtful of the news, have cleared the stage. Domitian and Parthenius are now 'somewhere else', in the fatal chamber the door to which – one of the stage doors at the Blackfriars theatre – is locked to prevent the emperor's escape, and subsequently, following the rapid and violent murder, broken open ('Force the doors!') by the returning tribunes, who discover the body and the conspirators. The play closes with the arrest of Domitia, identified, rather one-sidedly, as 'the ground / of all these mischiefs', the carrying off of Domitian's body, and the sententious observations of the First Tribune (Greville, having shifted costume following his last appearance as Latinus in 4.2) on the unlamented death of bad 'kings', actually so called. The application of Roman politics to seventeenth-century conditions seems explicitly drawn in the last moments of the play.

Much of the play, evidently, required careful ensemble work: the chaos of the final scene, for example, in which Domitian fights back before being felled, would have taken some collective working out so as not to have been *actually* chaotic. Large groups of actors form and reform throughout the performance of the play, while smaller group partnerships – the three actors, the three rejected women, the emperor and his lover – repeatedly appear together, and evidently they might have prepared scenes together before the entire production was brought together on stage. The effect of the early performances would have owed a great deal to the force and energy of the performers of the dominant parts, John Lowin and John Thompson. Joseph Taylor, for all his prominence at the opening of the play as a proud defender of the stage against carping authority and as leading man in the three inset plays, had a role otherwise characterized by rather timid submission to power; even his seduction by Domitia seems to happen because he feels himself, rather comically, to be under orders. In defending himself against her advances he urges her not to confuse him, the man himself, with his assumed stage parts, but Massinger does not give us much impression of what exactly Paris amounts to when off the stage. We have no record of Taylor's appearance, but we can imagine something of Lowin's physical presence as Domitian, looking backward, as it were, through his portrait of fourteen years later. A large, solid man, by no means handsome, and already considerably marked by age in 1626, Lowin was undoubtedly a convincing soldier-emperor, a commander of troops, with real physical threat inform-ing his sadistic power, but with enough tanned antiquity to animate a sensitive nerve about sexual competition (one of Othello's rationalizations of Desdemona's supposed unfaithfulness). No image of Thompson's appearance has survived; he was required to be a beauty, but the fictional assignment of that quality probably counted for a good deal; barring a ridiculous disproportion between the actual and the proposed, an audience accepts what it is told as part of the contract of playgoing. Far more important were Domitia's sheer force and passion; her will is more relentless than that of Domitian, and she brings him down. Thompson got the part because he was the senior player of female roles at the time of the play's production; if, as seems likely, he was in his later teens he could have been quite tall, hence possessing a physical presence matching Domitia's spirit. Yet he was also cast, we would guess, because he was judged to be up to the considerable demands of the part, and could play against Lowin and Taylor as an equal. Sheer seniority was not the only measure of casting; Honeyman, younger than Trigge, received the larger role of Domitilla, having been judged, no doubt, to be more suited to the smouldering resentment of that part.

All the female roles, in fact, are strong parts; none of the boys need have felt short-changed. There *are* decidedly minor roles among the adult parts, even without counting the mute guards and attendants required throughout the play, but there is also a fair spread of significant secondary parts, played by Sharpe, Pollard, Benfield, and Swanston. Parthenius, Sharpe's part, indeed, appears in more scenes than any other character, and his development is more varied: he is successively, even simultaneously, the seducer, the heavy, the concerned son, the obsequious follower, the recruit to resistance, and the crafty plotter. His doubts and temporizing are one index of a corrupt world, and his uncertain moral position at the end of the play a sign that Rome has not been entirely freed. Sharpe was charged with a subtler role than was Swanston as Aretinus, who is simply the relentless secret policeman. Parthenius is the man in the middle, as also in a muddle.

The Roman Actor, Joseph Taylor writes in his dedicatory poem to the 1629 edition of the play, is the 'best' of Massinger's tragedies. If his colleagues shared his opinion the play is likely to have been remounted after its 1626 premiere, although there are no surviving records to demonstrate that it was. Lowin and Taylor would no doubt have continued as progressively ageing versions of Domitian and Paris, but the crucial role of Domitia would have changed hands, as did that of the Duchess of Malfi. The constant and intense work by the actors of the King's men on new plays and revivals remains largely inaccessible to us; the cast list and the surviving text of *The Roman Actor* afford one glimpse of it.

CHAPTER 6

Conclusion

I love the quality of playing, ay; I love a play with all
My heart, a good one, and a player that is
A good one too, with all my heart.
                         Brome, *The Antipodes*, 1.5.72–4.[1]

That the theatre of Alleyn, Burbage, Lowin, Perkins, and Taylor established
a tradition is evident from Restoration attitudes to the stage of half a century
earlier. The gap between the old theatre and the new was roughly the same
as that between the work of contemporary playing at the Royal Shakespeare
Theatre in Stratford-upon-Avon, say, and the legendary foundational period
under Peter Hall in the early 1960s, but without the unbroken continuities
we might observe if we were telling that particular later history. Some older
playgoers can vividly remember the players and productions of the early
RSC, a blank, or at most a collection of written and photographed records,
to modern playgoers in their twenties. Even the RSC has seen considerable
change in personnel, artistic policies, and playing spaces over fifty years, but
evidently without a radical change in national government, a damaging civil
war, and an authoritarian ban on the art it exists to practise, all of which
were experienced by theatre people and theatre lovers in the middle of the
seventeenth century. The recovery of the theatre after 1660 was marked
on the one hand by the presence of some significant figures who had known
the older conditions, including the new managerial leaders Sir William
Davenant and Sir Thomas Killigrew, and the actors Michael Mohun,
Charles Hart, Theophilus Bird, and George Jolly, among others, and on
the other by the absence of the theatre-based tradition of training boys
for playing. No apprentices had been learning the art of stage playing for
eighteen years when the theatres began to operate once more – three generations or so of specialization in female roles – and Edward Kynaston was
an exceptional presence on the new London stage, for a brief period only.
The court and some of the actors had spent the interregnum in continental

174

Europe, where women actors took female roles on stage with evident skill and success, and the new liberalism of the court-supported theatre fairly immediately brought the English stage into conformity with the practice of Europe at large. Thus the paternal model of training and the generational division of the acting troupe together disappeared, and do not seem to have been lamented; the style of playing the older plays consequently was adjusted as adult women took on the parts of Beatrice or Desdemona, and became considerably nearer to modern conditions in the theatre. As the old repertory was valued and continued to be played, however, particularly the plays of Shakespeare, Jonson, and Fletcher, so too its stage history was valued, leading to such stories as the direct succession of playing parts stretching back to Shakespeare and Burbage.

Acting style evidently would also have changed over the period from Edward Alleyn's adolescence to John Lowin's old age; Lowin was in actuality as well as in Restoration legend a living link with the theatre of the later sixteenth century. Born in London in the same year that James Burbage opened the Theatre in Shoreditch, Lowin might have watched the Queen's men, and the famous Richard Tarlton, as a boy; he is very likely to have watched Alleyn in the years following. The contact of individual actors with a variety of playing styles over a lifetime still persists, although now perhaps seems less marked than it did in rather earlier generations. David Waller, for example, who ended his career as an associate artist of the Royal Shakespeare Company, played a famous working-class, tubby, clownish Bottom in the legendary production of *A Midsummer Night's Dream* directed by Peter Brook in 1970. He was then fifty years old, and some twenty years earlier he had been at the Old Vic, acting with Donald Wolfit and directed by Tyrone Guthrie, in another remarkable artistic context, but of a radically different style from that created by Brook, his designers, and the predominantly young and athletic cast of the 1970 *Dream*. Early modern theatrical styles did not vary in such ways. The production and staging of plays were run primarily by the actors, and conceptual frameworks for the design, lighting, and directorial approach to the play, in the modern fashion, were unknown. A play was approached as a story told to an audience, and its chief semiotic medium was the costumed actors, speaking and moving. The telling of the story was partly determined by the genre and written style of the play, so that acting styles changed to accommodate changes in the ways of writing drama. At some point in the first half of the 1590s the rather older verbal extravagance and rhetorical elaboration of the Marlovian school became a target for literary parody and mockery, as a sign of being over the top, so that acting that accommodated to that style, observing its particular decorum of emphasis and bravura display, became tarred with the same brush as being *outré*, *passé*, and so last year. 'Rampum, scrampum, mount tufty Tamburlaine', ran John Marston's parodic pentameter line (not quite in regular metre), spoken by one of the Paul's Boys performers in the Induction to Marston's play *Antonio and Mellida*, mocking the performance of one of his fellows in what the Grocer's Wife in the Induction to *The Knight of the Burning Pestle* calls a 'huffing part'.[2] Huffing and puffing also characterizes the style of Ancient Pistol, amateur of the theatre theatrical: 'Shall packhorses / And hollow pampered jades of Asia, / Which cannot go but thirty mile a day, / Compare with Caesars, and with Cannibals, / And Troiant Greeks?' (*2 Henry IV*, 2.4.162–6). The joke is Shakespeare's rather than Pistol's; Pistol and his like-minded playgoing associates continued to find the older heroic plays thrilling theatrical fare, so that the style suiting such writing *in performance* never truly died out, though it continued to be sneered at by the sophisticated. Richard Fowler of Prince Charles's men, Snarl in *Holland's Leaguer*, was to emerge as a favourite exponent of the older heroic-military style at the Red Bull and Fortune playhouses in the later 1630s and early 1640s.[3]

In so far as Edward Alleyn was the celebrated lead in many of the older plays which fairly rapidly came to seem dated, if only in the eyes and ears of those attuned to different kinds of poetic rhetoric, so has he often been taken to represent the old school in acting, and Burbage, by contrast, the new. This is something of a caricature, and relies too much on the evolution of dramatic writing as we can now observe it, and the chance of what little survives from once extensive repertories of plays. To caricature the approach itself, Alleyn was adequate to the strong colours and broad brush of Marlowe, but it required a Burbage to do justice to the subtle palette and brushwork of a Shakespeare. Both actors, rather, played in a varied repertory of material, suiting their range of styles to the play at hand. Neither *The Fair Maid of Bristow* nor *The Merry Devil of Edmonton*, in both of which we can reasonably guess Burbage took larger parts, are distinguished plays; this fact does not lessen our assessment of the actor's evident skill and range. That Alleyn never had the material Burbage did – the great Shakespearean parts of the decade following 1600 – is an accident of history; had their positions been reversed there is very little to suggest, I think, that Alleyn would not have been as powerful and compelling a Hamlet or Othello as was his great colleague. Alleyn chose to retire from the stage in the first year or two of the seventeenth century not because his star had fallen but certainly because he had other business to attend to; generally he seems to have been more socially and financially ambitious than his famous coeval, and perhaps had less tolerance, as he grew older, for the tough and often frustrating life of the player. Not a few actors have regarded their art with a mixture, variously combined, of passion and impatience.

The sense of tradition that Restoration actors and dramatists alike possessed, defining their place with reference to almost a hundred years of English theatrical activity, in fact developed fairly early in that period. Hamlet's remark about the value of players as memorializers, 'the abstract and brief chronicles of the time' (*Hamlet*, 2.2.523–4), might be compared with Thomas Nashe's enthusiasm for the vivid effect of living theatre, which brings legend and history to immediate life before us. In *Pierce Penniless* (1592) he writes of how it would 'have joyed brave Talbot (the terror of the French) to think that after he had lain two hundred years in his tomb, he should triumph again on the stage';[4] the passage even manages to quote a phrase from the play of *1 Henry VI* itself. Conscious of the stage's role in animating the legendary past, Shakespeare included in *Julius Caesar* a remarkable reflective moment following the assassination, first spoken by the players of the Chamberlain's men in the roles of the chief conspirators; Burbage, it is likely, as Brutus:

Cassius ... How many ages hence
  Shall this our lofty scene be acted over
  In states unborn and accents yet unknown!

Brutus How many times shall Caesar bleed in sport,
  That now on Pompey's basis lies along
  No worthier than the dust!

Cassius So oft as that shall be,
  So often shall the knot of us be call'd
  The men that gave their country liberty.   (3.1.111–18)

As players became Talbot, Brutus, Cassius, or Aeneas so they became invested with presences beyond their private individual selves, and so Burbage was memorialized both as himself and as the men he had impersonated on the stage. The lofty scenes in which he had appeared in turn became invested with his presence, of which subsequent performers of the roles were conscious. Furthermore, the stage itself could memorialize performance. A mere year after Richard Tarlton's death his colleague Robert Wilson wrote the play *The Three Lords and Three Ladies of London* for performance by the Queen's men. Early in the action a group of three pages encounter a ballad-seller and his wares, about which they question him. Young aristocratic know-nothings, they have never heard of Tarlton, and do not recognize his picture – a broadside woodcut print, with verses below it – when it is shown to them. Honesty, as the ballad-seller is called, has to explain why

Tarlton should be remembered, providing an irony the audiences of the
play's first performances would have appreciated as a good joke: how could
he ever be forgotten?

Wilson's play perhaps marks the start of a new consciousness of the
accomplishments of English theatrical art. Tarlton otherwise lived on for a
long time in folk memory and in popular print through the medium of jest-
books, collections of funny stories with a variable basis in fact (Figure 6).
Less associated as he was with stage roles that continued to be performed,

6 Woodcut of Richard Tarlton performing a jig, 1613. The picture is possibly
the same as that used on the stage as a property in 1589

his afterlife was necessarily different from that of Richard Burbage. In his *Apology for Actors* of 1612 Thomas Heywood memorialized in print reputations of which he had only heard, from older members of audiences who had seen performances he himself had not. '*Knell, Bentley, Mills, Crosse, Laneham,* and others; these, since I never saw them, as being before my time, I cannot as an eye witness of their desert give them that applause which no doubt they worthily merit, yet by the report of many judicial auditors their performance of many parts have been so absolute that it were a kind of sin to drown their worths in Lethe, and not commit their almost forgotten names to eternity.'[5] If the work of these men was obscure to Heywood, how much the more so to us; we have very little idea even of the parts played by Knell and Bentley, the two most prominent of Heywood's group. Yet Heywood, conscious of the remarkable achievements of the theatre by the date he wrote, wished to remember and honour those who had come before his generation.

Heywood's sense of the continuity of the theatre is also plain in his prologue to the 1630s performance of *The Jew of Malta*, praising Alleyn as the incomparable originator of the leading role, and commending its current player, Richard Perkins, and his modesty in forbearing to 'exceed' or even 'equal' the performance of his former master. Perkins and Heywood had no doubt seen Alleyn play Barabas; only their contemporaries, those in their fifties or later forties, in the audience of the Cockpit in the early 1630s can have shared in their experience, and might have had something to say about Perkins's success relative to his eminent predecessor. The reception of the later performance of the play, framed in a repertory and consequent expectations from an audience quite different from the theatrical context of forty years earlier, we can calculate to have been different from that of its earliest showings, but quite how the playing style of its performers might have differed is, as always, hard to define. The repertory of Queen Henrietta's men at the Cockpit included a good deal of fashionably up-to-date comedy, reflecting the social world of the audience more closely than did the adventurous, exotic, and romantic plays staged at the Rose in the 1590s. Yet Perkins and his colleagues also played tragedy and history, as we have seen, and Heywood's own plays formed one link in their repertory with older styles of playwriting. If the smaller and more intimate space of the Cockpit encouraged a rather quieter and more subtle style of playing, and if Perkins's portrait suggests he may have favoured a sensitive and introspective approach to his stage roles, yet the demands of the text of *The Jew of Malta* are such that the part of Barabas has to be played with brio and energy, charming the audience with ironic complicity. Different as the performances of Alleyn and Perkins are likely to have been, they would have differed in degree rather than in any fundamental approach to the role of Barabas itself – Alleyn perhaps more fiery and physically dangerous, as a tall, long-legged, vigorous man, and Perkins perhaps the more detached and ironic, rather more weary, grinning more subtly, and biting with the more surprising force (see *The Jew of Malta*, 2.3.20–1). My reimagining, evidently, is based on my sense of the differing bodily presence of the two men; as is still the case, the size, shape, physiognomy, and vocal colour of individual performers would have given a particular quiddity to the parts they played.

The tradition represented by an accumulated older repertory, marked by continuing periodic revivals, is particularly notable in the case of the King's men, still acting the heroics and antiheroics of Prince Hal and Sir John Falstaff forty years after their first appearance on the stage, and generally playing seasons with a fair proportion of older pieces popular with audiences. Malvolio's cross-garters were guaranteed to fill the playhouse in the Stuart years, we are told. We might think that a certain freight of older plays acted as a brake on changes in the style of playing. Consciously connected to a glorious past as the company was, enshrined particularly in the Shakespeare Folio of 1623, Lowin, Taylor, and Shank perhaps strove to maintain a conservatory style in the performance of those Shakespeare plays that continued to be acted, preserving something of the quality of the Burbage years. Attempting to 'fix' a style of performance, however, leads to a rather inert style, as happened in modern times, following Bertolt Brecht's death in 1956, with the remounted productions of the Berliner Enemble. To stay vital, older plays need to be in dialogue with playing styles of the time of their revival, and it is hard to imagine that the plays of Shakespeare, changing casts as they inevitably did, and set within a developing repertory of new plays from the time of Shakespeare's death in 1616 for another twenty-six years, could not have subtly shifted in the ways in which they were played. Such aspects as the speed of delivery, the accenting of the verse, or prose, and the emphasis given to particular characters or entire scenes, all may have altered. The part of Roderigo in *Othello*, for example, might have suggested certain real-life models to both actor and audience in 1604, yet might have carried rather different suggestions for portrayal and reception in the changed social and political world of the 1630s. If Shakespeare 'was not for an age, but for all time', part of his recurring appeal in the theatre has been that the plays are largely friendly to local and temporal associations.

The quality of English playing not only was a source of pride within England itself, but was recognized in the international culture of Europe. Neither Alleyn nor Burbage ever played outside their native shores, as far as we know, but Kemp certainly did, and may have been in touch with some foreign players on the European mainland, leading to such stories as that told by Nashe, quoted in Chapter 4. The chief success of those English troupes that travelled to Europe was achieved in the German-speaking lands, the cognate language evidently being of some sort of help to the comprehension of audiences. The English traveller Fynes Morrison recounts the success in 1592 of even second-rank English players at Frankfurt (am Main) – a chief international exchange, at the time of its markets. 'So as I remember that when some of our cast despised stage players came out of England into Germany, and played at Frankfurt at the time of the mart, having neither a complete number of actors nor any good apparel, nor any ornament of the stage, yet the Germans, not understanding a word they said, flocked wonderfully to see their gesture and action.'[6] The careers of not a few English players, in fact, were committed for long periods to travel in Europe, and to occasional patronage by continental courts. From 1611 the court of the Palatinate at Heidelberg had a British princess, King James's daughter Elizabeth; her son Karl Ludwig (Charles Louis) resumed patronage of English players in the 1650s, following the disruptions of war and exile. That war, beginning at Prague and Heidelberg in 1618, disrupted the work of English players in Germany for thirty years; by its end those uprooted by civil war in England itself moved back into touring their old routes, and entertained the ambassadors to the Treaty of Westphalia at Münster and Osnabrück.

Travel to elsewhere in Europe was less rewarding, but players made occasional visits to Paris, as French troupes also visited London during the reign of King Charles I, a cultural exchange facilitated by the King's marriage to a French princess, Henrietta Maria (Henriette Marie), in 1625. Her brother Louis, King of France from 1610, had seen English actors at the French court as a very young boy, in 1604, probably a troupe led by John Thare, a player with Worcester's men and an associate of Robert Browne the touring player, who had a few years earlier rented the Hôtel de Bourgogne, a celebrated Parisian theatre space, for performances over a period of several months.[7] In September 1604 the three-year-old future King gravely observed a tragedy performed by the English players – perhaps a version of *Richard III* – and some days later, his guardian recorded, tried out his own enactment of what he had seen and heard. 'He says he wants to play at acting. "Monsieur," say I, "How will you speak?" He replies "Tiph, toph," making his voice deep.'[8] The training of a prince might have included the example of stage kings. Playhouses in London itself were a favourite site for foreign visitors unfamiliar with such places in their native cities. Thus the Swiss gentleman Thomas Platter saw *Julius Caesar* at the Globe in 1599, and the famous Spanish ambassador Count Gondomar, himself subsequently turned into a character appearing on stage at the Globe in Thomas Middleton's play *A Game at Chess*, visited the Fortune playhouse in 1621 and was entertained there after the show by the players.

The social place of players in the later sixteenth to the mid seventeenth century was on the one hand well defined, on the other somewhat ambiguous. No player we know of, I have observed, came from a gentry family and none were university graduates, yet several were from reasonably well off families in the middling ranks of society: Nathan Field was the son of a clergyman, and his brothers became respectively a publisher and a bishop. A good number of actors came from families in trade occupations, and not a few apprenticed within the 'great companies' of London. Leading players were of a social rank equal to the respectable citizens of London, many of whom witnessed their wills and were named as friends and legatees. At the bottom of the acting profession, as is still the case, many journeyman actors would have been scratching an existence, and living on the margins of poverty. A small number of actors made a good deal of money, usually by doing something other than simply acting, including buying in to theatrical property; a number, like Alleyn, Lowin, and Taylor, received posts in the royal household establishment of a rank higher than that shared with their colleagues. The status of all major playing troupes as liveried servants, either of a powerful aristocrat or a member of the royal family, gave them a certain cachet, and some privileges, such as freedom from arrest under common law for such alleged offences as debt, a common circumstance for those players who managed company expenditures, frequently on credit. As the King's, Queen's, or prince's servants, players held a minor status in the royal household, as Grooms of the Chamber, and an annual allowance of scarlet livery cloth, rather than wages, from which their ceremonial costumes were made.

They also carried letters patent, especially when they travelled, giving them royal permission to perform their plays throughout the kingdom, an endorsement of their business from the highest levels of authority. Such a political alignment with the Crown became a less flexible asset as the Crown's authority fell further and further into question in the 1630s, while local administrative independence – the freedom of local mayors and burgesses to make their own decisions about players and their permission to perform and draw audiences – was always an issue of some delicacy. By 1642, however, all London players who were permanent members of playing troupes were sworn servants of the Crown, and technically bound by oath to support the King's cause. As they did so – and not all of them did – they became enemies of Parliament, and the constitutional crisis directly affected all players' business. London was immediately seized, and subsequently held, by the Parliamentary party, and the city administration taken over by its partisans. For the active years of the ensuing war, 1642–6, there was no place for playing in London; older actors retired completely or bided their time, while a number of younger men joined the King's armies, Michael Mohun and Charles Hart particularly distinguishing themselves as royalist officers. Their reputation in the Restoration was that of both distinguished players and loyal and courageous royalists.[9]

Before the enforced extreme politicization of the profession, the older strand of moralistic criticism of the stage tended to characterize players as *arrivistes*, pretending to a status higher than that to which they belonged, particularly resented for 'jetting it' in silks and satins.[10] Actors' portraits – those of Alleyn, Lowin, and Perkins – belie this charge. Off stage, it seems, actors dressed in the sober black of respectable London citizens of the middle rank, without any extravagance of costume or personal decoration. That they might have worn rich and valuable stage clothes outside the theatre was even precluded by contractual agreement, such as that signed in 1614 by Robert Dawes, player, for the managerial team of Philip Henslowe and Jacob Mead.[11] The rather unsophisticated charge of borrowed feathers confuses stage costume, which certainly could be elaborate and expensive, and the display and bravura of certain stage parts, with the respectable and neighbourly off stage existence of the great majority of players. The church of St Giles Cripplegate today memorializes Edward Alleyn in a stained-glass window, as a repeated benefactor of the parish in which the Fortune play-house stood, and from the profits of which place Alleyn contributed funds to poor relief through the church, as his Christian profession urged him to do.

Quite why boys or men became players seems in some cases plain, where family affiliation or parents' choice of apprenticeship gave some individuals an early immersion in the art, in which they then proved to be gifted. Other careers speak of personal inclination later in life: an admiration of the stage combined with some boredom with one's career path as a goldsmith or a grocer, say, leading to conversations with the players. Most people in that category, it seems, had made such a jump by their early twenties. Many players were London born; others were brought to the city by apprentice-ship of one kind or another, which was evidently regarded by many provincial parents as an entrée to a more prosperous career. Shakespeare's own way into the profession of player, however it was done, was unusual, as was his maintaining his chief household quite remote from London, as he appears to have done. The stage probably suggested itself as option to rather more young men after it become culturally more prominent in the 1580s, partly as a result of the changes in style of playwriting, and consequently of playing, and partly through the influence of stars such as Tarlton and Alleyn. Tarlton is supposed to have inspired Armin, and Alleyn's example no doubt was a stimulus to many others. The passports of those wishing to enter the theatre later in life than the median age of apprenticeship must have been validated by talent or money, and preferably both. As it was possible to buy one's way into membership of London trade companies, 'by redemption', so cash must have been a persuasive medium in negotiation with the players, especially if talent was not abundantly apparent. The jokey audition conducted by Kemp and Burbage in *2 Return from Parnassus* is a facetious version of interviews that must have taken place in fact, more soberly, and possibly with the entire troupe of sharers present. A group of people who had to work closely together daily would have been rightly cautious about whom they might be admitting to their fellowship.

Actors' careers were significantly different from those of their modern counterparts in being conducted in such closed contractual groups for an extended period, sometimes a considerable stretch of years. John Lowin saw more changes within the personnel of the King's men than did any other member of that troupe, yet even he worked with Richard Burbage for sixteen years, and with Joseph Taylor for twenty-three. Such close contact for a protracted time is virtually unknown in the modern Western theatre – although some of the actors in the Piccolo Teatro of Milan might have experienced something like it – and we might compare it with the position of musicians in a string quartet, groups which occasionally remain together for many years without any change in membership, and come to know one another's playing very well, aspiring to play as one. That analogy cannot be pushed too far, since Lowin and Taylor appeared among a group of as many as twenty others (e.g., in *The Roman Actor*), and the ensemble as a whole changed, perhaps in the case of minor hired actors – wage-earners but free agents – fairly often. Where modern actors might bond as a cast for the rehearsal and run of a play, generating a certain amount of off stage friendship over coffee, in bars, and at parties, actors of early modern companies saw one another in play after play, season after season, and spent most of the daylight hours of each working day together, apprentices never escaping the circle, since they lived in the household of their masters. London actors tended to congregate in dwelling places in the same districts, historically associated with playhouses: the parishes of St Saviour Southwark, St Leonard Shoreditch, St Botolph Aldgate, St Giles Cripplegate, and St James

Clerkenwell all had communities of actors, who would have seen one another as neighbours, as well as on the stage. Relationships by marriage – that of William Browne and his brother-in-law Thomas Bond, for example – further tied together the social network within which players lived and worked, as did rentals and other arrangements producing extended households: the junior player George Jolly was living in the house of his senior partner Matthew Smith (Agurtes in *Holland's Leaguer*) in White Cross Street, near to the Fortune playhouse, in 1640, for example.[12] The community of players was, then, in many cases exactly that. Men and youths who worked together in the playhouses saw a good deal of one another in the rest of their daily life, and that they chose to cultivate close friendships is apparent in the provisions of the wills they made, in which working colleagues are nominated as among the most intimate friends of the dying man. Fellow players are not infrequently witnesses to and executors of their colleagues' wills.

Players then constituted a quite significant artistic community within certain districts of London, commonly outside the walls of the city rather than within them, and contributed to the changing social mix of the extended city as a whole. Their commitment to an economy of leisure and entertainment reflects a general growth in the city's population and some changes in its constitution. In the seventeenth century newly fashionable districts in the west, notably around Covent Garden, catered to the increasing observation of a London 'season' by the moneyed classes, of which playgoing was a part. The theatre before 1642 remained democratic, however. If the Cockpit and the Blackfriars playhouses saw plenty of aristocratic and gentry spectators among their audiences, the cheaper playhouses to the north, the Fortune and the Red Bull, continued to draw crowds, as did the Globe on the south bank of the river.

The professionalization of the English theatre, lamented by one conservative commentator in early 1590, in the style of nostalgia for 'Merrie England', when playing was a leisure activity open to all,[13] was in some senses restrictive. As the players took as their model of organization the London companies of which a number were members, so they took on the template of controlled access to the right to practise a particular trade, open chiefly by serving prolonged training in apprenticeship: a closed shop, in short, and a lesser version of 'lordship', in which masters commanded dependent servants. Andrew Gurr has characterized the foundation of the Chamberlain's and Admiral's companies in 1594 as a deliberately limited 'duopoly' in the London theatre world, whereby roughly twenty master players were in control of who might enter their ranks, sharing in the art of stage playing and the profits arising from it. In fact, it seems that other troupes of players found room to operate, although their patterns of organization appear to have followed those of the leading companies.

Even before the high tide of professionalism, a chief route into the theatre was training with an established player. In 1529 one George Maller, officially a glazier (a trade much in request at the court of King Henry VIII, incidentally), took on an apprentice called Thomas Arthur, 'him to teach in playing of interludes and plays, whereby he might attain and come to be one of the King's players', a condition which rather suggests that Maller himself was of that number. Arthur, however, induced three of Maller's covenant servants, 'being expert in playing', to leave and set up a small touring troupe (of four players, presumably), hindering Maller in his 'science of playing' and earning money independently, none of it reverting to the master. Maller further complains that Arthur was not a very good player, or didn't apply himself, but he evidently possessed individual entrepreneurial skills.[14] The anecdote illustrates, sixty-odd years before the disagreement between Alleyn and Perkins, that independent talent might have found ways around restrictive professional controls. In a theatrical market, good players were always worth money, and might find their own ways to realize their worth.

The activity of playing, its very name suggests, was a pleasurable and light-hearted pursuit; players did not perform actions and speak words 'in earnest', but rather 'in jest': 'they do but jest, poison in jest' Hamlet sharply reminds Claudius, who is concerned about possible 'offense' in the play they are watching (*Hamlet*, 3.2.232–5). True poisoning, and true offence, have occurred elsewhere. Players undoubtedly drew pleasure from what they did, sharing in giving pleasure to audiences through their art, and experiencing the exhilaration and satisfaction, individually and as a team, of performances that were especially successful and enthusiastically received. Yet that what they did was work, and exacting, difficult, and not entirely predictable work, we are reminded by other language in plays, prologues, and epilogues. Lowin, a servant of the public as well as the Crown, had 'labour'd' to please them over the course of thirty years, in the phrasing of Davenant's prologue, cited in Chapter 4. 'And we'll *strive* to please you every day', sings Feste to the audience at the end of *Twelfth Night* (5.1.408, my emphasis). The prologue to *Romeo and Juliet* offers a contract: if the audience listens and pays attention carefully, 'What here shall miss, our *toil* shall *strive* to mend' (line 14, my emphases). Preparing the play had already taken a certain amount of toil, in learning lines and in rehearsal, including careful preparation of the fight scenes, but when performance before an audience began, the toil of communal attention in making scenes work as they should, and in keeping a check on the audience's engagement with the action and speech on stage, was that of the mental and muscular energies engaged in stage playing: disciplined, concentrated, focused, and exhausting. How the kind of work involved in playing was seen in Shakespeare's day is apparent from Philostrate's disparaging comments as he attempts to dispel Theseus' growing interest in the 'tedious brief scene' of Pyramus and Thisby as the choice for a wedding revel at the end of *A Midsummer Night's Dream*. Asked who the players are, he replies 'Hard-handed men who work in Athens here / Which never labor'd in their minds till now'. Bottom and his companions are adept enough at their own occupations, using their hands, but the imaginative mental work of players is beyond them, both in the mechanics of line learning, and crucially in the sympathetic creation of character and emotion in action and speech, through the exercise of what Hamlet calls 'conceit'. They have 'toiled their unbreathed [under-exercised] memories', and are likely to give performances 'Extremely stretch'd, and conn'd with cruel pain', and hence likely to inflict some pain on the audience (5.1.56–81). The prologue to Shakespeare and Fletcher's *Henry VIII*, addressing the audience, insists on the end of the actors' work: 'Think ye see / The very persons of our noble story / As they were living.' To aim for any lesser kind of show, featuring 'fool and fight', would involve, the speaking actor says, 'forfeiting / Our own brains' (lines 17–27). Players used their brains to bring fictional or historical persons to life in the presence of their audiences, in a shared imaginative act of speech, action, and thought. Their art can now only be reimagined, yet the testimony to its power remains in what has been left behind, not least in the magnificent range of dramatic texts sixteenth- and seventeenth-century players first brought to life in the theatre.

Appendix: Principal actors 1558–1660

The following list compiles brief biographies of all professional actors with careers of reasonable prominence between the beginning of Queen Elizabeth's reign and the Restoration of King Charles II. It excludes school, university, inns-of-court, and chorister amateurs, but includes those in the transitional period of the Chapel troupe who became professionals within the Children of the Queen's Revels; individuals who were principally theatre musicians (e.g., Ambrose Beeland) have also been excluded. In compiling it I have relied, with gratitude, on similar lists and dictionaries by preceding scholars, attempting to reflect recent research as fully as I can. Birth and death dates are given where known; the abbreviation *fl.* (for the Latin *floruit* = flourished) indicates the period of ascertainable theatrical activity of a given subject.

ADAMS, JOHN, *fl.* 1576–88. Sussex's company as leading actor in 1576; founder member of the Queen's men, 1583, possibly still acting until 1591. Mentioned in *Bartholomew Fair* as comic stage partner of Tarlton.

ALLEN, RICHARD, *fl.* 1613. As performer with Children of the Queen's Revels, acted in *Epicoene* and *The Coxcomb*; possibly passed to Lady Elizabeth's company.

ALLEN, WILLIAM, *fl.* 1614–47. Leading actor with Queen Henrietta's company at the Cockpit from 1625, Allen had possibly been an apprentice or trainee under Christopher Beeston. Briefly a member of the King's men (by early 1641); a Royalist officer in the civil wars.

ALLEYN, EDWARD, 1566–1626. One of two legendary tragic actors of the late sixteenth century, Alleyn began acting in his teens, and retired before he was forty. In 1583 he was a member of the Earl of Worcester's company, and a member of the Admiral's troupe by 1589, emerging in 1594 as leader of the reconstituted Admiral's men at the Rose playhouse, until a temporary retirement from playing in 1597, returning to play for a few years at the new Fortune playhouse in 1600. Allied by marriage to Philip Henslowe (m. Joan Woodward, Henslowe's stepdaughter, 1592), in the seventeenth century his energies were given to joint ventures in theatre management and the royal office of Master of the Bears, and to his College of God's Gift, Dulwich, opened in 1617.

ALLEYN, RICHARD, *fl.* 1594–1601. No relation to the famous Edward, Richard Alleyn was a member of the Queen's men in 1594, and with the Admiral's men from 1597 until his death in late 1601, with a reasonably prominent position in the company.

ARMIGER, EDWARD, 1612–37. Armiger was acting by the age of seventeen, as a member of a touring troupe associated with the Red Bull, led by William Perry and Richard Weeks. In the mid 1630s he was married, living in London, and possibly acting at the Fortune, but had moved to playing in Dublin by later 1637, where he died.

ARMIN, ROBERT, *c.* 1568–1615. A legendary comic performer, Armin, the son of a tailor, came from King's Lynn, and moved to London to serve an apprenticeship as a goldsmith. It was completed by 1591, but Armin chose not to claim his freedom of the company until 1604, after he had established himself as a player. Beginning with a provincial troupe patronized by Lord Chandos, Armin moved to the Chamberlain's men about 1599, and became principal comic player following the departure of Kemp. Possibly sick and infirm in the last years of his life, and not performing after 1610; also playwright and author.

ATTWELL, GEORGE, *fl.* 1590–9. Member of Strange's men, possibly then of Queen's men. Author and probable performer of at least one jig.

ATTWELL, HUGH, *c.* 1592–1621. Member of Queen's Revels by 1609, playing La Foole in *Epicoene*; Prince Charles's company by 1616. New Year in Middleton's *Masque of Heroes*, Inner Temple, January–February 1619. Elegy by fellow player William Rowley speaks of a six-year struggle with a fatal condition.

AXEN, ROBERT, *fl.* 1630–9. Member of Queen Henrietta's company at the Cockpit by 1630, with named parts in three published cast lists; member of King and Queen's Young Company in 1639.

BARKSTED, WILLIAM, b. *c.* 1590, *fl.* to 1616. Member of Queen's Revels by 1609, playing Morose in *Epicoene*; subsequently of Lady Elizabeth's and Prince Charles's company. Poet and dramatist. References to him recur until 1638, but he possibly left the stage in 1616.

BASSE, THOMAS, 1585–1634. Member of Lady Elizabeth's company in 1611; Queen Anne's by 1617. No records of his playing activity after 1622, though he still moved in theatrical circles, marrying (probably) Dorcas Woodgate, stepdaughter of his Queen's fellow Robert Lee (*q.v.*).

BAXTER, RICHARD, 1593–>1665. Baxter had the longest and most varied career of any of his contemporaries, beginning as a teenaged hired player at the Red Bull, 1605–6, moving to the King's men as a minor player in the 1620s, acting in Europe in 1646, and remaining a member of actors' agreements to revive playing in London in the later 1640s, and occasionally acting surreptitiously. He re-emerged as a player with the Restoration King's company under Killigrew, but seems not to taken parts after he was seventy; he died within a year or two following that anniversary.

BEESTON, CHRISTOPHER, alias HUTCHINSON, 1580–1638. Probably began with the Chamberlain's men, apprenticed with Augustine Phillips; played in *Every Man In His Humour* in 1598. With Worcester's men in 1602, translated to Queen Anne's company in 1603, moving to Red Bull playhouse at its opening in 1605–6. Beeston succeeded to chief managerial position at the death of Thomas Greene in 1612. Having made a socially advantageous marriage to Jane Sands (or Sandys) in 1602, Beeston had probably acquired some money, leading to his building of the indoor Cockpit playhouse in Drury Lane in 1616, one of the two principal London theatres by the 1630s. Thereafter he possibly did not do a great deal of playing, severing himself from the Queen's group, and concentrating on management and training of new companies.

BEESTON, WILLIAM, c. 1606–82. Son of Christopher, was trained in playing under his father, but his precise place in any company in the earlier part of his career is not clear. He inherited and expanded his father's managerial ambitions, being involved with the management of the Salisbury Court playhouse in 1632. By 1637 he was playing with the King and Queen's Young Company at the Cockpit, and he succeeded to his father's role as Governor of that troupe. During the interregnum he continued theatrical investment, refitting the Salisbury Court theatre, but lost the war for patronage in 1660, and was reduced to minor theatrical ventures for the final decades of his life.

BELTE, THOMAS, *fl.* 1595–1604. Apprenticed to John Heminges of the Chamberlain's men in late 1595 for a nine-year term, Belte was probably then in his younger teens and began on stage in female roles, and hence is likely to have appeared in the contemporary Shakespearean comedies, although he is not named in any cast lists. A 'T. Belt' has two parts, one female, in the plot of *2 Seven Deadly Sins*; if this was Heminges's boy the performance of that play requires redating from its older assignment to c. 1590.

BENFIELD, ROBERT, c. 1583–1649. Benfield perhaps began with the Queen's Revels company, but came to them as a man of twenty-five (in

1608) rather than a youth. Moved to Lady Elizabeth's company, and to King's men about 1615; named in numerous cast lists, 1616–32. With the exception of his playing Antonio in *The Duchess of Malfi* when he was about forty, Benfield remained a middle-rank player, his role in *The Roman Actor* being typical of his other known parts.

BENTLEY, JOHN, 1553–85. Bentley, probably born in Halifax, Yorks., had presumably emerged as a leading tragic player in his twenties, qualifying him to be chosen for the Queen's men in 1583, of which troupe he was a leading player for two years. We know nothing of his earlier career, or his stage roles, though his reputation was as one of the chief stars of the stage before Alleyn. He was involved in an affray at a performance by the Queen's players at the Red Lion Inn in Norwich in June 1583, when he seems to have been chiefly responsible for the death of a riotous member of the audience; he was imprisoned for a period.

BIRCH (BURGH), GEORGE, *c.* 1597–1625? George Burgh, so spelt, was apprenticed to John Heminges in 1610 for a term of eight years, playing, probably, Lady Would-Be and Dol Common in revivals of *Volpone* and *The Alchemist* in his late teens (a manuscript list of parts calls the actor *Richard* Birch). He married Richard Cowley's daughter Elizabeth in early 1619, shortly before the senior actor's death, and his name subsequently appeared in numerous cast lists. His own career was perhaps cut short by the bad plague epidemic of 1625.

BIRD, THEOPHILUS, 1608–63. The son of William Bird (below), veteran player at the Fortune, under whom he probably first trained, Theophilus was in his mid teens at his father's death, and was recruited by Christopher Beeston, and continued playing female roles with Queen Henrietta's company at the Cockpit until 1630. At some time in the next few years he married Beeston's daughter Anne, becoming part of the extended Beeston theatrical clan. He was a member of the King and Queen's Young Company from 1637, but in early 1641 transferred to the King's men. Remained involved with interregnum playing groups, and in Beeston theatre business (with William). Bird joined the King's company in the Resoration, acting for a season or two in the company of his son-in-law, Michael Mohun.

BIRD, WILLIAM, alias BOURNE, *fl.* 1597–1624. Bird was in Pembroke's company in 1597, but transferred to the Admiral's in that year, and spent the rest of his career with that troupe, under its successive titles, most of it in playing at the Fortune playhouse. He spoke the part of Zeal from the New World Pageant in Fleet Street during the entry celebration for James I in 1604. A leading member of the Palsgrave's company 1616–21, he appears to have retired from the stage in the last year or two of his life, but remained living alongside the Fortune; friend and associate of Edward Alleyn.

BLANEY, JOHN, *fl.* 1609–25. Blaney was with the Queen's Revels company, and in the cast of *Epicoene*, by 1609, and with Queen Anne's company at the Red Bull by 1616; he was living in the district of the playhouse in 1623. In 1625 he played Asambeg in Massinger's *The Renegado* at the Cockpit, as a member of Queen Henrietta's men. No further records of his activity survive after that date.

BOND, THOMAS, 1602–>44. Bond first emerges as a minor player in 1622, in connection with the Red Bull; further association with that playhouse is indicated by his marriage in 1627 to Susan Hunter, daughter of Robert Browne (1) and Susan Baskerville. Founder member of Prince Charles's troupe, 1631–2; played Miscellanio in *Holland's Leaguer*, 1631, Salisbury Court playhouse. Free of Founders' Company, by patrimony, 1632(?). Lord Chamberlain's records indicate Bond's continuing career through 1630s, at the Red Bull; his widow (probably) remarried in 1644.

BOWYER, MICHAEL, 1599–1645. Born in Kidderminster, Worcs., Bowyer was apprenticed, probably in his earlier teens, to an unnamed touring company led by William Hovell (*q.v.*). By 1621 Bowyer had attained freedom as a player, was married, and living in London. A leading player with Queen Henrietta's company at the Cockpit from 1625, with identified parts in several published cast lists, in 1637 or thereabouts he transferred to the King's men, devoting his remaining professional career to playing at the Blackfriars and the Globe. Friend and associate of Richard Perkins, to whom he left an annuity in his will.

BROWNE, ROBERT (1), *fl.* 1580s–1603. More than one player with the common name of Robert Browne was active, and living in the district of Southwark, in the late sixteenth century, making for confusion. This list distinguishes two people, the first a leading member of the Earl of Derby's company, and a lessee of the Boar's Head playhouse in Whitechapel, established in 1599. In 1592 Browne married a young woman named Susan Shore; together they founded a family theatrical empire which was to last to Susan's death in 1649. Browne died, evidently as a youngish man, in 1603, leaving his widow with five children and his playhouse investments.

BROWNE, ROBERT (2), 1563–1622. The second Browne was involved in a wide variety of theatre enterprises from 1583 onwards; as a player he was best known as a principal leader of touring troupes into continental Europe between 1590 and 1620. Browne's second wife was Cicely Sands, sister of Jane, wife of Christopher Beeston: the two men were brothers-in-law. He was a neighbour and friend of the King's player William Sly, who left him 'his part of the Globe' at his death in 1608. Such connections perhaps had to do with Browne's becoming a patentee of the Queen's Revels troupe in 1610. He had died by mid 1622, when his widow remarried to the player William Robins.

BROWNE, WILLIAM, 1602–34. Son of Robert (1) and Susan Browne; stepson of Thomas Greene, who died when he was ten but may have had some early influence on his playing. A hired player with Queen Anne's men from his teenage years, his unpaid wages were one item of dispute between his mother and members of the company in the early 1620s. Founder member of Prince Charles's troupe in 1631–2, he played Philautus in *Holland's Leaguer*. Died young, willing (stage?) clothing to his colleague and brother-in-law, Thomas Bond. His widow Anne remarried to the bookseller and theatre entrepreneur John Rhodes.

BRYAN, GEORGE, *fl.* 1586–96. A touring player in Denmark and Germany in 1586–7, Bryan was subsequently a member of Lord Strange's company, and then of the Chamberlain's company by 1596. Shortly afterwards Bryan appears to have retired from playing to take up a court post as Groom of the Chamber, which he held until at least 1613. He has parts in the plot of *2 Seven Deadly Sins*, and is named as an original actor in Shakespeare's plays in the Folio of 1623.

BURBAGE, JAMES, *c.* 1530–97. A foundational figure in the business of Elizabethan theatre, and of the family-based playhouse ownership that assured the success of the companies in which his sons were involved, Burbage was a freeman of the Joiners' Company, presumably by the early 1550s, and probably took up playing within the next decade. By 1572 he was the head of the Earl of Leicester's players, but his retreat from full-time playing probably coincided with his enterprise with his playhouse, the Theatre, opened in 1576. Burbage acquired the site of the Blackfriars playhouse in 1596, but was unable to exploit it at that date as a venue for his son Richard's troupe.

BURBAGE, RICHARD, 1569–1619. Trained under his father, James, Richard Burbage began as a player in his teens. In the early 1590s he was at various times a member of Strange's, Sussex's and Pembroke's companies; in 1594 a foundational member of the Chamberlain's men, acting with that troupe (becoming the King's company in 1603) until his death in early 1619. Leading player, he premiered in the majority of Shakespeare's plays, and in many other plays now unknown. With Alleyn, one of the models for 'the actor' during and following his lifetime. Dramatized as a character in *2 Return from Parnassus*, acted at Cambridge *c.* 1600.

BURT, NICHOLAS, *fl.* 1636–69. Restoration legend places Burt as Shank's apprentice at Blackfriars, then as an actor of female roles under Beeston at the Cockpit, suggesting he may have been born about 1620. He served in the wars with Hart and Shatterell in Prince Rupert's Regiment of Horse, and by 1648 was involved with actors attempting to revive playing, and was arrested, with Lowin and Taylor, at a performance of Fletcher's *Rollo* at the Cockpit. At the Restoration a member of the King's company, acting principal parts with Charles Hart and Michael Mohun.

CANE, ANDREW, 1589–>1659. Cane served an apprenticeship of nine years as a goldsmith to his brother, gaining his freedom in 1611 and apparently immediately moving into business on his own account, which he continued to pursue until his death. He evidently took up playing, concurrently, at some time in the next decade: by 1622 he was a 'chief player', with experience at both the Fortune and the Cockpit, a member of the Palsgrave's company, and possibly of the King and Queen of Bohemia's. He was a leader of the new Prince Charles's company in 1631, playing Trimalchio in *Holland's Leaguer*, and performing for a further eleven years at the Red Bull and the Fortune. Renowned in popular legend as a clown and performer of jigs, Cane had a fame that lived on well into the Restoration.

CARTWRIGHT, WILLIAM, *fl.* 1598–1636. Cartwright entered the Admiral's company in 1598, and remained with it in its subsequent incarnations, performing at the Fortune playhouse for more than twenty years and living in White Cross Street, by the playhouse, in 1623. In later years, Cartwight was associated with the King's Revels troupe at Salisbury Court; about 1634 he performed Claudius in Nathaniel Richards's *Messalina*.

CARTWRIGHT, WILLIAM, JR, 1606–86. Son of William Cartwright the elder, likely to have begun in female roles at the Fortune, under the supervision of his father; by the 1630s a member of the King's Revels troupe at Salisbury Court, emerging as a leading player with the King's company after 1660, and playing, among other roles, Falstaff. Joined the amalgamated company in 1682, and acted for a season or two more. A large collection of books and pictures, including numerous actors' portraits, willed to Dulwich College at his death.

CLARK, HUGH, *c.* 1609–48>. Clark's first roles were leading female parts with Queen Henrietta's company, 1626–30. If he was the Hugh Clark christened at St Andrew Holborn early in 1609, he was seventeen when he played Gratiana in Shirley's *The Wedding*, and twenty-one when he played Bess Bridges in Heywood's *The Fair Maid of the West*. That he may have married Judith Browne in 1627 might seem a little unlikely, but it was possibly a theatrical alliance: Judith was the daughter of Robert Browne (2), and stepdaughter of William Robins, chief player in Clark's company. Clark joined the King's men in 1641, possibly picking up some of the younger parts Taylor had abandoned: he may have played Philaster, for example. Clark remained in touch with fellow players into the later 1640s.

CLAY, NATHANIEL, *fl.* 1615–30. A member of touring troupes of various kinds, Clay, as a fellow sharer, was given theatrical property in the 1615 will of William Hovell (*q.v.*). He was subsequently associated with the Children of Bristol (1618), and a branch of the King's Revels company, in Reading, Berks., 1630.

CLUN, WALTER, *c.* 1620?–64. Restoration legend has it that Walter Clun, with Charles Hart, trained as a female specialist at the Blackfriars before 1642; he possibly played Arethusa in *Philaster*. Clun was certainly a member of Prince Charles's troupe, acting in continental Europe 1644–6, and subsequently a party to actors' agreements in London in 1648. At the Restoration Clun joined the King's company, acting leading roles with great success, including Iago, and Subtle in *The Alchemist*. His career was cut short by his murder, by robbers, in 1664.

CONDELL, HENRY, *fl.* 1598–1627. Condell had joined the Chamberlain's men by 1598, when he played in *Every Man In His Humour*. He appeared as himself (and probably in another role) in *The Malcontent* in 1604; other known roles are Mosca in *Volpone*, Surly in *The Alchemist*, and the Cardinal in *The Duchess of Malfi*. Continued playing until 1619, remaining a sharer in company property, and friend of numerous players. With John Heminges, active in the production of the 1623 Folio of Shakespeare's works, and also in the parish affairs of St Mary Aldermanbury, near the Guildhall, where he was buried in December 1627.

COOKE, ALEXANDER, *c.* 1583/4–1614. Cooke was apprenticed to John Heminges in January 1597 for an eight-year term, which means he should have been free of his bonds in early 1605. Presumably he was, since he seems to have married about then, and was the father of a son, Francis, the following October. Like Armin, he delayed claiming his freedom, finally becoming a freeman grocer in March 1609. Cooke is likely to have played female roles with the Chamberlain's/King's troupe for at least a few years; from 1605, we may take it, he became a full member of the company, playing adult roles in the plays in which he is listed after that date: *Volpone*, *The Alchemist*, *Catiline*, and *The Captain*; his name also appears in the Shakespeare Folio as a principal actor. He died early in 1614, aged not much more than thirty, entrusting Heminges and Condell with the safe management of money left to his young children.

COOKE, WILLIAM, *fl.* 1632–44. Cooke was a minor member of Prince Charles's company by 1632, and was sworn as a full member in 1635. He did not stay, however, since in 1638 he was in Dublin, acting at the Werburgh Street playhouse. He possibly remained there until the outbreak of war; he performed with other English players at the Hague in 1644–5.

COWLEY, RICHARD, *fl.* 1593–1619. Strange's men in 1593, probably founder member of new Chamberlain's company in 1594, although never, apparently, a sharer. Played Verges in *Much Ado About Nothing*, probably to Kemp's Dogberry: possibly indicative of his rank in parts. Named in the Folio as initial performer of Shakespeare.

COX, ROBERT, 1604–55. Cox attended Merchant Taylors' School, from 1618, and hence attained some classical learning. As a no longer young man he was admitted to the troupe at the Cockpit in 1639; he was subsequently a member of the company of actors formed by Richard Baxter in 1648, and was active in surreptitious playing, arrested at a show at the Red Bull in 1653. His posthumous fame came as the supposed 'contriver and author' of the 'drolls', published in 1660 and 1672. How true that may be depends on how far one is inclined to believe Francis Kirkman, who made the claim almost twenty years after Cox's death.

DOWNTON, THOMAS, *fl.* 1592–1618. Downton was with Strange's company in 1593, Pembroke's in 1596, and joined the Admiral's as a hired man in 1597, rising quickly to take on parts formerly played by the temporarily absent Alleyn. By 1617 he was a leader of the troupe, then the Palsgrave's company, but in 1618 he retired from the stage, buying himself freedom of the Vintners' Company, marrying the wealthy widow of a vintner, Jane Easton, and taking over the business of running the Red Cross tavern, Clerkenwell. He died in 1625.

DREWE, THOMAS, *c.* 1586 – *c.* 1627. From about 1613, when he was in his later twenties, Drewe was a player with Queen Anne's men at the Red Bull. He claimed to have left the company at the end of 1618, although he appears amongst the players provided with black cloth for Queen Anne's funeral procession in May 1619. Later that year he claimed freedom of the Fishmongers' Company by patrimony, as the son of George Drewe, fishmonger. He remained a member of the company for the remaining seven years until his death, although how active he was in business is not apparent. Also an author and dramatist.

DUTTON, JOHN, *c.* 1548–1614. John Dutton and his brother Lawrence were active in the theatrical world of the 1570s, and retired in the early 1590s. Both were freemen of the Weavers' Company, and had presumably served apprenticeships in the 1560s. John Dutton, probably the younger of the two, was successively a member of Lincoln's, Warwick's, and Oxford's men, and a founding member of the Queen's men in 1583. At his retirement from playing, John Dutton took on administrative positions in the Weavers' Company, indicating he was a man of some wealth and standing.

DUTTON, LAWRENCE, *fl.* 1571–98. Lawrence may have preceded his brother into the business of playing. Associated with Lord Lane's, Lincoln's, Clinton's, Warwick's, and Oxford's troupes over a ten-year period from the early 1570s, Lawrence Dutton joined his brother as a player in the Queen's men in 1589, no doubt repairing the losses of a number of that troupe's initial complement. He does not appear to have taken up the path of bourgeois prosperity pursued by his brother later in life.

ECCLESTON, WILLIAM, 1590–1624>. Hired man with King's company from 1609, playing Kastril in *The Alchemist*, and in *Catiline*; tranferred to Lady Elizabeth's in 1611, returning to King's 1613–14, thereafter appearing in actor lists and other company records until the early 1620s.

EDMONDS, JOHN, *fl.* 1594–1621. Edmonds was apprenticed to Thomas Pope, although probably free of his bonds by 1600; Pope left him a share of clothing and arms in his will of 1603. Edmonds subsequently married another legatee of Pope, Mary Clarke, and thus acquired a share in the Globe. His own career seems patchy. He was named as a joint licensee of the touring group the Children of Bristol in 1618, and he moved in the same circles as the touring players Clay and Hovell: he owed money to Joan Hovell, widow of William, at her death in 1620.

FENN, EZEKIEL, 1620–39>. Fenn played leading female roles with Queen Henrietta's company at the Cockpit from the age of fifteen at the furthest, when he took the role of Sophonisba in *Hannibal and Scipio* (1635). His first male part, four years later, was the subject of a poem by Henry Glapthorne. He was then a member of the King and Queen's Young Company, and probably remained with them until 1642. There are no indications of a continuing theatrical career thereafter.

FIELD, NATHAN, 1587–1620. Field was a thirteen-year-old pupil of St Paul's School under Richard Mulcaster when he was impressed to join the Children of the Chapel, playing in Jonson's *Cynthia's Revels* and *The Poetaster*. Chief player with the Children of the Queen's Revels, his roles included the first Malevole in *The Malcontent*, and Bussy in Chapman's *Bussy D'Ambois*, taken over or reclaimed from the Paul's Boys repertory. Founder member and leading actor of Lady Elizabeth's company, 1613–15; King's company, 1615–19. Among other roles in his last years, played Face in partnership with Burbage's Subtle in *The Alchemist*. Protégé of Ben Jonson; dramatist, poet, and author of at least one prose tract.

FOWLER, RICHARD, *c.* 1585–1643. Fowler was probably a young man when he appeared as a member of the Palsgrave's company at the Fortune in 1618; he was living in Redcross Street, in the playhouse district, in 1623. In 1631 he joined the new company of Prince Charles, playing Snarl in *Holland's Leaguer* at the Salisbury Court playhouse. In the next decade he gained renown at the Red Bull for 'conquering parts', perhaps continuing the tradition of heroic playing in the style of Alleyn, as it had been passed down through the Fortune players.

GARLAND, JOHN, *fl.* 1583–1616. Founder member of Queen's men; may have remained with them for twenty years. Lennox's company by 1605, Duke of York's/Prince Charles's from 1610; played at Norwich in 1615, and retired the year following. He died in 1624, probably at some advanced age (Henslowe had called him 'old Garland' twenty years earlier), and with considerable property in land at Mile End and Stratford.

GOAD, CHRISTOPHER, *fl.* 1630–40. Possibly a member of Queen Henrietta's company before he appears in the cast of *The Fair Maid of the West*, acted in 1630, he acted smaller roles in that play and others. By 1634 he had moved to the King's Revels company, and probably remained with them until 1642.

GOODALE, THOMAS, *c.* 1557–1610>. Goodale was with Berkeley's men in 1581; he took minor parts in *2 Seven Deadly Sins* and *Sir Thomas More*. In 1593 he perhaps had some connection with the Admiral's company, entering a bond, with two other actors, to Edward Alleyn. The son of another Thomas Goodale, mercer, Goodale the player was also a freeman of the Mercers' Company by patrimony.

GOUGH, ALEXANDER, 1614–55>. Son of Robert Gough (below), perhaps Alexander Gough's first stage part was the female role of Caenis in *The Roman Actor*, played when he was twelve. He continued in female roles until he was at least eighteen, when he played the witty female lead, Lillia-Bianca, in a revival of Fletcher's *The Wild-Goose Chase*, opposite Joseph Taylor as Mirabell. Gough remained with the company until 1642, and was engaged in surreptitious playing in the later 1640s. Gough wrote dedications to several plays published in the 1650s.

GOUGH, ROBERT, *fl.* 1590–1625. Gough is named in the plot of *2 Seven Deadly Sins*, whatever the date of that ambiguous document, playing a female role. He was apprenticed for some period to Thomas Pope, who left him a share of arms and 'wearing apparel' in his will, 1603. By 1605 he was the brother-in-law of Augustine Phillips, married to that actor's sister Elizabeth, and he witnessed Phillips's will in May of that year; Gough perhaps succeeded to Phillips's place in the King's company. He played

Memphronius in *The Second Maiden's Tragedy* (1611); he had a minor part in *Sir John van Olden Barnavelt* (1619). In 1621 he became a royal messenger, and in 1624 was sent to summon Thomas Middleton's son, in the absence of the man himself, to answer questions before the Privy Council in the *Game at Chess* affair.

GRADWELL, HENRY, *c.* 1607–51. In 1631 Gradwell played Capritio in *Holland's Leaguer*, as a member of the new troupe, Prince Charles's men. There is no indication that he left the troupe before 1642, but he has no other profile as a player.

GREENE, JOHN, 1578–1626>. John was the younger brother of Thomas Greene (below), the famous clown of the Red Bull. Renowned as a touring actor in Europe, Greene led troupes in company with Robert Browne (2) from 1606, travelling from the Baltic to Austria. A portrait of Greene as 'Nemo', or Nobody, costumed as the figure from the play *Nobody and Somebody*, survives in Austrian archives. In 1617 he was in Prague for the fateful coronation of Elector Frederick as King of Bohemia, and then moved to Vienna; in 1626 he played in Dresden. Received money and a seal ring in the will of his brother Thomas, 1612.

GREENE, THOMAS, 1573–1612. Born at Romford, Essex, the son of John Greene the elder. Worcester's/Queen Anne's men in 1603, playing at the Boar's Head and the Curtain. Married Susan Browne, widow of Robert (1), probably in 1604. Chief investor in the Red Bull playhouse, and leading player there at its opening, *c.* 1605. Popular comedian, renowned as Bubble in *Greene's Tu Quoque*. He had perhaps been engaged in a European tour with his brother immediately before his death in August 1612, since an epigram about him four year later says that he 'new come from sea, made but one face, and died'. His will was witnessed by his colleagues Christopher Beeston, Richard Perkins, and Thomas Heywood.

GREVILLE, CURTIS, *fl.* 1622–34. Greville may have had early connections with either the Palsgrave's or the Lady Elizabeth's companies, but by 1626 he was with the King's men, taking the relatively modest part of Latinus in *The Roman Actor*; his largest known part in his King's career was that of the goldsmith Mountain in *The Soddered Citizen*, *c.* 1630. In 1634 he had moved to the King's Revels troupe at Salisbury Court, where he probably remained until 1642.

GUEST, ELLIS, *fl.* 1625–34. A member of touring troupes, under a variety of names, playing at Norwich, Leicester, and Reading, in the roughly ten-year period defined above.

GUNNELL, RICHARD, *fl.* 1613–34. A player and playwright with the Palsgrave's company at the Fortune, Gunnell moved increasingly into theatre management. As playing at the Fortune became increasingly diffi-cult in the mid 1620s, Gunnell retired from appearing on stage, and with William Blagrave established the Salisbury Court playhouse, and its pro-jected company of trainee boy actors, in 1629. Died intestate, and in some debt, in 1634; his heirs were still attempting to settle his affairs in the 1650s. Friend and associate of Edward Alleyn; none of Gunnell's work as a dramatist has survived.

HALL, WILLIAM, *fl.* 1632–64. William Hall claimed late in his career to have apprenticed with Andrew Cane, although he was never formally bound through the Goldsmiths' Company. He was probably a young man in 1632, when he became Cane's colleague as a member of Prince Charles's troupe. By 1634 he had moved to the King's Revels troupe, and spoke in the Lord Mayor's Show in October of that year. He fought in the civil wars, as a Captain of Foot at Bristol and other places; in 1646 he was with a touring group of players in Paris. After 1660 he had a place in the King's company, and sued them about a pension he felt due to him in 1663–4.

HAMMERTON, STEPHEN, *c.* 1614–48>. Hammerton was born in Yorkshire, and first apprenticed, possibly in his home territory, to the travelling manager William Perry. Perry evidently recognized his talent, brought him to London in 1629, and transferred him, for a price, to William Blagrave, Revels officer and entrepreneur at the Salisbury Court playhouse. The Blackfriars scouts also got wind of Hammerton, and arranged an entirely new London apprenticeship for him, as a merchant taylor, running until late 1639. Thus secured, he began to perform female roles at the Blackfriars: Oriana in *The Wild-Goose Chase* in 1632. By 1640, following his freedom, he was renowned as the handsome *jeune premier*. He signed the dedication to the Beaumont and Fletcher Folio in 1647, and entered a bond for debt, with his colleagues, in the following year.

HART, CHARLES, 1625–83. Probably the son of William Hart, a minor player with the King's company, Hart is supposed to have apprenticed with Richard Robinson, and to have played female parts at the Blackfriars, presumably in the final years of that theatre's career; Hart was not fully seventeen when the theatres were closed. He may have played Euphrasia in *Philaster*. Despite his youth he joined the King's army, in the company of his fellows Burt and Shatterell, rising to the rank of Captain in Prince Rupert's Regiment of Horse. After the surrender of Oxford in 1646, Hart and his fellows travelled to play in Paris, returning to London by 1648 when they entered agreements to revive playing. Hart's principal career began as a leading player of the King's company in 1660, lasting for a further twenty years.

HEMINGES, JOHN, 1566–1630. Born in Droitwich, Worcs., Heminges apprenticed in London as a grocer, from 1578 to 1587. His company affiliation was to be subsequently employed for his attaching a series of apprentices to the playing troupe of which he was long a member (ten, from 1595 to 1628). Heminges's playing career may have begun with the Queen's men (he married the widow of William Knell, *q.v.*); in 1593 he was with Strange's men, and probably moved to the Chamberlain's men at the establishment of that troupe in 1594. He played in all the major Jonson plays staged by the company, taking Corbaccio in *Volpone*, and he must have been a chief player in most of Shakespeare's plays, although we know none of his parts. He retired from playing in the second decade of the seventeenth century, but remained a financial manager of company affairs, and master of apprentices. With Condell, editor of the Shakespeare Folio of 1623, and active parish administrator of St Mary Aldermanbury, London.

HEYWOOD, THOMAS, 1573–1641. Heywood's 'time of residence at Cambridge' probably occurred for a year or two in his teenage years, say around 1590; he did not graduate. His first recorded appearance as a player is in 1598, when he joined the Admiral's men at the Rose playhouse; he began to write plays about the same time. In 1602 he was a sharer with Worcester's men, subsequently Queen Anne's men, and probably did not act after the dissolution of that troupe, finally, in 1619. His friendship with Beeston and Perkins assured that he continued to provide occasional material, as a writer, for the Cockpit throughout the 1630s.

HOBBES, THOMAS, *fl.* 1610–36. Member of Duke of York's/Prince Charles's troupe from 1610. Transferred to King's about 1625; played Calistus in *Believe as You List*, 1631.

HOLCOMBE, THOMAS, *fl.* 1616–25. Holcombe may have begun playing with the King's men, perhaps under the supervision of John Shank, who claimed to have acquired him for the company, before he was formally apprenticed to John Heminges, in 1618, for a term of eight years, which Holcombe did not see out, dying in 1625. That he was rather older than the average apprentice (sixteen at the start of his bonds, say) is indicated by his fathering a child, born in July 1624, and presumably preceded by his marriage, strictly in contravention of his status as apprentice. He is named as a player in six of the Beaumont and Fletcher plays acted during his time with the King's men. His widow Frances remarried to Ellis Worth (*q.v.*) in the year after his death.

HONEYMAN, JOHN, 1613–36. Honeyman was John Shank's boy, and perhaps was new to the King's men when he acted Domitilla in *The Roman Actor* in 1626. He acted female roles until 1629, when he was sixteen; he moved to minor male roles thereafter, and when he was twenty he was sworn as a full member of the company, but his career was brief: in April 1636 he died, and was buried at the church of St Giles Cripplegate.

HOVELL, WILLIAM, 1560–1615. At his death Hovell was an established resident of Southwark, neighbour and tenant of Philip Henslowe, but any evidence of his involvement in London theatre business has yet to appear. He was a touring player, and manager of touring groups: at Norwich in June 1615 with William Perry and Nathan May, and in December, when he made his will, absent from a troupe somewhere on the road which included the actors Nathaniel Clay, John Podger, and another two unnamed sharers (Perry and May?), in addition to Hovell's two apprentices, Michael Bowyer and William Wilson.

JEFFES, ANTONY, 1578–1648. Jeffes began as a boy player, on tour in Germany with Robert Browne (2), 1592–7. He was then with the Admiral's men, and took the parts of Young Mahamet in *The Battle of Alcazar*, and Linus and Moor in *1 Tamar Cam*, at the Fortune in the early 1600s. Within the next decade he retired from playing, buying his freedom of the Brewers' Company in 1605, and becoming active as a brewer for the remaining half of his life.

JEFFES, HUMPHREY, 1576–1618. Older brother of Antony, associated with the Chamberlain's and Pembroke's companies before he joined the Admiral's men in 1597, remaining with them for the rest of his life. With his brother appeared in *The Battle of Alcazar* (Muly Mahamet Xeque) and *1 Tamar Cam* (Otanes).

JEWELL, SIMON, *fl.* >1592. We know very little about Jewell's career, but his will of August 1592 reveals him to have been a member of Pembroke's troupe, and gives information about the sharing and travelling arrangements within that group of actors. He left to his colleague Robert Nichols 'all my playing things in a box and my velvet shoes'.

JOHNSON, WILLIAM, *fl.* 1572–88. Johnson was with Leicester's troupe in the early 1570s, and joined the Queen's men in 1583. In Tarlton's will of 1588 he was appointed one of the wards of Tarlton's young son Philip. Despite this manifestation of trust, Johnson may have been something of a scapegrace, if not without a sense of humour. His illegitimate daughter born in 1587 was christened Comedia.

JOLLY, GEORGE, 1613–>83. Jolly is likely to have begun acting with Prince Charles's company in the 1630s: by 1640 he is identified in parish records as a 'player' living in the house of his probable fellow Matthew Smith. Within the next few years, following the outbreak of war, he embarked on a remarkable career of European touring as an actor-manager that lasted until the Restoration. He evidently learnt German, at latest by the 1650s, and hired German performers for his troupes, both men and women. Returning to London in 1660, he was remarkably rewarded with a third royal patent to run a company, contested by the other patentees, Killigrew and Davenant: the compromise was that Jolly was to run the training theatre, the Nursery. In fact, Jolly seems to have thrown himself into provincial touring, playing frequently at Norwich, and to have remained in harness until his death.

JONES, RICHARD, *fl.* 1583–1624. With Worcester's company in 1583; travelled with Robert Browne (2) in the Netherlands and Germany, 1592–3. Admiral's 1594–5; period with Pembroke's; returned to Admiral's 1597–1602. From 1615 in Germany, in Warsaw 1617 as a musician; in 1622 employed in the court of the Duke of Wolgast as a musician. Returned to England in 1623, but was seeking return to Germany in the following year.

JONSON, BEN, 1572–1637. Jonson's career as a player was brief. An unreliable account of it was given by John Aubrey; probably Jonson was a minor player with the Admiral's or Pembroke's company (or both) in 1597–8. In September 1598 he fought a duel with the player Gabriel Spencer, then a chief member of the Admiral's, and killed him: Jonson was ultimately pardoned. His playing was retired for full-time writing with the success of the *Humour* plays for the Chamberlain's men in 1598 and 1599.

JORDAN, THOMAS, *c.* 1614–85. Jordan was associated with the King's Revels troupe, and played Lepida, Messalina's mother, in Richards's *Messalina*, *c.* 1634, and Captain Penniless in his own play *Money is an Ass*, *c.* 1635; he was with a group of touring players at Norwich in 1635. He may have moved to the theatre in Dublin in the late 1630s to early 1640s, and possibly was involved in some surreptitious interregnum performance in London. A poet and pageant writer as well as dramatist, Jordan's chief success came after the Restoration: he devised the Lord Mayor's Shows from 1671 to 1684.

JUBY, EDWARD, *fl.* 1594–1618. Juby was a founder member of the reconstituted Admiral's men, probably then a young man, and died shortly after signing a renewed lease on the Fortune playhouse as a member of the Palsgrave's men. He was the King in *Frederick and Basilea*, Bessa and Avero in *The Battle of Alcazar*, and Pitho and a Moor in *1 Tamar Cam*.

KEMP, WILLIAM, *fl.* 1585–1602. A legendary entertainer of the late sixteenth century, Kemp remained his own man, avoiding prolonged association with any one company of fellow players. In 1585 he was a comic player in the Earl of Leicester's household, and accompanied his patron on the expedition to the Netherlands in 1585–6. Later in 1586 he was in Denmark, in the court of Frederick II. Only in 1592–4 is he traceable again in London, when he played with Strange's men, joining the Chamberlain's company at its foundation in 1594, remaining with them for five years, and playing a number of Shakespearean comic roles. In February–March 1600 he danced his famous morris dance from London to Norwich; in 1601 he travelled through Germany and Italy to Rome, perhaps leading a troupe of players for some of the time. In 1602 he was back in London and joined Worcester's men, but was not a member of the troupe after that year. He may have died in 1603, but his evident elusiveness throughout his life renders that conclusion tentative. Author of numerous jigs, in print by 1596; dramatized as a character, with Burbage, in *2 Return to Parnassus*, Cambridge, *c.* 1600.

KENDALL, WILLIAM, *fl.* 1597–1615. Kendall joined the Admiral's troupe as a hired man in late 1597, and may have continued in that position for another couple of decades; his name never appears in the successive company licences. He played several parts in *The Battle of Alcazar*, and was, it seems, challenged by William Fennor to an improvisation contest at the Fortune playhouse about 1614, in which he chose not to engage.

KNELL, WILLIAM, *fl.* 1583–7. Knell was probably a founder member of the Queen's men, and played heroic parts in their plays: he was fairly certainly the title character in *The Famous Victories of Henry V*. Like his colleague Bentley, Knell wielded his sword off stage as well as on, but with results fatal to himself. He was killed in a quarrel with his colleague John Towne, on tour at Thame, Oxon., in June 1587; the jury ruled that Towne had acted in self-defence. Knell's widow Rebecca remarried to John Heminges in March 1588.

LACY, JOHN, *c.* 1615–81. Born near Doncaster, Yorks., Lacy went to London in 1631 as the apprentice of John Ogilby, then in business as a dancing master. He was with the Young Company at the Cockpit by 1639, and probably stayed with them until 1642. During the wars Lacy served as lieutenant and quartermaster in the regiment of the Earl of Macclesfield, campaigning particularly in South Wales in 1644–5. Lacy had a prominent career as a comic actor and dancer with the King's company from 1660, as well as being a successful playwright. He is supposed to have known Ben Jonson during the playwright's final years, and advised him on northern dialect.

LANEHAM, JOHN, *fl.* 1572–91. Laneham was with Leicester's players from at least 1572 to 1574. He joined the Queen's men at their foundation in 1583 and was with them until at least 1591. He was a witness to his colleague John Bentley's will in August 1585.

LEE, ROBERT, *c.* 1569–1629. Lee was perhaps with Strange's men as a young actor in 1590, possibly had some connection with the Admiral's in the later nineties, but joined Worcester's/Queen Anne's troupe soon afterwards, and led a touring branch of the company between 1616 and 1623, as well as playing at the Red Bull and at court. His will reveals that he was related by marriage to his former colleague Richard Baxter (*q.v.*)

LONG, NICHOLAS, *fl.* 1612–22. Long probably apprenticed with William Hovell (*q.v.*), who called him 'sometime my servant' in his will of 1615, and released him from debt. Like Hovell, Long specialized in leading touring troupes in association with various other individuals, bearing the names of the Queen's Revels and Lady Elizabeth's, possibly flags of convenience for shifting personnel. Buried at St Giles Cripplegate, London, as a 'player', in February 1622.

LOVEDAY, THOMAS, *c.* 1616–65>. Loveday was with the King's Revels troupe by 1635, when he visited Norwich to play. A contemporary of Thomas Jordan, he appeared as Clutch in that actor's *Money is an Ass*, *c.* 1635. In 1644 he was with a troupe of English players at the Hague, and in London, joining a player's agreement, in 1648. In 1660 a founder member of the King's company.

LOWIN, JOHN, 1576–1653. Lowin had one of the longest and most distinguished careers in the Shakespearean period. A friend of Alleyn and Burbage, he was an accomplished player in his own right, with a style he could modulate to take in parts from Sir Epicure Mammon in *The Alchemist* to Bosola in *The Duchess of Malfi*. Apprenticed as a goldsmith in 1593, he joined Worcester's company as a player in 1602, after his bonds were served. Though his freedom was never registered, that he was regarded as a member of the Goldsmiths' Company is indicated by his performance as Leofstan in the Goldsmiths' Lord Mayor's pageant *Chrusothriambos* in 1611. He was with the King's company by 1603, taking a part in *Sejanus*. Lowin continued to act until 1642, and at least once after that date, when he was arrested in 1648, but in the 1630s he assumed, with Taylor, more of the leadership and management of the company. The story retailed by James Wright in *Historia Histrionica* that Lowin died poor as an innkeeper in Brentford, Middx., is hard to credit; Lowin should have made a good deal of money from his shares in the company and its playhouses. He was, at least, buried in London, at the church of St Clement Danes in August 1653.

MANNERY, SAMUEL, *c.* 1615–48. As the orphaned son of Nicholas Mannery, gentleman, Samuel Mannery was apprenticed to Thomas Goodwin, farrier, for a nine-year term in 1629. Goodwin practised as a musician, and may have been connected to the Salisbury Court playhouse, where Mannery appeared as the Bawd, a female role, in *Holland's Leaguer* in late 1631. Following the period of his service to Goodwin, Mannery joined the Young Company at the Cockpit, by 1639, and probably remained with them for the remaining three years of theatrical activity.

MARBECK, THOMAS, 1577–1603>. With Admiral's in 1602, and may have remained with the troupe as a minor player. Married the widow of Richard Alleyn (*q.v.*) in 1602.

MASSEY, CHARLES, *fl.* 1597–1625. Massey played Tamar in *Frederick and Basilea* with the Admiral's men in 1597, and became a sharer the following year, continuing with the troupe under its various titles to the end of his life. Shareholder in the Fortune playhouse, friend of Alleyn, and playwright: none of his work survives. Probably a victim of the virulent plague outbreak of 1625, he died in the parish of St Giles Cripplegate, and was buried at the church.

MAY, EDWARD, *fl.* 1631–41. May took the role of Fidelio in *Holland's Leaguer* in 1631, a reasonably large part that indicates he was by then an established actor, but he does not subsequently appear among the men sworn as the Prince's players in May 1632. By 1635 he appears to have joined the King's Revels company; possibly the author of commendatory verses addressed to Thomas Jordan, then a colleague, in 1637.

MOHUN, MICHAEL, *c.* 1620–84. By his own account, Mohun began acting in 1634, probably playing female roles with Queen Henrietta's men at the Cockpit, and joining the Young Company in 1637, graduating to male roles, including, by report, Bellamente in Shirley's *Love's Cruelty*. In 1642 he became a soldier, and had a distinguished military career, was wounded and twice imprisoned, and emerged from the conflict as Major Mohun, a title he retained in his Restoration career on the stage. Performing again in exile in the Netherlands in 1659, Mohun returned to London late in that year, began acting with the King's company, and was a distinguished principal player until late in his life.

MOORE, JOSEPH, *fl.* 1611–40. With Lady Elizabeth's company from 1611, largely with a touring branch, it appears. About 1620 he temporarily withdrew from active playing, running an inn in Chichester, but was with the troupe at the Cockpit in 1622, and acting, we may suppose, in *The Changeling*, performed in that year. He continued to lead touring groups for the next decade. By 1635, at the latest, he had joined Prince Charles's company, and assumed a leading role, with Cane and Worth, in company affairs from that date onwards.

MUNDAY, ANTHONY, 1560–1633. Like Jonson's, Munday's career as a player was neither long nor successful, but he appears to have tried playing in his early twenties, after beginning as a printer's apprentice and then travelling to Rome. There is no indication of Munday's affiliation with a troupe. A decade later he was a chief collaborating dramatist, with a variety of other writers, in supplying plays to the Admiral's men; from 1605 he was the deviser of a series of Lord Mayor's Shows. Also writer in a variety of other genres.

NEWTON, JOHN, 1584?–1625? In 1610 Newton was a member of the Duke of York's/Prince Charles's men. In 1611 he was playing at the Boar's Head and Curtain playhouses, by his own representation earning a pound a week: no small sum. In the same year he married the widow Joan Waters at the church of St James Clerkenwell, perhaps not with her entirely free consent. In early 1619 he took the role of 'A Fasting Day', 'a lean, spiny, rascal' in Middleton's *Masque of Heroes*, performed at the Inner Temple, in company with his fellows Hugh Attwell, William Rowley, and Joseph Taylor. Possibly a victim of the 1625 plague, although the extant burial record at St Giles Cripplegate (3 August) names 'William Newton Player', otherwise unknown.

OSTLER, WILLIAM, *c.* 1588–1614. Ostler was a member of the Children of the Chapel by 1601, performing in *The Poetaster*, and as a member of the Queen's Revels in Jonson's entertainment *The Key Keeper*, performed at the opening of the New Exchange in 1609. With the King's men in 1610, playing in *The Alchemist*; he was recorded as a cast member of various other plays, and played the first Antonio in *The Duchess of Malfi*. He married John Heminges's daughter Thomasine in 1611, living in the parish of St Mary Aldermanbury, hence perhaps as part of Heminges's extended household. Buried at the church in December 1614. Celebrated as 'the Roscius of these Times' in verses by John Davies, 1611.

PALLANT, ROBERT, *fl.* 1590–1619. Pallant appears to have been something of a freelance actor, without a major stake in any company: with Strange's men about 1590, Worcester's in 1602, and a variety of companies 1603–19. Friend of Heywood, contributing commendatory verses to *An Apology for Actors*, 1612; visited Philip Henslowe on his deathbed, January 1616.

PALLANT, ROBERT, JR, 1605–24>. The son of the elder Robert Pallant, christened at St Saviour Southwark on 28 September 1605. In February 1620, after his father's death, he was apprenticed as a grocer to John Heminges, for an eight-year term. He played Cariola in a revival of *The Duchess of Malfi* within the next three years. No other records of his career survive, although he was still with the King's men, as we would expect, in 1624.

PARR, WILLIAM, *fl.* 1602–20. A member of the Admiral's troupe in 1602, Parr remained with the troupe until at least 1620. Minor roles in *1 Tamar Cam*; friend of Edward Alleyn.

PATRICK, WILLIAM, *fl.* 1622–36. There were two William Patricks, father and son, active in the King's men, and it is difficult to disentangle the records about them in the 1630s, although they mostly seem to refer to Patrick senior. The older William Patrick, a hired actor, played Palphurius Sura in *The Roman Actor*, 1624, and had three parts, possibly, in *Believe as You List*, 1631; he is listed in players' passes in 1636, and may have played in *Philaster* in the early 1640s.

PATRICK, WILLIAM, JR, *c.* 1616–40>. Patrick was the last of Heminges's apprentices, bound for a term of twelve years in 1628, which extended beyond his master's death two years later, and would have been subject to some kind of renegotiation. He perhaps stayed with the company under other formal supervision, apart from that which might have been offered by his father.

PAVY, SALOMON, 1588–1602. Pavy was supposed to have been recruited to the Chapel children from an apprenticeship, *c.* 1600; he played in *Cynthia's Revels* and *The Poetaster*. His death, 'scarce thirteen', in 1602 was immortalized in Ben Jonson's 'Epitaph on S. P.' (1616).

PENN, WILLIAM, *fl.* 1609–36. Penn began with the Queen's Revels troupe, and was in the cast of *Epicoene* in 1609. Prince Charles's company, 1616–25. King's from 1625; played Julio Baptista in Massinger's *The Picture*, 1629, two parts in *Believe as You List*, and Clephis in *The Swisser*, both 1631. In the 1632 revival of *The Wild-Goose Chase* he played Nantolet.

PENNYCUICKE, ANDREW, 1620–58>. Reconstruction of Pennycuicke's career has to be based largely on his own assertions in dedications to plays published in the 1650s, which are not entirely consistent. It seems most likely that he had been an apprentice with Queen Henrietta's troupe in the early 1630s, and passed to the Young Company in 1637; he appears to have known Theophilus Bird. In his dedication to Davenport's *King John and Matilda*, published 1655, he claims to have played the second title role, of some 166 lines, which is unassigned in the actor list; if he premiered in the part he is likely to have been between twelve and fourteen at the time.

PERKINS, RICHARD, *c.* 1579–1650. A leading player with at least forty-two years on the stage, Perkins was attached to Edward Alleyn to play at the Rose with the Admiral's men for three years from November 1596; the following April Perkins left to play at the Swan, with Pembroke's company. Alleyn sued him, and won judgement; whether Perkins returned, as the law required him to, remains moot, although the fragmentation of the players at the Swan in later 1597 makes it likely that he rejoined the Admiral's. By 1602, as an independent adult, Perkins was with Worcester's men, and remained with that troupe until it dissolved, 1617–19. He probably played Flamineo in Webster's *The White Devil* at the Red Bull in 1612, and was praised by the author in the published text. Perkins continued to play at the Bull through the early 1620s, and may briefly, 1623–5, have moved to the King's men – the records remain rather puzzling. In 1625 he certainly joined the newly established Queen Henrietta's company at the Cockpit as a leading player, and remained there for a dozen years, taking several identifiable parts, reviving Marlowe's Barabas in the early 1630s. His final years on stage were spent as a member of the reorganized Queen's troupe playing at Salisbury Court. He lived in retirement for eight years, aided by an annuity left to him by his colleague Michael Bowyer; it was probably in that period that his portrait, now at Dulwich, was made.

PERRY, WILLIAM, *c*. 1580–1648. Perry is called a player in various records, but it is not clear that he ever was; rather he seems to have been a leader and manager of touring troupes of largely young players. He apprenticed in London as a draper, and became free in 1604. His own apprentices became part of the touring Lady Elizabeth's company active in 1613, of which Perry held a share of the patent, and the company was reincarnated under another name in 1617. In 1629 he was granted a licence for a touring group called the Red Bull company, and he continued to tour, from York to Canterbury, through the 1630s. Perry's activities in Yorkshire no doubt led to his recruitment of Stephen Hammerton in 1629, transferred to William Blagrave for the Salisbury Court boy troupe. In 1641 he seems to have tried his luck at the Werburgh Street playhouse in Dublin, but was back in England the following year. He died poor, if he was the William Perry buried at St James Clerkenwell in June 1648.

PHILLIPS, AUGUSTINE, *fl.* 1590–1605. Strange's men from the early 1590s; probably a founding member of the new Chamberlain's men in 1594, and remained with the troupe to his death. Sardanapalus in *2 Seven Deadly Sins*, in the cast of Jonson's two *Humour* plays, 1598 and 1599, and presumably played in the Richard II play at the Globe, 'old and long out of use', commissioned by conspirators in the Essex rebellion, February 1601, on the circumstances of which he subsequently testified to the conciliar enquiry. He was in the cast of *Sejanus* in 1603. Author of 'Phillips's Jig of the Slippers', entered in the Stationers' Register 1595. His will of May 1605 leaves money to several colleagues, including Shakespeare, and 'my servant' Christopher Beeston. Samuel Gilburne 'my late apprentice' was willed clothing, Phillips's sword and dagger, and a bass viol; James Sands, his current apprentice, was to have his cittern, bandore, and lute, once he had served his years. The training of a player involved more than action and accent.

PIG, JOHN, *fl.* 1593–9. Boy apprentice with Edward Alleyn, Strange's and Admiral's companies. Touring with Alleyn in 1593; played title role in *Alice Pierce*, 1597, Andreo in *Frederick and Basilea*, unspecified role in *Troilus and Cressida* (*c.* 1599 – not the Shakespeare play).

PODGER, JOHN, *fl.* 1615. Possibly of Devonshire origin and born in the 1580s, Podger was a fellow player in the provincial troupe to which William Hovell (*q.v.*) was also attached. In his will Hovell left jointly to Podger and his colleague Nathaniel Clay his share in the troupe's costume stock, and a horse, which probably carried the costume basket. Podger's obscurity is a reminder of the many players who did not cast a shadow in official records.

POLLARD, THOMAS, 1597–1653. Pollard was born in Aylesbury, Bucks., and became an apprentice to John Shank, possibly around 1610, when Shank was with Prince Henry's/Palsgrave's company. Shank moved to the King's men by 1616, and Pollard with him. Pollard's name appears in numerous casts from that date onwards; he was presumably free of his bonds around 1618, and rose in the ranks of the company thereafter; he was a sharer by 1624. His named roles are Silvio in *The Duchess of Malfi*, Aelius Lamia and Stephanos in *The Roman Actor*, Ubaldo in *The Picture*, Brainsick in *The Soddered Citizen*, Berecinthius in *Believe as You List*, Timentes in *The Swisser*, Pinac in *The Wild-Goose Chase*, and the speaker of the epilogue to *The Cardinal*. He also appears to have taken the title part in Fletcher's *The Humorous Lieutenant*, possibly from its first production (1619), and may have played Pharamond in *Philaster*. His reputation as a witty comic performer seems to have been cultivated off stage as well as on: about 1633 he belonged to a circle of wits and drinkers called 'The Order of the Fancy'. He remained active in company business up to the late 1640s, a member of the group attempting to revive King's playing, and among the cast of *Rollo* arrested at the Cockpit in 1648. Theophilus Bird later claimed that Pollard died rich, partly as a result of misappropriating company stock after 1642. Pollard's estate, at least, was willed to his younger sister, Anne Perrin.

POPE, THOMAS, *fl.* 1586–1603. Visiting player in Denmark and Germany, 1586–7. Strange's men 1593, Chamberlain's from 1594. Arbactus in *2 Seven Deadly Sins*; in the casts of Jonson's *Humour* plays, 1598 and 1599; apparently clown roles were within his range. Held shares in the Curtain and Globe playhouses; willed his apparel and arms jointly to his former apprentices Robert Gough and John Edmonds.

PRICE, RICHARD, *fl.* 1610–27. Price spent his entire career playing at the Fortune theatre (or theatres, since the building was burnt and rebuilt in 1622), as a member of Prince Henry's troupe and its successors. In 1623 he was living in White Cross Street, near the playhouse.

PULHAM, GEORGE, 1579–1611. Born near Stowmarket, Suffolk, member and sharer of Queen Anne's troupe at his death, he had perhaps been a player for a decade or so. He names 'my trusty friend' Christopher Beeston his executor in his will of May 1611. He was godfather of Beeston's son Robert, to whom he left money, as he did to Beeston's other children and to the daughters of Robert Browne (2).

READE, EMANUEL, *fl.* 1613–17. Lady Elizabeth's in 1613, when he had parts in *The Coxcomb* and *The Honest Man's Fortune*; Queen Anne's by 1616. Friend of Christopher Beeston. Moved to Ireland *c.* 1617, and abandoned playing.

READE, TIMOTHY, 1606?–>54. A renowned comic actor by the 1630s, Reade began with Queen Henrietta's company as a boy or youth, playing the female role of Cardona in Shirley's *The Wedding* in 1626, and stayed with the company after they moved to Salisbury Court in 1637. Reade apparently took over the part of Antonio in *The Changeling*, and practised some of the old gags of Tarlton's generation. In the prologue to Goffe's *The Careless Shepherdess* (1638?) a staged audience member called Thrift remarks 'I never saw Reade peeping through the curtain / But ravishing joy entered my heart.' Reade was arrested at a surreptitious performance of *A King and No King* at Salisbury Court in 1647 (playing Bessus, perhaps?). He died within the next few years.

REASON, GILBERT, *fl.* 1610–25. Duke of York's/Prince Charles's men; touring with provincial branch of the company 1617–25. His name appears, cast as a Priest of the Sun, in a theatrically marked copy of the old play *A Looking Glass for London and England*, perhaps played on tour between the above dates.

REEVE, RALPH, *fl.* 1603–17. Reeve led a troupe of players in Germany, 1603–9. In 1611 he led a touring branch of the Children of the Queen's Revels; he was acquainted with several people in the management of that company. He was involved in the abortive scheme to build a new playhouse at Puddle Wharf, Porter's Hall, 1613–17, with Philip Rossiter and Philip Kingman. The King's player Robert Benfield was his 'dear friend', and made executor of his will in 1617; Kingman was a witness.

REYNOLDS, ROBERT, *c.* 1590–1640>. Reynolds married Jane Browne, daughter of Robert Browne (2), 20 November 1614, at the church of St Michael Cornhill, London. He was perhaps by then a member of Queen Anne's company, from which he withdrew in 1617; by then he had begun to tour in Germany with his father-in-law. He also joined with John Greene, but by the later 1620s had established himself as a leader, and was playing in German. His great success was the clown character Pickleherring (Pickelhäring), who could 'twist [his] face in a thousand ways'.

RICE, JOHN, 1590?–1630>. John Rice was called 'a very proper child' when, dressed as an angel, he delivered a speech by Ben Jonson at an entertainment for the King in Merchant Taylors' Hall in 1607. He could not have been a particularly young child, however, since by 1611 he had left his apprenticeship with the King's men to join Lady Elizabeth's company as an adult player. He is likely to have been one of those youthful actors who had a long career in female roles, since in 1610 he floated on the River Thames, in the company of Richard Burbage as Amphion, as the 'fair and beautiful nymph' Corinea, in a welcoming ceremony for Prince Henry. He had rejoined the King's men by 1619, taking two roles in *Sir John van Olden Barnavelt* and playing the Marquis of Pescara in *The Duchess of Malfi*'s revival. He was with the company for ten years, but then took holy orders. He received a bequest in John Heminges's will as 'clerk of St. Saviour's'; as a 'loving friend' of Heminges he was also made, with Cuthbert Burbage, an overseer of the will. The friendship extended over at least twenty-three years: Heminges had directed Rice in his angelic address to King James.

ROBINS, WILLIAM, *fl.* 1616–45. Occasionally called Robinson, leading to confusion with other players of that name. Queen Anne's 1616–19; continued with the regrouped company of the Revels at the Red Bull; on tour in 1625. Joined Queen Henrietta's company in 1625, and remained until 1636, after which he joined the King's men. Renowned as a comic player by the 1620s. Played Carazie in *The Renegado*, Rawbone in *The Wedding*, Clem in *1* and *2 The Fair Maid of the West*, and probably Antonio in *The Changeling*. He and his wife Cicely (née Sands) were willed memorial rings by the player Thomas Basse in 1634. It was Robins who as 'Major Robinson' was killed by Parliamentary forces in the taking of Basing House, Hampshire, in October 1645, as was his son.

ROBINSON, JOHN, *fl.* 1634–41. Most of career with King's Revels company at Salisbury Court and Fortune playhouses; may have moved to Prince Charles's in 1640 when that company tranferred to the Fortune. Saufellus in *Messalina*, *c.* 1634; contributed verses 'to his friend Mr. Nathaniel Richards', the author, in the published text of the play, 1640. Married Elizabeth, widow of Richard Gunnell, after 1634, with whom he had a son, John; his nuncupative will of April 1641 was given in the presence of Richard Fowler and Roger Nore, two players with Prince Charles's men.

ROBINSON, RICHARD, *c.* 1596–1648. Robinson was probably Richard Burbage's apprentice, and was with the King's men from at least 1611, when he acted the Lady in *The Second Maiden's Tragedy*. His fame as a female-role specialist was celebrated by Ben Jonson in *The Devil is an Ass* (1616), a King's play in which Robinson no doubt had a part. In March 1619, by which time he was likely free of his bonds, he witnessed Richard Burbage's will, and three and a half years later he married Winifred, Burbage's widow (31 October 1622, church of St Mary Magdalene, Old Fish Street, London), inheriting such wealth and shares as Burbage had passed to his wife. The family remained living in traditional Burbage territory, in Shoreditch. Robinson played the Cardinal in the revival of *The Duchess of Malfi*, Aesopus in *The Roman Actor*, Count Orsinio and a Hermit in *The Deserving Favourite*, Lentulus in *Believe as You List*, and LaCastre in *The Wild-Goose Chase*. Charles Hart, by report, was his apprentice at the end of Robinson's career.

ROGERS, EDWARD, *fl.* 1625–6. Boy player with Queen Henrietta's men in opening seasons: Donusa in *The Renegado* and Millicent in *The Wedding*.

ROWLEY, SAMUEL, *c.* 1575–1624. Samuel and William Rowley were brothers, Samuel probably the elder. From 1597–1613 Samuel Rowley was a player with the Admiral's men and their successors: parts in *Frederick and Basilea*, *Fortune's Tennis*, *The Battle of Alcazar*, and *1 Tamar Cam*. Author of *When You See Me You Know Me* (1604), in which he no doubt played, and of several plays for the Palsgrave's troupe in the earlier 1620s. Married to Alice Coley in 1594, he lived in the Whitechapel district for much of his life; willed land and leases to his family, including a married daughter aged twenty-four.

ROWLEY, WILLIAM, *c.* 1585–1626. Willed 'all my books' by his (elder?) brother Samuel in 1624, William Rowley may have begun playing with Queen Anne's troupe about 1607, but first appears in records as a player in 1609 with the Duke of York's company, and he stayed with Prince Charles's company until 1621; by 1623 with King's. Known for fat, clownish parts; probably Rowley himself was of some girth. Played Plumporridge in Middleton's *Masque of Heroes* (Inner Temple), Jaques in his own play *All's Lost by Lust*, and the Fat Bishop in *A Game at Chess*. Playwright, alone and in collaboration (e.g., with Middleton on *The Changeling*), from 1607 until his death. Died February 1626 in Clerkenwell, leaving a widow, Grace.

SACKVILLE, THOMAS, *fl.* 1592–1628. Sackville's principal career as a player was conducted as a touring actor in Germany and elsewhere in Europe, for about fifteen years. In 1592 he was in a troupe led by Robert Browne (2), and in 1597 at Wolfenbüttel, in the court of Duke Henry Julius.

Specializing in a clown role, called John Bouset, Sackville played in various German cities over the next several years, and evidently prospered. By 1608, when Thomas Coryat encountered him at the Frankfurt fair, he had entered the business of a merchant and goldsmith, and ceased playing. He remained in Germany to his death.

SAVILLE, ARTHUR, 1617–39>. Saville was apprenticed to Andrew Cane (*q.v.*) in August 1631 for a term of eight years. He played Quartilla in *Holland's Leaguer* later in that year, and presumably continued to take other roles in Prince Charles's company's plays in subsequent years. He was freed as a goldsmith in 1639, and appears to have had no further theatrical career.

SHAKESPEARE, WILLIAM, 1564–1616. Shakespeare's beginnings as a player are the stuff of myth rather than verifiable fact. He may have been a member of Strange's, Pembroke's, and Sussex's companies between 1592 and 1594, a period of some fluidity in company affiliations, and seems to have been among the founding group of the Chamberlain's men in 1594. He was certainly in the cast of *Every Man In His Humour* in 1598, and of *Every Man Out of His Humour* in 1599: he was also in *Sejanus* in 1603. He is listed first, above Burbage, in the list of 'principal actors' in his own plays in the 1623 Folio. Otherwise we have no reliable indication of the parts he took nor of how soon he withdrew from stage playing, which he did within the first Jacobean decade.

SHANK, JOHN, *c.* 1570–1636. Shank described himself as a freeman of the Weavers' Company, though we have no indications of when or under whom he apprenticed. By his own account he had been a member at the start of his career of the Queen's and Pembroke's companies; by 1610 he was with Prince Henry's men, and transferred to the King's men *c.* 1613. Old enough to have observed Tarlton on stage, Shank was known for his clowning and performance of jigs and themes, although his style may have changed about 1612, when verses about the theatres and their players announced that Shank had given up singing 'his rhymes'. His identifiable parts with the King's men are not very revealing; he was Hilario in *The Picture*, Hodge in *The Soddered Citizen*, and possibly a Servant in *The Wild-Goose Chase*. He trained or recruited several apprentices, including Pollard, Thompson, Honeyman, Holcombe, Trigge, and, by report, Burt. Shareholder in the Blackfriars and Globe; playwright and author of jigs. A long-time resident of the parish of St Giles Cripplegate, he was buried at the church in January 1636.

SHANK, JOHN, JR, 1616–55. Son of John Shank senior, above. A member of the touring Red Bull company in 1635, joined Prince Charles's troupe in 1640, playing at the Fortune. 'Lieutenant Shanks' was in the

Parliamentary, rather than Royalist, forces in October 1642, but not whole-heartedly: he was imprisoned for deserting a skirmish.

SHARPE, RICHARD, *c.* 1600–32. Apprenticed to John Heminges for an eight-year term in early 1616, Sharpe played the title role in the revival of *The Duchess of Malfi* (between 1620 and 1623), and was thus playing female roles in the Fletcher plays in the actor lists among which his name appears from 1616 onwards. Free of his bonds in early 1624, he became a sharer in the King's company, playing Parthenius in *The Roman Actor*, Ferdinand in *The Picture*, Lysander in *The Deserving Favourite*, Witworth in *The Soddered Citizen*, and King of the Lombards in *The Swisser*.

SHATTERELL, EDWARD, 1620–64>. Younger brother of Robert Shatterell, below. There are no records of the younger Shatterell's playing in London before 1642, but he may have done so, since in 1644–5 he was a member of a touring troupe of English players at the Hague. In May 1659, rather jumping the gun on the resumption of playing, Shatterell and Anthony Turner were charged with 'the unlawful maintaining of stage plays and interludes' at the old Red Bull playhouse. With his brother he became a member of the King's company in 1660, but did not have a prominent or long-lasting career.

SHATTERELL, ROBERT, 1616–1684. Possibly the more talented of the two Shatterell brothers, Robert perhaps began as a boy player with Queen Henrietta's company in the early 1630s; married in 1634, in 1639 he was with the Young Company at the Cockpit, a colleague of Burt and Mohun. With Burt and Hart he served in Prince Rupert's Regiment of Horse during the wars in England, effectively over in 1646. Later that same year Shatterell, with Hart, was in a troupe under Prince Charles's patronage playing in Paris. By 1648 they had both returned to London, and entered into agreements planned to revive playing. Shatterell was at the Cockpit in the period immediately following the resumption of playing in 1660, and then became a member of the King's company, with numerous prominent roles, remaining a sharer until 1680.

SHAW, ROBERT, *fl.* 1597–1603. Shaw was with Pembroke's men at the Swan in 1597; by November, with his colleagues, all of whom had long professed 'the art of stage playing', in a dispute with the owner, Francis Langley. Shaw joined the Admiral's men at the Rose, and stayed with them until 1602. Possibly a playwright; certainly in possession of at least one playbook, offered on option to Admiral's, 1602.

SHERLOCK, WILLIAM, *fl.* 1616–38. Possibly first an apprentice of Christopher Beeston, Sherlock was in residence as keeper of the Cockpit from some time close to the establishment of that theatre; he was probably born in the early 1590s. By 1622 he was a chief player in Lady Elizabeth's company, and probably joined Queen Henrietta's company at its inception, and was a leader of the troupe by 1634. In 1637 he moved with the restructured company to Salisbury Court, and probably remained with them until 1642. His identifiable roles are Lodam in *The Wedding*, Ruffman in *1* and *2 The Fair Maid of the West*, Brand in *King John and Matilda*, and Maharbal in *Hannibal and Scipio*.

SINCLER, JOHN, *fl.* 1590–1604. Early associations with Strange's and Pembroke's companies; probably a founding member of the Chamberlain's men in 1594, remaining for a period of ten years but never becoming particularly prominent. Appeared in *2 Seven Deadly Sins, 3 Henry VI, The Taming of the Shrew*, and *2 Henry IV*; he played a naïve member of the audience in the 1604 Induction to *The Malcontent*, but his name does not appear in the actor lists of any of the Jonson plays.

SINGER, JOHN, *fl.* 1583–1611. Possibly a player by the early 1570s, and hence born roughly twenty years earlier, Singer was in the founding group of the Queen's men in 1583, and with them at Norwich that summer, in a costume of a black doublet and 'with a player's beard upon his face', joining John Bentley in a fatal attack on a riotous member of the audience at the Red Lion inn. In 1594 he joined the Admiral's troupe, and was with them until 1603 when he appears to have taken a court post as Groom of the Chamber. Played in *Fortune's Tennis* and *1 Tamar Cam*. Linked by Dekker with Tarlton and Kemp, Singer had a reputation as a stage fool or clown, speaking 'boorish'. Author of at least one play, 1603.

SLATER, MARTIN, *c.* 1560–1625>. Slater was apprenticed as an iron-monger to Richard Smith in 1581, and freed in 1587. He continued to pay quarterage dues to the Ironmongers' Company for the rest of his life. He perhaps became a player soon after attaining his freedom, and for a number of years seems to have been averse to prolonged association with any one troupe: he joined the Admiral's company in 1594 and stayed with them until 1597. In 1599 he was in Scotland in some kind of association with the player Lawrence Fletcher, who subsequently joined the King's men. In 1603 he was in London performing with Hertford's troupe, and in 1606 he was with a touring branch of Queen Anne's company, not entirely, it appears, with the approval of Thomas Greene, then running the main troupe in London; Slater was one of the sharers in the new Red Bull playhouse. In 1608 he was part of the management of the Children of the Queen's Revels at Whitefriars, and was named as a patentee of the Children of Bristol in 1618. For the next seven years Slater toured with a troupe using the name of (the late) Queen Anne as patron.

SLY, WILLIAM, *fl.* 1590–1608. Strange's men *c.*1590–4; appeared in *2 Seven Deadly Sins*. Probably founding member of the Chamberlain's company of 1594, remaining with them to his death. Appears in the actor lists of both Jonson's *Humour* plays, *Sejanus*, and *Volpone*, and in that of the players of Shakespeare in the 1623 Folio. Played a foolish audience member in the 1604 Induction to *The Malcontent*, looking for the famous Globe actors, including himself. His will of August 1608 demonstrates a close relationship with the family of Robert Browne (2); Cicely Browne was his executrix, and Robert was left his share in the Globe.

SMITH, ANTHONY, *fl.* 1616–31. Smith was with Prince Charles's company in 1616, but ten years later was with the King's men as a hired actor playing smaller roles. He was Philargus in *The Roman Actor*, Gerard in *The Deserving Favourite*, Clutch in *The Soddered Citizen*, and Asprandus in *The Swisser*.

SMITH, MATTHEW, *fl.* 1631–42. An established actor with the King and Queen of Bohemia's company by 1631, Smith had probably been playing with them at the Fortune playhouse for at least a year or two beforehand. In later 1631 he joined the newly formed Prince Charles's troupe at the Salisbury Court playhouse, taking the role of Agurtes in *Holland's Leaguer*, and remaining with the troupe as a principal player in their subsequent moves to the Red Bull and the Fortune, Smith perhaps ending his playing career where he had begun it. Resident of White Cross Street in 1640.

SPENCER, GABRIEL, 1576–98. Probably a quarrelsome young man (he had killed a man in a fight in 1596), Spencer met his match in the equally truculent Ben Jonson, who killed him in a duel with rapiers in later 1598. With Shaw, Spencer had left the Pembroke's group at the Swan in 1597 to join the Admiral's troupe. Despite his youth, Spencer perhaps showed signs of considerable early promise as a player. Henslowe wrote to Alleyn, who was out of London, on 26 September 1598 with 'hard and heavy' news: 'I have lost one of my company which hurteth me greatly.' Spencer, even at twenty-two, was no bit player.

SPENCER, JOHN, *fl.* 1604–23. A prominent leader of travelling troupes, particularly in northern Germany, in the first quarter of the seventeenth century, Spencer received patronage from the Elector of Brandenburg, and performed in the major cities of the Prussian area, including Königsberg, Gdańsk, and Berlin, subsequently travelling to Leipzig and Nuremberg. With John Greene, he was in Prague in 1617 for the coronation of Frederick of the Palatinate as King of Bohemia. After 1620 Spencer lost his patronage at the Prussian court, and disappears from German records within the next three years. Spencer, like Robert Reynolds, developed a clownish stage persona, first Hans Leberwurst (John Liversausage) and subsequently Hans Stockfisch (Poor John, in Trinculo's sense). Any career as a player he may have had in England remains undiscovered.

STRATFORD, ROBERT, 1618–31>. Son of William, below, christened at church of St Giles Cripplegate in April 1618. Taken into the company of his father's former colleagues as a boy performer in 1631, when he was thirteen, he played Triphoena in *Holland's Leaguer*, and presumably continued to play female roles with the company for a few years more. He might have been an independent adult actor by 1639 or so, but there are no surviving indications of such a career.

STRATFORD, WILLIAM, *fl.* 1610–25. A player at the Fortune throughout his known career, Stratford was with Prince Henry's troupe in 1610, and remained with it, signing Richard Gunnell's bond to continue playing there in 1624, with his colleagues Andrew Cane and Richard Fowler. He and his family lived near the playhouse, at the upper end of White Cross Street, in 1623. He died in August 1625, probably a victim of the plague epidemic which hit the parish of St Giles Cripplegate particularly hard, and was buried at the church.

STUTVILLE, GEORGE, *fl.* 1622–40. A minor player with the Revels company at the Red Bull in 1622–3, Stutville was probably then quite young; perhaps he was born around the beginning of the seventeenth century. He was a member of Prince Charles's company in 1632, but moved company twice in the early thirties, arriving among Queen Henrietta's men at the Cockpit by 1635: he played a Soldier and Bostar in *Hannibal and Scipio*. He then passed to the Young Company, and was in trouble in 1640, with William Beeston and Michael Mohun, over the performance of an unlicensed play. In the same year he contributed introductory verses to a book by 'his worthy friend' Thomas Heywood.

SUMNER, JOHN, *fl.* 1625–51. Sumner was a chief player at the Cockpit, and then at Salisbury Court, with Queen Henrietta's men from their establishment, and a friend and colleague of Richard Perkins, with whom Sumner is reported to have 'kept house' in Clerkenwell in their final years. He played Mustapha in *The Renegado*, Marwood in *The Wedding*, the Duke of Florence in 2 *The Fair Maid of the West*, Young Bruce in *King John and Matilda*, and Himulco in *Hannibal and Scipio*.

SWANSTON, EILERT, *c.* 1598?–1651. By 1622 Swanston was a chief player with Lady Elizabeth's company at the Cockpit; in 1624 he joined the King's men, with which troupe he remained for the rest of his career, rising in profile within the company as its leaders, Lowin and Taylor, got older.

He played Aretinus in *The Roman Actor*, Ricardo in *The Picture*, Count Utrante in *The Deserving Favourite*, Chrysalus in *Believe as You List*, Alcidonus in *The Swisser*, and Lugier in *The Wild-Goose Chase*; later reports and notes credit him with the parts of Othello, the title role in *Philaster*, and Bussy in *Bussy D'Ambois*. He was one of the actors negotiating for a fuller share of holdings in playhouse stock in 1635; thereafter he is named with Lowin and Taylor as leading players of the troupe. Legatee of colleague Richard Benfield's will of 1639, where he is named, with Pollard, as a 'gossip'; perhaps Benfield had been godfather to one of Swanston's children. After 1642, by report, Swanston aligned himself with Parliament, and remained in London; he was buried at the church of the parish he had long inhabited, St Mary Aldermanbury, in June 1651.

SWINNERTON, THOMAS, *fl.* 1603–28. With Queen Anne's company from 1603, Swinnerton made an early investment in the Red Bull playhouse, which probably brought him some profit in the following years. From 1616 he led touring groups, on his own and in association with a variety of other actors, including Lee and Slater, with Norwich and Leicester as favourite destinations.

TARLTON, RICHARD, *c.* 1555–88. Like Armin but unlike Kemp, as far as we know, Tarlton served as a London apprentice in his youth, to the haberdasher Ralph Boswell; Tarlton became a freeman of the Haberdashers in later 1576. While still an apprentice, it seems, Tarlton had begun to write and publish ballads, a popular form that undoubtedly spread his growing fame; simultaneously he began as a player with Sussex's troupe, establishing a reputation that led to his being chosen as a founding player of the Queen's men in 1583, with which group he remained for the rest of his short career: a dozen years in total. Tarlton's evidently remarkable gifts as a comic performer, improviser, and song-and-dance man led to a remarkable legend that lived on beyond the memories of those who witnessed his performances. He was also an athlete and trained fencer, graduating as a Master of Defence in 1587. Many of the stories about him are apocryphal, but speak to the extremely powerful effect of his rather more than a decade on the stage, and of the amusement and affection he generated. In addition to his career as a player, Tarlton was a playwright and ballad-writer, and also pursued other business. In 1584 he was translated from the Haberdashers' to the Vintners' Company, the better to carry on his activity as a tavern-keeper.

TAYLOR, JOSEPH, 1586?–1652. A player by 1610, when he was with the Duke of York's troupe, moved to Lady Elizabeth's in 1611, returning to Prince Charles's men, as by then they were, in 1616; in 1619, after performing Doctor Almanac in Middleton's *Masque of Heroes* at the Inner Temple in January–February with his Prince's colleagues, he became a member of the King's troupe, and entered the most prominent part of his career. A leading player in tragic and comic roles, he played Ferdinand in the revival of *The Duchess of Malfi*, Paris in *The Roman Actor*, Mathias in *The Picture*, the Duke in *The Deserving Favourite*, Antiochus in *Believe as You List*, Arioldus in *The Swisser*, and Mirabell in *The Wild-Goose Chase*. Roles he is reputed to have played are Hamlet, Iago, Mosca in *Volpone*, Face in *The Alchemist*, Truewit in *Epicoene*, Amintor in *The Maid's Tragedy*, and Arbaces in *A King and No King*. He was playing the title part in Fletcher's *Rollo* when arrested at the Cockpit in 1648. As a leading representative of the company Taylor had frequent contact with Sir Henry Herbert, Master of the Revels, and he cultivated other court contacts. Helping the Queen with her preparations for the amateur production of *The Shepherds' Paradise* in 1633, he was rewarded with the gift of the costumes, designed by Inigo Jones, which he employed in a lavish revival of Fletcher's *The Faithful Shepherdess* at court the following season. Favour at court no doubt led to his appointment as Yeoman of the Revels in 1639. Shareholder in Globe and Blackfriars playhouses.

THARE, JOHN, *fl.* 1598–1612. Thare, or Thayer, was active in touring troupes as well as in London playing. He was with Worcester's troupe at the Rose in 1602–3, handling payments to property and costume suppliers, and appearing several times in Henslowe's accounts. In 1598 he had been in Paris, and had rented the theatre in the Hôtel de Bourgogne for four months, June–September, to play in the afternoons; he was to provide 'the men, costumes, tapestries, and other requisites' suitable to staging the plays. He was perhaps in Paris again in 1604, playing for the court. The previous year he had been in Germany, with Robert Browne (2) at Frankfurt, and at Ulm and Augsburg later in the year. Thare perhaps joined Queen Anne's men at the Red Bull in the last years of his life. Richard Perkins later testified that Thare had held a share in the company, and had died about 1612.

THOMPSON, JOHN, *c.* 1608–34. John Shank claimed to have brought Thompson to the King's men; he was with them from about 1620, taking female roles for a remarkably extended period, up to the time of his marriage and freedom as an adult player (1631). He was a full member of the troupe by 1633, but died at the end of the following year. He played Julia in the revival of *The Duchess of Malfi*, Domitia in *The Roman Actor*, Honoria in *The Picture*, Cleonarda in *The Deserving Favourite*, Miniona in *The Soddered Citizen*, and Panopia in *The Swisser*.

TOOLEY, NICHOLAS, alias WILKINSON, *fl.* 1603–23. An apprentice of Richard Burbage, to whose will in 1619 he was a witness, Tooley did not become a full member of the King's troupe until late in 1603 at the earliest. Played Corvino in *Volpone*, Ananias in *The Alchemist*, and Forobosco and one of the madmen in the revival of *The Duchess of Malfi*. Lodging with the family of Cuthbert Burbage at time of his death; bequests to several colleagues; Condell, with Burbage, made executors.

TOWNE, JOHN, *fl.* 1583–1617. A founding member of the Queen's men, Towne killed his fellow player William Knell in self-defence during a fight at Thame, Oxon., in 1587. In 1594 he witnessed a loan from Philip to his nephew Francis Henslowe to buy his share as a new member of the Queen's troupe. Died early 1617, resident of parish of Allhallows Barking.

TOWNE, THOMAS, *fl.* 1594–1612. Admiral's from foundation of the troupe; stayed with them to his death. Played Myron-Hamec in *Frederick and Basilea*, Stukely in *The Battle of Alcazar*, three roles in *1 Tamar Cam*, and in *1 Honest Whore*. His will of August 1612 leaves three pounds to his 'very good friends and fellows' in the playing company to hold a supper in his memory. Possibly a cousin of John Towne the player; a man of that name then resident in Hackney was bequeathed five pounds.

TOWNSEND, JOHN, *fl.* 1611–34. Member and leader of Lady Elizabeth's company, usually of a touring provincial branch, frequently in Norwich, 1616–28. By 1634 Townsend was a member of a touring group of the King's Revels.

TRIGGE, WILLIAM, *c.* 1611–52>. Trigge became the apprentice of John Heminges in December 1625, for a term of twelve years. At Heminges's death in 1630 John Shank may have taken over as Trigge's master, but in 1631 Trigge petitioned the Mayor's Court about his status, and in 1632 was granted the freedom of the Grocers' Company, as the son of Robert Trigge, grocer. Trigge was cast in female roles up to that year. He played Julia in *The Roman Actor*, Corsica in *The Picture*, Modestina in *The Soddered Citizen*, Selina in *The Swisser*, and Rosalura in *The Wild-Goose Chase*. In 1636 he was a minor adult player with King's, and perhaps dissatisfied with his progress he moved to the Young Company at the Cockpit, by 1639, probably remaining there until 1642. Later that year he was called 'Captain Trigge', soldier in the King's army. He evidently survived the war; he and his wife were residents of the parish of St Giles Cripplegate in the early 1650s.

TUNSTALL, JAMES, *c.* 1555–99. In his nuncupative will Tunstall described himself as citizen and saddler of London, a status he acquired by patrimony from his father Henry. He acted with Worcester's men in 1583, with the older Admiral's troupe 1590–4; joined the newly constituted

Admiral's in 1594 and remained with them until at least 1597. Parts in *Frederick and Basilea*. Long-time resident of parish of St Botolph Aldgate; buried at the church 10 December 1599.

TURNER, ANTHONY, *fl.* 1622–59. With Lady Elizabeth's company at the Cockpit in 1622, probably joining Queen Henrietta's troupe at its formation in 1625, moving to Salisbury Court in 1637 and playing until 1642. Played Justice Landby in *The Wedding*, probably Bashaw Alcade in *1* and *2 The Fair Maid of the West*, Old Bruce in *King John and Matilda*, and Piston in *Hannibal and Scipio*. May have contributed dedication, as 'A. T.', with Pennycuicke, to the published text of William Heminges's *The Fatal Contract* (1653), in which play he had acted, *c.* 1638. With Edward Shatterell, involved in a rather too early attempt to revive playing at the Red Bull, May 1659.

UNDERWOOD, JOHN, *c.* 1587–1625. Underwood was with the Chapel children by 1600, and played in *Cynthia's Revels* and *The Poetaster*. In 1608, with William Ostler, he moved to the King's men, and the rest of his career was spent in that troupe. He played Delio and one of the madmen in the first and second productions of *The Duchess of Malfi*, Bonario in *Volpone*, Dapper in *The Alchemist*, and is included in the actor lists of many other plays, including that in the Shakespeare Folio. He was 'very weak and sick' when he made his will in October 1624; he died in the first month of 1625. He left shares in the Blackfriars, Globe, and Curtain playhouses; his 'loving friends' Condell, Heminges, and Lowin were nominated executors and overseers. He died a widower with five small children; one of his sons was called Burbage Underwood.

VERNON, GEORGE, *fl.* 1624–30. Vernon was a hired player with the King's company, taking smaller parts. He played a Creditor in the revival of *The Honest Man's Fortune*, and a Lictor in *The Roman Actor*, and appears in King's records until 1629.

WADE, JOHN, *fl.* 1617–71. Wade was a leading player in continental Europe for much of the seventeenth century; there are no records of any playing he may have done in his native country. He may in fact have trained as a musician, possibly under George Vincent, who had perhaps appeared in *2 Seven Deadly Sins*. In 1617 Vincent was at the Polish court in Warsaw, and Wade with him, as was Richard Jones (*q.v.*). Wade was at the Polish court for about two years. The European wars seem to have interrupted his activities, but from 1643 he was active as a player, from Stockholm and Riga to Prague and Vienna, sometimes in association with his countrymen William Roe and George Jolly. His last recorded appearance was at Dresden in 1671, when he must have been an old man.

WAMBUS, FRANCIS, *fl.* 1611–28. Leader of a provincial branch of Lady Elizabeth's company, frequently at Norwich. Imprisoned there for a month in April–May 1624 for defying the civic authorities; Wambus posted a playbill announcing the imminent performance of 'an excellent new comedy called *The Spanish Contract*' (now otherwise unknown), and lost the subsequent argument with the mayor. A further appeal to the authority of the Master of the Revels was also unavailing.

WILBRAHAM, WILLIAM, *fl.* 1626–44. With Queen Henrietta's company by 1626; touring in Norwich in 1635; in 1640 held a mortgage on the Cockpit playhouse, as security of a loan of 150 pounds to Elizabeth Beeston, indicating some prosperity. Played Isaac in *The Wedding* and possibly a role in *1 Fair Maid of the West*, although the cast list seems confused over the parts assigned respectively to Wilbraham and Turner.

WILSON, JOHN, 1595–1674. Apprenticed to John Heminges in 1611 for eight years; freed as a grocer in later 1621. He was primarily a singer and musician, and wrote songs for masques and many plays of the King's men, although he also appeared in musical parts on stage: as 'Jacke Wilson' his name survives in the Folio text of *Much Ado About Nothing*, in which he played Balthasar at some time during his decade or so with the company. A guest, and possibly a performer, at Edward Alleyn's wedding anniversary dinner in 1620. He subsequently became a city musician, a member of the King's Music, and Professor of Music at Oxford in 1656.

WILSON, ROBERT, *fl.* 1572–1600. With Leicester's troupe 1572–81; founder member of Queen's men, 1583, until 1592–3. Playwright during and after his playing career.

WINTERSEL, WILLIAM, *c.* 1620?–79. Wintersel is supposed to have performed at Salisbury Court before the wars, presumably while still a young man or youth, possibly as a member of Queen Henrietta's men. He was certainly playing in Paris in 1646, and from 1648 was in London, continuing as a signatory to the actors' agreements that attempted to keep professional activity alive. At some time in the 1640s he married Margaret Gunnell, daughter of Richard, and thus came into shares in the Salisbury Court playhouse and its business. When acting resumed Wintersel began at the Red Bull, and he was possibly part of Turner and Shatterell's venture as early as 1659. Therafter he joined the King's company, and was a principal player and shareholder for almost a further twenty years.

WORTH, ELLIS, 1587–1659. Worth had a long career in the theatre. He was with Queen Anne's company by 1612, becoming a member of the Players of the Revels at the Red Bull after 1619; by early 1624 seems to have had some connection with Prince Charles's company, but is otherwise unrecorded in the later 1620s. In 1626 he married Frances, widow of the King's player Thomas Holcombe. He resurfaces as a founding member of the new Prince Charles's company in 1631–2, playing Ardelio in *Holland's Leaguer*, and remaining with the company throughout the remaining decade as a leading player, with Andrew Cane. Early in 1638 he claimed freedom of the Merchant Taylors' Company by patrimony, as the son of Henry Worth 'late merchant taylor deceased'. Worth perhaps entered London business after 1642: he took on his own son as his only apprentice in 1647. His will speaks of reasonable means; he was buried at the church in which he had probably been christened, St Giles Cripplegate, 19 April 1659, 'in the middle aisle by my relations there lying'.

WRIGHT, JOHN, 1614–55>. The son of John Wright the elder, baker of the parish of St Giles Cripplegate, Wright was apprenticed to Andrew Cane for eight years from September 1629. In 1631 he played Millicent, opposite his master as Trimalchio, in *Holland's Leaguer* at the Salisbury Court playhouse. That Wright continued to perform with Prince Charles's company through the rest of his apprenticeship is indicated by his presence in the Young Company at the Cockpit in 1639, two years after his bonds had been served. He did not claim his freedom as a goldsmith until it had become more valuable than being a player (or perhaps a soldier), early in 1646, while Cane was still with the royal court in Oxford. At the Goldsmiths' Company court he was granted his freedom, 'his service certified by Ellis Worth', citizen and freeman. Wright was perhaps involved in some interregnum entertainment, but does not appear among any Restoration records of players.

Notes

1. Milhous and Hume, 'New Light', p. 409 (modernized); Bentley, *Profession of Player*, p. 122; Wickham *et al.* (eds.), *English Professional Theatre*, p. 442.
2. Thomas Heywood, prologue to *The Jew of Malta* (London, 1633), sig. A4^v.
3. See entries on Lowin and Perkins in Matthew and Harrison (eds.), *Oxford Dictionary of National Biography* (all further references cited as *ODNB*) which are illustrated with the portraits; the entry on Burbage is not illustrated and specifically excludes any mention of the portrait, the author of the biography, Mary Edmond, evidently regarding it as spurious. The picture is, however, reproduced in many books about the Shakespearean stage – see, for example, Gurr, *Shakespearean Stage*, p. 62 – and is illustrated and discussed in the catalogue by Waterfield *et al.*, *Mr. Cartwright's Pictures*.
4. The size and composition of troupes in the earlier Tudor period is examined by Bevington in *From Mankind to Marlowe*: see Chapter 5, particularly pp. 74–9. The growth of theatrical enterprise in the earlier Elizabethan period is the concern of Ingram in *Business of Playing*.
5. See Rutter, *Documents*, pp. 72–5.
6. All quotations from Shakespeare are from *The Riverside Shakespeare*: *Midsummer Night's Dream*, 1.2.40; *1 Henry IV*, 2.4.387. Although 'veins' of playing might suggest particular 'lines' or 'types' followed by particular actors, as argued by Baldwin in *Organization*, 'vein' had a wide range of contemporary usage, and is otherwise not much used with reference to playing. It might, for example, mean 'mood' ('I am not in the giving vein to-day', *Richard III*, 4.3.116), or 'literary style' ('Let me hear Mr. Shakespeare's vein', *1 Return from Parnassus*, quoted in *Riverside Shakespeare*, Appendix C, p. 1961, modernized).
7. Both the original Latin of the letter, from Henry Jackson to William Fulman, both of Corpus Christi College, Oxford, and an English translation are given in *Riverside Shakespeare*, Appendix C, p. 1978: 'But truly the celebrated Desdemona, slain in our presence by her husband, although she pleaded her case very effectively throughout, yet moved us more after she was dead, when, lying on her bed, she entreated the pity of the spectators by her very countenance.'
8. See *Riverside Shakespeare*, Appendix C, pp. 1966–8.

CHAPTER I   SHADOWS, JESTS, AND COUNTERFEITS

1. On the general context of opposition to the theatre, and detailed discussion of the Shakespearean period and its critical polemics, see Barish, *Anti-Theatrical Prejudice*.
2. Jonson, *Complete Plays*, vol. IV.
3. Diderot, *Paradox of Acting*. It was first published, as *Paradoxe sur le comédien*, in 1830.
4. On the contemporary use of the term, see especially Foakes, 'Player's Passion'. Roach's *Player's Passion* usefully traces the growing understanding of human psychology as it influenced the discourse about acting, up to the nineteenth century, and has a valuable chapter on the early period. The limitation of the approach is that it tends to describe the older theories of humours, spirits, and passions as if they were universally assented to, rather than regarded variously with some scepticism, and subject to a considerable range of interpretation.
5. See, for example, the actor Ian Richardson on playing Malcolm in *Macbeth* in 1967. 'In the England scene when I hear the news about Macduff's children, in order to get myself into the right emotional state I have quickly to flash a kaleidoscope set of pictures through my mind of my own children and what my emotions would be if something ghastly happened to them.' Evans, 'Shakespeare', pp. 124–5.
6. See Astington, 'Actors and the Body'.
7. Ezekiel Fenn, for example, an actor with Queen Henrietta's men at the Cockpit playhouse in the 1630s, was celebrated by the poet and dramatist Henry Glapthorne in 1639 in a poem on his first acting a man's part, at the age of nineteen. Theophilus Bird, born in 1608, was still playing female roles at the age of twenty-two; Alexander Gough, born in 1614, played the leading character Lillia-Bianca in Fletcher's *The Wild-Goose Chase* in 1632, when he was eighteen; William Trigge played women until the age of twenty-one or so, and John Wright, apprentice of Andrew Cane, played the leading role of Millicent, opposite his master as Trimalchio, in *Holland's Leaguer* (1631), when he was seventeen. See Kathman, 'How Old'.
8. Aristotle, *History of Animals*, vol. III, p. 415.
9. *Ibid.*, pp. 415–17.
10. The quoted speech does not appear in the version of the play published in quarto format in 1600. For theoretical discussion of the variant texts of *Henry V* see recent editions by Gary Taylor (Oxford University Press, 1982) and Andrew Gurr (Cambridge University Press, 1992).
11. This scene was not included in the first printed versions of the play, and it may have been either censored or tactfully cut by the actors in performance, since the replacement of a living monarch was a politically sensitive subject.
12. See the exhibition catalogue *Mr. Cartwright's Pictures*, cited in note 3 of the Introduction.
13. Quoted in Nungezer, *Dictionary*, p. 74 (modernized).
14. Kyd, *Spanish Tragedy*, pp. 134–5.

15. The account of Jan de Witt, translated from the original Latin in Wickham *et al.* (eds.), *English Professional Theatre*, p. 441.
16. The phrase was drawn from line 333 of Horace's *Ars Poetica*, which reads 'Aut prodesse volunt aut delectare poetae' (Poets want to give either benefit or pleasure).
17. Prologue to *Every Man in His Humour* (1616), line 24.
18. Milhous and Hume, 'New Light', p. 506 (modernized).

CHAPTER 2   PLAYING AND EDUCATION

1. All references to Jonson's plays are to the text of *Complete Plays*.
2. Cressy, *Education*, pp. 9–10.
3. See *Riverside Milton*, pp. 977–86.
4. Beaumont, *Knight of the Burning Pestle*.
5. See Munro, *Children*.
6. Whitelocke, *Liber Famelicus*, p. 12 (modernized).
7. Quoted in Motter, *School Drama*, p. 86.
8. Chambers, *Elizabethan Stage*, vol. II, pp. 8–76.
9. Lancashire, 'St. Paul's Grammar School'.
10. Motter, *School Drama*, p. 50.
11. White, *Theatre and Reformation*, pp. 100–5.
12. Gibson (ed.), *Kent*, vol. I, pp. lxvii, 191, 193; vol. II, p. 927.
13. Somerset (ed.), *Shropshire*, vol. I, pp. 209–10; vol. II, pp. 375–6.
14. Baldwin, Clopper, and Mills (eds.), *Cheshire including Chester*, vol. I, pp. xxii–xxiii, 182; vol. II, pp. 646–7.
15. Quoted in Simon, *Education and Society*, p. 362.
16. Hoole, *New Discovery*, pp. 142–3.
17. See Baldwin, *William Shakespere's*, vol. II, p. 29.
18. Cicero, *De Oratore*, I.v.18, vol. I, pp. 14–15; I.xxxix.132, vol. I, pp. 92–3 (English translations somewhat adapted).
19. Marston, *Antonio and Mellida*, Induction, lines 1–4, etc.
20. Cicero, *De Oratore*, III.lviii.223, vol. II, pp. 178–9.
21. *Ibid.*, III.lviii.221, vol. II, pp. 176–7.
22. Quintilian, *Orator's Education*, vol. I, pp. 236–7.
23. *Ibid.*, pp. 240–1.
24. The full Ciceronian formulation is 'Optimus est enim orator qui dicendo animos audientium et docet et delectat et permovet. Docere debitum est, delectare honorarium, permovere necessarium' (The best orator is thus he who in speaking instructs, delights, and moves the minds of his auditors. Instruction is an obligation, delight a favour, and the moving of the feelings a necessity). Cicero, *De Optime Genere Oratorum*, pp. 356–7 (my translation).
25. Wilson, *Art of Rhetoric*, pp. 242–3.
26. Alan Brown, 'Bull, John', *ODNB*, vol. VIII, pp. 591–3.
27. See the petition of William Hunnis addressed to the Privy Council in November 1583. Among other burdens, Hunnis observes that 'there is no

allowance nor other consideration for those children whose voices be changed, who only do depend upon the charge of the said Master until such time as he may prefer the same with clothing and other furniture, unto his no small charge'. Ashbee (ed.), *Records*, vol. VIII, pp. 39–40 (modernized).

28. Roger Bowers, 'Westcote, Sebastian', *ODNB*, vol. LVIII, p. 256.
29. *Ibid.*, pp. 255–7.
30. Wickham *et al.* (eds.), *English Professional Theatre*, p. 309.
31. Ashbee (ed.), *Records*, vol. VI, p. 46 (modernized).
32. Bowers, 'Playhouse'.
33. Bowers, 'Westcote, Sebastian', *ODNB*, vol. LVIII, p. 256.
34. Honigmann and Brock (eds.), *Playhouse Wills*, p. 49 (modernized).
35. Ashbee (ed.), *Records*, vol. VI, p. 8 (modernized).
36. Ashbee and Harley (eds.), *Cheque Books*, vol. II, p. 59 (modernized).
37. See Munro, *Children*.
38. Wickham *et al.* (eds.), *English Professional Theatre*, p. 402.
39. Astington, *English Court Theatre*, pp. 192–7.
40. If the Marprelate 'defence' was run in some organized, if undercover, fashion, Paul's Boys may have been a chosen tool in the war on Martin, and fallen victim to a subsequent decision to put an end to all the rather unpredictable mudslinging which, as far as we can now guess, characterized the exchange.
41. See Lyly, *Endymion*, pp. 57–9.
42. Lyly, *Campaspe*, p. 35.
43. Wickham *et al.* (eds.), *English Professional Theatre*, p. 511.
44. Chambers, *Elizabethan Stage*, vol. II, pp. 46–7.
45. Eccles, 'Martin Peerson'.
46. For example, the Earl of Leicester and Archbishop Laud were Chancellors of Oxford, and Lord Burghley Chancellor of Cambridge.
47. Nelson, *Early Cambridge Theatres*, pp. 39–40.
48. Elliott *et al.* (eds.), *Oxford*, vol. I, p. 541 (modernized).
49. Gordon McMullan, 'Fletcher, John', *ODNB*, vol. XX, pp. 107–13.
50. Elliott *et al.* (eds.), *Oxford*, vol. I, pp. 340–81.
51. *Ibid.*, vol. II, p. 613.
52. See Nelson, *Early Cambridge Theatres*, pp. 16–37.
53. Marston, *Jack Drum's Entertainment*, act five, in *Plays*, vol. III, p. 234.
54. Leonard W. Cowie, 'Palmer, John', *ODNB*, vol. XLII, p. 505.
55. Venn and Venn, *Alumni Cantabrigienses*, vol. IV, p. 149.
56. William Barker, 'Fraunce, Abraham', *ODNB*, vol. XX, pp. 888–9.
57. Venn and Venn, *Alumni Cantabrigienses*, vol. II, p. 195; vol. IV, p. 59.
58. Narrative of Miles Windsor, in Elliott *et al.* (eds.), *Oxford*, vol. I, p. 133 (modernized).
59. *Ibid.*, p. 130 (modernized).
60. Orrell, *Theatres*, pp. 24–38; Elliott *et al.* (eds.), *Oxford*, vol. II, pp. 765–71.
61. Elliott *et al.* (eds.), *Oxford*, vol. I, p. 283.
62. *Ibid.*, vol. II, p. 892 (modernized).
63. Nelson, *Early Cambridge Theatres*, pp. 16–37.

64. Elliott *et al.* (eds.), *Oxford*, vol. II: account of Antony Wood, p. 886 (modernized); pp. 772–89.
65. All references are to the text of *Three Parnassus Plays* (modernized).
66. Prest, *Inns of Court*, p. 154.
67. Quoted *ibid.*, p. 92.
68. See *ibid.*, pp. 5–17.
69. The account of Gerard Legh, quoted in Green, *Inns of Court*, p. 69.
70. Hughes, *Misfortunes of Arthur*, p. 19. On the staging of the play, see also Astington, *English Court Theatre*, pp. 106–7.
71. Green, *Inns of Court*, pp. 40–5.

CHAPTER 3   APPRENTICES

1. See Bevington, 'Theatre as Holiday'.
2. Dekker, *Shoemakers' Holiday*, scenes 18, 19, 21.
3. The documents of the London companies in the sixteenth and seventeenth centuries have survived in varying states of completeness and detail, and generally the so-called 'Great Companies', representing the wealthier and larger trades, have preserved more. Inevitably, not all records of apprenticeship and freedom, including those of boys and men connected to the theatre, are now extant. See Kathman, 'Grocers'.
4. Henslowe, *Diary*, pp. 81, 230.
5. Berry, 'The Player's Apprentice'.
6. Quoted in Watson, *English Grammar Schools*, p. 192.
7. See Pilkinton (ed.), *Bristol*.
8. British Library, MS c.106.cc.3.
9. Merchant Taylors' Court Book, 30 January 1638, Guildhall Library microfilm 329.
10. See Astington, 'John Rhodes'.
11. See Wickham *et al.* (eds.), *English Professional Theatre*, pp. 221–8; Gurr, *Shakespeare Company*, Appendix 3.
12. Thomas Pollard was christened at the church of St Mary, Aylesbury, on 11 December 1597. His younger sister Anne was christened in the same church on 29 May 1600. She stayed in the Aylesbury area, and at the time of her brother's death was married to a man called Richard Perrin: they inherited Pollard's estate. See Honigmann and Brock (eds.), *Playhouse Wills*, p. 235; International Genealogical Index.
13. Wickham *et al.* (eds.), *English Professional Theatre*, p. 224.
14. Honigmann and Brock (eds.), *Playhouse Wills*, p. 186.
15. See Astington, 'Succession of Sots'.
16. We might think that if *The Knight of the Burning Pestle*, featuring a Grocer and his stagestruck apprentice, includes some joking at the expense of Hemings, then *A Midsummer Night's Dream*, with its histrionic weaver who enjoys ranting in old-fashioned verse, might similarly glance at Dutton.
17. Two particular John Shanks might have seen Tarlton in his heyday. The first was christened at the church of St Mary the Virgin, Dover, in March 1563. This

man would have been old for an apprentice when the Queen's men began; he would have been seventy-two in 1635. A second John Shank was christened on 30 April 1570 at the church of Kelsale in Suffolk, 'the son of Henry Shank and Joan his wife'. He would have been exactly the right age for apprenticeship in 1583, and sixty-five in 1635. See International Genealogical Index.

18. Honigmann and Brock (eds.), *Playhouse Wills*, pp. 96–8.
19. He was christened at the church of St Botolph, Colchester, on 29 January 1561, the son of John Hovell (Parish Book, Essex Record Office). At his death he left property and bequests to brothers and sisters (or half-brothers and half-sisters) in Essex and other parts of East Anglia. Honigmann and Brock (eds.), *Playhouse Wills*, pp. 98–101.
20. *Ibid.* (modernized).
21. *Ibid.*, pp. 118–19.
22. Galloway (ed.), *Norwich*, p. 143.
23. September 1599: 'The xxix^th day was Christened Michell the sonne of John Bowyer' (Parish Book of All Saints Kidderminster, Worcester County Record Office).
24. Pilkington (ed.), *Bristol*, pp. 203–4.
25. Wasson (ed.), *Devon*, p. 188 (modernized).
26. Falstaff in *1 Henry IV*, 2.2.85.
27. Bentley, *Jacobean and Caroline Stage*, vol. ii, p. 386. Hereafter cited as *JCS*.
28. *Ibid.*, p. 431.
29. *Ibid.*, vol i, p. 168 (modernized).
30. Answer of Richard Gunnell, suit of Babham vs Gunnell, 1632, cited in Bentley, 'Salisbury Court Theatre'.
31. Some of them perhaps were among the players named in later records of the company, post-1634. See *JCS*, vol. i, pp. 283–301.
32. Wickham *et al.* (eds.), *English Professional Theatre*, p. 269.
33. *Ibid.*, p. 271.
34. In his will of 1605 Phillips left thirty shillings as a bequest to Beeston, as he also did to his 'fellows' Shakespeare and Condell; Beeston, however, is called 'my servant'. This both indicates that Beeston was no longer a colleague (he was then in Queen Anne's company) and recalls an earlier bond of apprenticeship. See Honigmann and Brock (eds.), *Playhouse Wills*, p. 73.
35. *JCS*, vol. i, p. 325 (modernized).
36. See Matusiak, 'Christopher Beeston'.
37. *JCS*, vol. ii, pp. 433–4.
38. Brome, *Dramatic Works*, vol. i, p. 272 (modernized).
39. Quoted in Hotson, *Commonwealth*, p. 96.
40. Dryden, *John Dryden*, p. 144, lines 76–8. On the Nursery, see Hotson, *Commonwealth*, pp. 176–96
41. See Astington, 'Jolly, George', *ODNB*, vol. xxx, pp. 425–6.
42. The original Latin of the legal document states that Alleyn 'retinuisset *pre-dictum* Ricardum ad des*er*viendum eidem Edwardo'. KB 27/1343/1, quoted from Mateer, 'Edward Alleyn', Appendix A.

43. Perkins's portrait, painted towards the end of his life, shows him to have had quite sensitive and delicate features, particularly when compared to the bluff and burly John Lowin (Figures 1 and 2). Perkins may indeed, as a teenager, have had a quite convincingly feminine stage countenance, set off by wig and costume.
44. Henslowe, *Diary*, pp. 118, 164, 167, 241.
45. See King, *Casting*.
46. *Ibid.*, pp. 59, 122.
47. Contractual legal agreements governing the agreed servitude, for stipulated wages and other conditions, of one individual to another for a term of years were common. Philip Henslowe contracted adult actors to play at his play-houses in this fashion, and Edward Alleyn secured the service of Richard Perkins for a three-year term with such a document. Legal minors – those under the age of twenty-one, as Perkins was in 1597 when he entered Alleyn's service – would technically have required the agreement, and signature, of a parent or guardian to the contract.
48. Kathman, 'Grocers', pp. 6–12.
49. Kathman, *ibid.*, and 'Reconsidering'.
50. Chambers, *Elizabethan Stage*, vol. ii, p. 421.
51. Riddell, 'Some Actors'.
52. *Ibid.*, p. 213 (modernized).
53. Kathman, 'How Old?', pp. 231–2.
54. *Ibid.*, p. 235.

CHAPTER 4   PLAYING MANY PARTS

1. See King's survey of modern scholarship in *Casting*, pp. 4–5.
2. 'The Prologue, to the Stage, at the Cock-Pit', lines 1–11. Marlowe, *Doctor Faustus and Other Plays*. All quotations from Marlowe refer to this text unless noted otherwise.
3. In his dedicatory poem to the Shakespeare Folio of 1623, 'To the Memory of my Beloved, the Author, Mr. William Shakespeare, and What He Hath Left Us'.
4. The printed text of the first part of *Tamburlaine* has rather more than 2,000 lines, of which the title part claims 820-odd; the second play is almost 300 lines longer than the first, and Tamburlaine's role has 874 lines.
5. See Henslowe, *Diary*, p. 36.
6. See Gurr, *Shakespeare's Opposites*, pp. 22–4.
7. All quotations refer to Chapman, *Blind Beggar*, with my modernization of spelling.
8. Gurr, *Shakespeare's Opposites*, pp. 59–71, 218; Henslowe, *Diary*, pp. 31–3.
9. All quotations refer to *Look About You*, with my modernization of spelling.
10. See pp. 166–208.
11. Beaumont, *Knight of the Burning Pestle*, Induction, lines 85–6.
12. Quoted in Nungezer, *Dictionary*, pp. 223–4 (modernized).
13. Henslowe, *Diary*, p. 278 (modernized).

14. See Kathman, 'Reconsidering'; McMillin, 'Building Stories'.
15. See Greg, *Dramatic Documents*, 'Commentary' volume, pp. 94–104.
16. Mateer, 'Edward Alleyn'.
17. Honigmann and Brock (eds.), *Playhouse Wills*, p. 73. Phillips's will was dated 4 May 1605, and finally proved two weeks later.
18. Q1: '*enter Clowne and an other*'; Q2, F: '*Enter two Clownes*'.
19. See Jonson, *Bartholomew Fair*, Induction.
20. King's scheme, predicated on dividing the roles amongst nine principal players, three boys, and a group of supporting players taking minor parts, doubles Polonius and the First Clown, for a total of around 400 lines. He has the actor of Rosencrantz, at liberty after act four, assume the role of Osric (total 110–30 lines). See King, *Casting*, pp. 208–11.
21. See 'THE ACTORS NAMES', a list of dramatis personae following the text of *2 Henry IV*, and preceding the following play, *Henry V*.
22. See Dutton, *Mastering*, and Bawcutt, *Control*.
23. The second quotation is from the second line of the prologue to *Tamburlaine the Great*. In a preface 'To the gentleman readers', the publisher, Richard Jones, writes 'I have purposely omitted and left out some fond and frivolous gestures, digressing and, in my poor opinion, far unmeet for the matter, which I thought might seem more tedious unto the wise than any way to be regarded, though haply they have been of some vain conceited fondlings greatly gaped at, what times they were shown upon the stage in their graced deformities.' *Tamburlaine the Great*, A2^r (modernized).
24. *Knack to Know a Knave*, title page (modernized).
25. Kemp's foolery took place in the Netherlands in May 1586. Adams (ed.), *Household Accounts*, p. 374.
26. Thomas Nashe, *An Almond for a Parrot*, quoted in Nungezer, *Dictionary*, pp. 216–17 (modernized).
27. See Richards and Richards, *Commedia dell'Arte*, pp. 141–7.
28. See Knutson, *Repertory*, pp. 115–18, 174–5, 184–5; Astington, 'Globe'.
29. *Three Parnassus Plays*, *Pilgrimage*, lines 661–73 (modernized).
30. Cf. King's scheme for casting the play, in *Casting*, pp. 223–6.
31. See Greg, *Two Elizabethan*.
32. Riddell, 'Some Actors'.
33. Downes, *Roscius Anglicanus*, p. 55 (modernized).
34. James Wright, *Historia Histrionica* (1699), quoted in *JCS*, vol. II, p. 693 (modernized).
35. Riddell, 'Some Actors'.
36. References are to Webster, *Duchess of Malfi* (Revels edition).
37. Quoted in Webster, *Duchess of Malfi*, p. lviii.
38. The claim by Brandon Centerwall that Taylor had been a member of Paul's Boys before 1608 rests on a very insubstantial foundation, and I am not convinced by it. See Centerwall, 'Greatly Exaggerated Demise'.
39. See King, *Casting*, pp. 58–9.
40. King, *Casting*, p. 62 (modernized).

41. In early 1633 the Queen and her ladies were rehearsing Walter Monagu's pastoral play *The Shepherds' Paradise*, presented at Somerset House on 9 January 1633 in a custom-built scenic theatre designed by Inigo Jones. In the period beforehand it was reported that 'Taylor the prime actor at the Globe goes every day to teach them action.' See Feil, 'Dramatic References'.
42. Milhous and Hume, 'New Light'.
43. See King, *Casting*, p. 70.

CHAPTER 5   PLAYERS AT WORK

1. See Stern, *Rehearsal*.
2. See Harold Pinter's memoir 'Mac' (1966) about working as a young actor in the early 1950s with the actor-manager Anew McMaster (1894–1962), playing Shakespeare on tour in provincial Ireland. Pinter, *Poems and Prose*, pp. 75–84.
3. Marmion, *Holland's Leaguer*, A4ᵛ. All quotations have been modernized in spelling and punctuation.
4. See Bentley, 'Salisbury Court Theatre'.
5. Bawcutt, *Control*, p. 174.
6. *JCS*, vol. IV, p. 742.
7. *JCS*, vol. II; Astington, 'Career'; Kathman, *Biographical Index*.
8. Information about Bond, Browne, and Worth draws on my unpublished paper 'Tom Bond, Man of Property?' presented at the meeting of the Shakespeare Association of America in New Orleans, April 2004.
9. Kathman, 'Grocers', p. 27.
10. *Holland's Leaguer* as published gives little scope to display musical talent, although in 2.2 Fidelio (May) instructs Faustina (Godwin) to 'use all art for his content / With music, songs, and dancing' (D4ʳ) as part of a plan to free Philautus from his self-enclosed vanity. Nothing is subsequently made of this on stage.
11. Armin also was a freeman of the Goldsmiths, from 1604, and Lowin, who served an apprenticeship as a goldsmith, probably was. See Kathman, 'Grocers'.
12. Parsloe (ed.), *Wardens' Accounts*, pp. 295, 330, 332, 338.
13. One Robert Hewett was christened at St Bride's Church on 14 February 1613, and would have been almost nineteen at the time of *Holland's Leaguer*, a local youth who, we might guess, had become attached to the theatre, perhaps from its foundation in 1629.
14. Based on King, *Casting*, Table 28, pp. 138–9, with emendations.
15. Typographically the play has twenty-four divisions, with five scenes in four of the five acts and four scenes in act three. Probably these were in the manuscript, since the play seems to have been set in type from the book as corrected by Sir Henry Herbert (see *JCS*, vol. IV, pp. 745–8). Some of them, however, are (authorial?) French/Jonsonian divisions, marking the entry of a new character rather than a general clearing of the stage, the working definition of the end of a scene for the players. King's analysis follows playhouse practice, treating as one scene 1.1–1.4, 1.5–2.1, 2.4–2.5, 3.2–3.3, and 3.4–4.1, producing a total of seventeen scene units.

16. *Agurtes* . . . Recall your self
       Were you not formerly engag'd?
    Miscellanio No, never.
    Agurtes Not to mistress *Quartilla*?
    Miscellanio Faith, we have toy'd
       In jest sometime.
    Agurtes Let it be now in earnest.
       Make her amends. I know she loves you.   (L3ʳ)

    All the first-hand evidence against which one might judge these assertions is
    contained in 2.4/2.5, some stage or reading time back. Miscellanio and
    Quartilla do indeed flirt, in genteel fashion, in that scene, but neither seems
    particularly head-over-heels at the time, and there is certainly no follow-up,
    dramatized or reported. Quartilla's 'love', by her own account, takes in the
    male sex at large, and in numbers, and is not of the moony, romantic variety.
17. *Measure for Measure* is one influence on the play, here and in the brothel and
    comic trial scenes; *Much Ado About Nothing* also shows through in the arrests
    and examinations by the municipal constabulary.
18. A joke at least as old as *2 Henry IV*: see Falstaff, 2.4.48–52.
19. For example, the witches in *Macbeth*, in Davenant's adaptation, and the
    Nurse in Otway's adaptation of *Romeo and Juliet*, *Caius Marius*. See Hogan,
    Shakespeare.
20. Of the named actors Mannery is the freest, before dressing for the Bawd role,
    to take on the small part of the '*Boy*', unlisted in the dramatis personae and
    required for a few moments at the end of 1.5 and the beginning of 2.1; he has
    seven lines to speak. Since a 'Boy' is a bottom-end hierarchical position as
    much as a particular age and size, a surly, lumpy teenager will do as well as –
    may indeed be funnier than – a child.
21. If Stratford took 1 Whore and Saville 2 Whore, their respective line totals would
    have risen to 77 and 68. The evident candidate to play the Pander, who has 56
    lines spread over two scenes, would have been Robert Huyt, whose two
    appearances as Jeffrey came at opposite extremes of the length of the play.
    There is a long two-scene gap between the final exit of the Pander and the
    reappearance of Jeffrey.
22. The text is likely to have been printed from Massinger's manuscript, so one
    must be cautious about assuming that what the actors performed on the stage
    followed the printed version in every detail. See Massinger, *Plays and Poems*,
    vol. III, pp. 4–7.
23. See Ripley, *Julius Caesar*, pp. 13–22.
24. See Gurr, *Shakespeare Company*, pp. 193–4; Butler, 'Romans'.
25. Massinger, *Plays and Poems*, vol. III, p. 20.
26. Unpublished paper presented at the meeting of the Shakespeare Association of
    America, Philadelphia, 2006.
27. Robinson's six recorded parts in King's men's plays vary in length in this
    manner. Robinson seems to have settled into a middle-rank position in the

company, his youthful talent perhaps having ceased to develop; depending on the design of the play he was sometimes cast in smaller roles, calculated by line-count.

28. All quotations from and references to the text of *The Roman Actor* relate to the edition of A. K. McIlwraith, included in the anthology *Five Stuart Tragedies*.
29. Massinger, *Poems and Plays*, vol. v, p. 184.
30. Ovid, *Metamorphoses*, 14.698 ff.

CONCLUSION

1. Brome, *Antipodes*.
2. See Beaumont, *Knight of the Burning Pestle*, Induction, lines 72–5. In a further layer of parody, what Ralph produces in response to the request for him to do some huffing is a version of Hotspur's speech on honour from *1 Henry IV* (1.3.200 ff.), removed from its immediate context, where its extravagance is ironized.
3. See Astington, 'Playing the Man'.
4. *Riverside Shakespeare*, Appendix C, p. 1961 (modernized).
5. Heywood, *Apology*, E2^v (modernized).
6. Quoted in Chambers, *Elizabethan Stage*, vol. i, p. 343 (modernized).
7. Howarth (ed.), *French Theatre*, pp. 16–17.
8. Journal of Jean Héroard, *ibid.*, p. 88.
9. See Astington, 'Acting in the Field'.
10. See Stephen Gosson, *The School of Abuse* (1579), quoted in Chambers, *Elizabethan Stage*, vol. iv, pp. 203–5.
11. Wickham *et al.* (eds.), *English Professional Theatre*, p. 283.
12. *JCS*, vol. ii, p. 484. Jolly was then twenty-seven, Smith probably in his forties.
13. See the letter of Samuel Cox, secretary to Sir Christopher Hatton, in Wickham *et al.* (eds.), *English Professional Theatre*, pp. 168–9.
14. *Ibid.*, pp. 275–7.

Bibliography

Adams, Simon (ed.), *Household Accounts and Disbursement Books of Robert Dudley, Earl of Leicester* (Cambridge University Press, 1995).

Aristotle, *The History of Animals*, trans. A. L. Peck and D. Balme, 3 vols. (Cambridge, MA: Harvard University Press, 1965–91).

Ascham, Roger, *The Scholemaster* (1570; Menston: Scolar Press, 1967).

Ashbee, Andrew (ed.), *Records of English Court Music*, 9 vols. (Snodland: Andrew Ashbee; Aldershot: Scolar Press, 1986–96).

and John Harley (eds.), *The Cheque Books of the Chapel Royal*, 2 vols. (Aldershot: Ashgate, 2000).

Astington, John H., 'Acting in the Field', *Theatre Notebook*, 60 (2006), 129–33.

'Actors and the Body: Metatheatrical Rhetoric in Shakespeare', *Gesture*, 6 (2006), 239–57.

'The Career of Andrew Cane, Citizen, Goldsmith, and Player', *Medieval and Renaissance Drama in England*, 17 (2005), 37–55.

English Court Theatre, 1558–1642 (Cambridge University Press, 1999).

'The Globe, the Court, and *Measure for Measure*', *Shakespeare Survey* 52 (1999), 133–42.

'John Rhodes: Draper, Bookseller, and Man of the Theatre', *Theatre Notebook*, 57 (2003), 83–9.

'Playing the Man: Acting at the Red Bull and the Fortune', *Early Theatre*, 9 (2006), 130–43.

'The Succession of Sots, or Fools and their Fathers', *Medieval and Renaissance Drama in England*, 20 (2007), 225–35.

Baldwin, Elizabeth, Laurence M. Clopper, and David Mills (eds.), *Cheshire including Chester*, 2 vols. (University of Toronto Press, 2007).

Baldwin, T. W., *The Organization and Personnel of the Shakespearean Company* (Princeton University Press, 1927).

William Shakespere's Small Latin and Lesse Greeke, 2 vols. (Urbana: University of Illinois Press, 1944).

Barish, Jonas, *The Anti-Theatrical Prejudice* (Berkeley: University of California Press, 1981).

Bawcutt, N. W., *The Control and Censorship of Caroline Drama* (Oxford: Clarendon Press, 1996).

Beaumont, Francis, *The Knight of the Burning Pestle*, ed. Sheldon P. Zitner (Manchester University Press, 1984).

Bentley, G. E., *The Jacobean and Caroline Stage*, 7 vols. (Oxford: Clarendon Press, 1941–68).

The Profession of Player in Shakespeare's Time, 1590–1642 (Princeton University Press, 1984).

'The Salisbury Court Theatre and its Boy Players', *Huntington Library Quarterly*, 40 (1977), 129–49.

'The Troubles of a Caroline Acting Troupe: Prince Charles's Company', *Huntington Library Quarterly*, 41 (1978), 217–49.

Berry, Herbert, *The Boar's Head Playhouse* (Washington: Folger Shakespeare Library, 1986).

'The Player's Apprentice', *Essays in Theatre*, 1 (1982–3), 73–80.

Bevington, David, *From Mankind to Marlowe: Growth of Structure in the Popular Drama of Tudor England* (Cambridge, MA: Harvard University Press, 1962).

'Theatre as Holiday', in David L. Smith, Richard Strier, and David Bevington (eds.), *The Theatrical City* (Cambridge University Press, 1995), pp. 101–16.

Boas, Frederick S., *University Drama in the Tudor Age* (Oxford: Clarendon Press, 1914).

Bowers, Roger, 'The Playhouse of the Choristers of Paul's, *c.* 1575–1608', *Theatre Notebook*, 54 (2000), 70–85.

Bradley, David, *From Text to Performance in the Elizabethan Theatre* (Cambridge University Press, 1992).

Brinsley, John, *Pueriles Confabulatiunculae (1617)*, ed. R. E. Alston (Menston: Scholar Press, 1971).

Brome, Richard, *The Antipodes*, ed. Ann Haaker (Lincoln: University of Nebraska Press, 1966).

The Dramatic Works of Richard Brome, ed. R. H. Shepherd, 3 vols. (London: John Pearson, 1873).

Butler, Martin, 'Romans in Britain: *The Roman Actor* and the Early Stuart Classical Play', in Douglas Howard (ed.), *Philip Massinger: A Critical Reassessment* (Cambridge University Press, 1985), pp. 139–70.

Centerwall, Brandon, 'A Greatly Exaggerated Demise: The Remaking of the Children of Paul's as the Duke of York's Men (1608)', *Early Theatre*, 9 (2006), 85–107.

Cerasano, Susan P., 'The "Business" of Shareholding, the Fortune Playhouse, and Francis Grace's Will', *Medieval and Renaissance Drama in England*, 2 (1985), 231–52.

'Philip Henslowe, Simon Forman, and the Theatrical Community of the 1590s', *Shakespeare Quarterly*, 44 (1993), 145–58.

Chambers, E. K., *The Elizabethan Stage*, 4 vols. (Oxford: Clarendon Press, 1923).

Chapman, George, *The Blind Beggar of Alexandria*, ed. W. W. Greg (Oxford: Malone Society, 1928).

Cicero, *De Optime Genere Oratorum*, ed. H. M. Hubbell (Cambridge, MA: Harvard University Press, 1949).

De Oratore, ed. E. W. Sutton and M. Rackham, 2 vols. (Cambridge, MA: Harvard University Press, 1942).

Cohn, Albert, *Shakespeare in Germany in the Sixteenth and Seventeenth Centuries* (1865; New York: Haskell House, 1971).

Cressy, David, *Education in Tudor and Stuart England* (London: Arnold, 1975).

Dekker, Thomas, *The Shoemakers' Holiday*, ed. R. L. Smallwood and Stanley Wells (Manchester University Press, 1979).

Diderot, Denis, *The Paradox of Acting and Masks or Faces?*, trans. W. H. Pollock (New York: Hill and Wang, 1957).

Downes, John, *Roscius Anglicanus*, ed. Judith Milhous and Robert D. Hume (London: Society for Theatre Research, 1987).

Dryden, John, *John Dryden*, ed. Keith Walker (Oxford University Press, 1987).

Dutton, Richard, *Mastering the Revels* (Iowa City: University of Iowa Press, 1991).

Eccles, Mark, 'Elizabethan Actors I: A–D', *Notes and Queries*, 236 (1991), 38–49.

'Elizabethan Actors II: E–K', *Notes and Queries*, 236 (1991), 454–61.

'Elizabethan Actors III: K-R', *Notes and Queries*, 237 (1992), 293–303.

'Elizabethan Actors IV: S to End', *Notes and Queries*, 238 (1993), 165–76.

'Martin Peerson and the Blackfriars', *Shakespeare Survey* 11 (1958), 100–6.

Elliott, John R., Jr, Alan Nelson, Alexandra F. Johnston, and Diana Wyatt (eds.), *Oxford*, 2 vols. (University of Toronto Press, 2004).

Evans, Gareth Lloyd, 'Shakespeare and the Actors', *Shakespeare Survey* 21 (1970), 115–25.

Feil, J. P., 'Dramatic References from the Scudamore Papers', *Shakespeare Survey* 11 (1958), 107–16.

Fletcher, Alan J., *Drama, Performance, and Polity in Pre-Cromwellian Ireland* (University of Toronto Press, 1999).

Foakes, R. A., '"The Player's Passion": Some Notes on Elizabethan Pyschology and Acting', *Essays and Studies of the English Association* (1954), 62–77.

Fraunce, Abraham, *The Arcadian Rhetoric* (1588; Menston: Scolar Press, 1969).

Galloway, David (ed.), *Norwich, 1540–1642* (University of Toronto Press, 1984).

George, David, 'Early Cast Lists for Two Beaumont and Fletcher Plays', *Theatre Notebook*, 28 (1974), 9–11.

Gibson, James M. (ed.), *Kent: Diocese of Canterbury*, 3 vols. (University of Toronto Press, 2002).

Giese, Loreen L., 'Theatrical Citings and Bitings', *Early Theatre*, 1 (1998), 113–28.

Green, A. Wigfall, *The Inns of Court and Early English Drama* (New Haven: Yale University Press, 1931).

Greg, W. W., *Dramatic Documents from the Elizabethan Playhouses*, 2 vols. (Oxford: Clarendon Press, 1931).

Two Elizabethan Stage Abridgements (Oxford: Malone Society, 1922).

Gurr, Andrew, *Playgoing in Shakespeare's London*, 3rd edn (Cambridge University Press, 2004).

The Shakespeare Company, 1594–1642 (Cambridge University Press, 2004).

The Shakespearean Stage 1574–1642, 4th edn (Cambridge University Press, 2009).

Shakespeare's Opposites (Cambridge University Press, 2009).

Henslowe, Philip, *Henslowe's Diary*, ed. R. A. Foakes, 2nd edn (Cambridge University Press, 2002).

Heywood, Thomas, *An Apology for Actors* (London, 1612).

Hillebrand, H. N., *The Child Actors: A Chapter in Elizabethan Stage History* (Urbana: University of Illinois Press, 1926).

Hogan, C. B., *Shakespeare in the Theatre, 1701–1800*, 2 vols. (Oxford: Clarendon Press, 1952).

Honigmann, E. A. J., and Susan Brock (eds.), *Playhouse Wills, 1558–1642* (Manchester University Press, 1993).

Hoole, Charles, *A New Discovery of the Old Art of Teaching School*, ed. R. E. Alston (Menston: Scolar Press, 1969).

Hotson, Leslie, *The Commonwealth and Restoration Stage* (Cambridge, MA: Harvard University Press, 1928).

Howarth, William D. (ed.), *French Theatre in the Neo-classical Era, 1550–1789* (Cambridge University Press, 1997).

Hughes, Thomas, *The Misfortunes of Arthur*, ed. Brian Jay Corrigan (New York: Garland Press, 1992).

Ingram, William, *The Business of Playing: The Beginnings of the Adult Professional Theater in Elizabethan London* (Ithaca: Cornell University Press, 1992).

Jonson, Ben, *The Complete Plays of Ben Jonson*, ed. G. A. Wilkes, 4 vols. (Oxford: Clarendon Press, 1981–2).

Joseph, B. L., *Elizabethan Acting*, 2nd edn (London: Oxford University Press, 1964).

Kathman, David, *Biographical Index of English Drama before 1660*, http://shakespeareauthorship.com/bd/

'Grocers, Goldsmiths, and Drapers: Freemen and Apprentices in the Elizabethan Theater', *Shakespeare Quarterly*, 55 (2004), 1–49.

'How Old were Shakespeare's Boy Actors?', *Shakespeare Survey* 58 (2005), 220–46.

'Reconsidering *The Seven Deadly Sins*', *Early Theatre*, 7 (2004), 13–44.

King, T. J., *Casting Shakespeare's Plays* (Cambridge University Press, 1992).

A Knack to Know a Knave, ed. G. R. Proudfoot (Oxford: Malone Society, 1963).

Knutson, Roslyn, *The Repertory of Shakespeare's Company, 1594–1613* (Fayetteville: University of Arkansas Press, 1991).

Kyd, Thomas, *The Spanish Tragedy*, ed. J. R. Mulryne (London: Benn, 1970).

Lancashire, Anne, *London Civic Theatre: Drama and Pageantry from Roman Times to 1558* (Cambridge University Press, 2002).

'St. Paul's Grammar School before 1580: Theatrical Development Suppressed?', in John H. Astington (ed.), *The Development of Shakespeare's Theater* (New York: AMS Press, 1992), pp. 29–56.

Limon, Jerzy, *Gentlemen of a Company: English Players in Central and Eastern Europe 1590–1660* (Cambridge University Press, 1985).

Look About You, ed. W. W. Greg (Oxford: Malone Society, 1913).

Lyly, John, *Campaspe*, ed. G. K. Hunter (Manchester University Press, 1991).

Endymion, ed. David Bevington (Manchester University Press, 1996).

McIlwraith, A. K., *Five Stuart Tragedies* (London: Oxford University Press, 1953).

McMillin, Scott, 'Building Stories: Greg, Fleay, and the Plot of *2 Seven Deadly Sins*', *Medieval and Renaissance Drama in England*, 4 (1989), 53–62.

and Sally-Beth MacLean, *The Queen's Men and their Plays* (Cambridge University Press, 1998).

Marlowe, Christopher, *Doctor Faustus and Other Plays*, ed. David Bevington and Eric Rasmussen (Oxford: Clarendon Press, 1995).

The Jew of Malta (London, 1633).

Tamburlaine the Great (London, 1590).

Marmion, Shakerly, *Holland's Leaguer* (London, 1632).

Marston, John, *Antonio and Mellida*, ed. W. Reavley Gair (Manchester University Press, 1991).

The Plays of John Marston, ed. E. Harvey Wood, 3 vols. (Edinburgh: Oliver and Boyd, 1934–9).

Massinger, John, *The Plays and Poems of Philip Massinger*, ed. Philip Edwards and Colin Gibson, 5 vols. (Oxford: Clarendon Press, 1976).

Mateer, David, 'Edward Alleyn, Richard Perkins and the Rivalry Between the Swan and Rose Playhouses', *The Review of English Studies*, 60 (2009), 61–77.

Matthew, H. G. C., and Brian Harrison (eds.), *Oxford Dictionary of National Biography*, 60 vols. (Oxford University Press, 2004).

Matusiak, Christopher, 'Christopher Beeston and the Caroline Office of Theatrical "Governor"', *Early Theatre*, 11 (2008), 39–56.

Milhous, Judith, and Robert D. Hume, 'New Light on English Acting Companies in 1646, 1648, and 1660', *The Review of English Studies*, 42 (1991), 487–509.

Milton, John, *The Riverside Milton*, ed. Roy Flannagan (Boston: Houghton Mifflin, 1998).

Motter, T. Vail, *The School Drama in England* (London: Longmans, 1929).

Mulcaster, Richard, *Positions Concerning the Training Up of Children (1581)*, ed. William Barker (University of Toronto Press, 1994).

Munro, Lucy, *The Children of the Queen's Revels: A Jacobean Theatre Repertory* (Cambridge University Press, 2005).

Murray, J. T., *English Dramatic Companies, 1558–1642*, 2 vols. (London: Constable, 1910).

Nelson, Alan H., *Early Cambridge Theatres* (Cambridge University Press, 1994).

(ed.), *Cambridge*, 2 vols. (University of Toronto Press, 1989).

Nungezer, E., *A Dictionary of Actors* (New Haven: Yale University Press, 1929).

Orrell, John, *The Theatres of Inigo Jones and John Webb* (Cambridge University Press, 1985).

Parsloe, G. (ed.), *Wardens' Accounts of the Worhipful Company of Founders, 1497–1681* (London: Athlone Press, 1964).

Pilkinton, Mark C. (ed.), *Bristol* (University of Toronto Press, 1997).

Pinter, Harold, *Harold Pinter, Poems and Prose 1949–1977* (New York: Grove Press, 1978).

Prest, Wilfrid R., *The Inns of Court under Elizabeth and the Early Stuarts, 1590–1640* (London: Longman, 1972).

Quintilian, *The Orator's Education (Institutio Oratoria)*, ed. Donald A. Russell, 5 vols. (Cambridge, MA: Harvard University Press, 2001).

Rappaport, Steve, *Worlds Within Worlds: Structures of Life in Sixteenth-Century London* (Cambridge University Press, 1989).

Richards, Kenneth, and Laura Richards, *The Commedia dell'Arte: A Documentary History* (Oxford: Blackwell, 1990).

Riddell, James A., 'Some Actors in Ben Jonson's Plays', *Shakespeare Studies*, 5 (1969), 285–98.

Ripley, John, *Julius Caesar on Stage in England and America, 1599–1973* (Cambridge University Press, 1980).

Roach, Joseph R., *The Player's Passion: Studies in the Science of Acting* (Newark: University of Delaware Press, 1985).

Rutter, Carol Chillington, *Documents of the Rose Playhouse* (Manchester University Press, 1984).

Shakespeare, William, *The Riverside Shakespeare,* gen. ed. G. Blakemore Evans, 2nd edn (Boston: Houghton Mifflin, 1997).

Shapiro, Michael, *Children of the Revels: The Boy Companies of Shakespeare's Time and their Plays* (New York: Columbia University Press, 1977).

Simon, Joan, *Education and Society in Tudor England* (Cambridge University Press, 1966).

Somerset, J. Alan B. (ed.), *Shropshire*, 2 vols. (University of Toronto Press, 1994).

Stern, Tiffany, *Rehearsal from Shakespeare to Sheridan* (Oxford: Clarendon Press, 2000).

Thomson, Peter, 'Rogues and Rhetoricians: Acting Styles in Early English Drama', in John D. Cox and David Scott Kastan (eds.), *A New History of Early English Drama* (New York: Columbia University Press, 1997), pp. 321–35.

Shakespeare's Professional Career (Cambridge University Press, 1992).

Shakespeare's Theatre (London: Routledge & Kegan Paul, 1983).

The Three Parnassus Plays, ed. J. B. Leishman (London: Nicholson and Watson, 1949).

Venn, John, and J. A. Venn, *Alumni Cantabrigienses, Part 1*, 4 vols. (Cambridge University Press, 1922–6).

Wasson, John M. (ed.), *Devon* (University of Toronto Press, 1986).

Waterfield, Giles, *et al.*, *Mr. Cartwright's Pictures: A Seventeenth-Century Collection* (London: Dulwich Picture Gallery, 1987).

Watson, Foster, *The English Grammar Schools to 1660* (Cambridge, 1908).

Webster, John, *The Duchess of Malfi*, ed. John Russell Brown (London: Methuen, 1964).

White, Paul Whitfield, *Theatre and Reformation* (Cambridge University Press, 1993).

Whitelocke, James, *The Liber Famelicus of Sir James Whitelocke*, ed. John Bruce (London: Camden Society, 1858).

Wickham, Glynne, Herbert Berry, and William Ingram (eds.), *English Professional Theatre, 1530–1660* (Cambridge University Press, 2000).

Wilson, Thomas, *The Art of Rhetoric (1560)*, ed. Peter E. Medine (University Park: Pennsylvania University Press, 1994).

Index